Communicate What You Mean

A Concise Advanced Grammar

■ ■ ■ ■ ■ ■ ■ Second Edition

Carroll Washington Pollock

Revised by **Samuela Eckstut**

PRENTICE HALL REGENTS
A VIACOM COMPANY
Upper Saddle River, NJ 07458

Library of Congress Cataloging-in-Publication Data
Pollock, Carroll Washington.
    Communicate what you mean : a concise advanced grammar / Carroll
Washington Pollock ; revised by Samuela Eckstut. -- 2nd ed.
        p.   cm.
    Includes index.
    ISBN 0-13-520107-1
    1. English language--Textbooks for foreign speakers.   2. English
language--Grammar--Problems, exercises, etc.   I. Eckstut-Didier,
Samuela.   II. Title.
PE1128.P584   1997
428.2 ' 4--dc21

                                            96-53662
                                            CIP

Publisher: *Mary Jane Peluso*
Editor: *Sheryl Olinsky*
Development Editor: *Janet Johnston*
Production/Composition: *Jan Sivertsen*
Manufacturing Manager: *Ray Keating*
Art Director/Interior Designer: *Merle Krumper*
Additional Interior Design: *Jan Sivertsen*
Cover Design: *Paul Pullara*

PRENTICE HALL REGENTS
A VIACOM COMPANY

Published by PRENTICE HALL REGENTS
Prentice-Hall, Inc.
A Simon & Schuster Company
Upper Saddle River, New Jersey 07458

Photo Credits: pp. 65, 221: Page Poore   p. 92: Trans World Airlines   p. 116: Library of Congress   p. 182: U.S. Forest Service   p. 184: Alexis Seabrook   p. 212: Ken Karp p. 213: E.R. Kalmbach, Fish and Wildlfe Service (coyote); Laimute E. Druskis (sleeping student, also on p. 221); National Archives (destroyed building, also on p. 220); United Nations (grinning man)   p. 214: United Nations (man under arrest, also on pp. 220 and 221); Laimute E. Druskis (frightened woman)   pp. 220, 221, and 279: Irene Springer (judge in courtroom)   p. 228: Marc P. Anderson (winter street scene, also on p. 220)

Printed in the United States of America

10 9 8 7 6 5 4 3 2 1

ISBN 0-13-520107-1

Prentice-Hall International (UK) Limited, *London*
Prentice-Hall of Australia Pty. Limited, *Sydney*
Prentice-Hall Canada Inc., *Toronto*
Prentice-Hall Hispanoamericana, S.A., *Mexico*
Prentice-Hall of India Private Limited, *New Delhi*
Prentice-Hall of Japan, Inc., *Tokyo*
Simon & Schuster Asia Pte. Ltd., *Singapore*
Editora Prentice-Hall do Brasil, Ltda., *Rio de Janeiro*

CONTENTS

Lesson Ten

PART 5: PASSIVE VOICE   177

Lesson Eleven

PART 6: MODAL AUXILIARIES   192

Lesson Twelve

PART 7: CONDITIONAL SENTENCES   226

Lesson Thirteen

PREFACE

■ Underlying Concepts of the Text ■

The grammatical rules of a language do not tell us *what to say*. Rather, the grammatical rules of a language tell us *how to respond correctly* within the structural system of the language. Therefore, using a language is, to a large degree, a psychological activity in that a speaker's responses depend not only upon a knowledge of structure but also upon a knowledge of the events of a situation and the speaker's feelings toward those events. Students (at every level) must be expected to give semantically and situationally correct responses as well as grammatically correct ones.

Although "formal" studies of grammatical analysis and of meaning are often autonomous, encoding one's thoughts into a correct as well as situationally appropriate response is not. When speaking or writing, semantics and syntax work together to transmit meaning, and a message will be anomalous if there is a mistake in one or the other. For example, the student who says, "I have been arriving in the United States," understands the grammatical formation of the present perfect continuous tense, but the meaning of the verb *arrive* in this sentence limits us to an activity that occurs only one time.

■ Features of the Exercises ■

With few exceptions, the exercises are contextual; that is, they are built around a center of interest so that the student is talking about something rather than simply repeating or completing a series of unrelated statements.

Although the explanations are presented deductively, the exercises that follow provide oral as well as written practice. High-level students need just as much aural-oral practice with complex structures as do low-level students with more basic structures.

The exercises require that the student make a grammatically correct response as well as one that is semantically appropriate. For this reason, many of the exercises allow for a number of correct responses that reflect the particular way in which a student has perceived the situation or has understood what has previously been stated. The student must think instead of merely filling in the blanks. Students who are required only to fill in the blanks are not provided with an opportunity to reuse previously learned structures or vocabulary.

There is a "built-in" repetition of structures from lesson to lesson so that old, previously learned material is reviewed while new material is being practiced. This built-in redundancy also impresses upon the student the realization that several points of grammar operate simultaneously whenever we speak or write.

■ Special Features of the Text ■

At the beginning of each part, introductory remarks to the student provide a general idea of what is to be covered in that part. This feature grew as a result of students' questions over the years. Before each part is begun, these remarks should be read in class or assigned to the student to be read at home, but they should not be omitted.

Each part and some lessons conclude with a practice exam. This exam provides a final review of the material covered in the lessons, and it permits the teacher to identify any remaining weaknesses.

Tense Review

■ INTRODUCTION TO PART 1 ■ ■ ■ ■ ■ ■ ■ ■

There are times in speaking and writing when one tense is used predominantly; however, when speaking or writing, a person usually uses several different tenses and moves from one tense to the other correctly and quickly. As you review the tenses in this chapter, remember the following.

1. Grammar rules do not tell you what to say. Grammar rules tell you how to say something correctly. Real-life events and your feelings about these events will determine what you will communicate.

2. Certain verbs cannot be used in certain tenses because of the meaning of the verbs. You must think about the meaning of a particular verb as well as the meaning of the whole sentence before you use the verb in a particular tense. At all times *meaning* and *form* must fit. Look at the following sentence from a student composition.

   Incorrect: *My parents have sent me to Stanford University after my graduation from high school.*

   The form of the present perfect tense is correct—*have* + past participle—but the meaning of the word *sent* in this sentence refers to an activity that usually happens only one time and is then finished. How many times can you graduate from high school? After graduation, how many times can your parents send you to the same university for the first time?

   Correct: *My parents sent me to Stanford University after my graduation from high school.*

   As you review the tenses in Part 1, remember that the listener or reader does not know what you are going to say or write or how you feel about something until you say it or write it. Your choice of tense must correctly express the activities of a situation as well as your feelings about the situation. Your choice of tense must express what you wish to communicate.

Lesson One

■ 1-1 PRESENT TIME

▪ **Simple Present** ▪	▪ **Present Continuous** ▪

1. The simple present is used to make factual statements.

   *Martina **plays** tennis very well.*
   *Colombia **produces** good coffee.*
   *Roberto **is** from Colombia. His father **owns** a coffee plantation.*

1. The present continuous is used to express a single activity or a series of activities happening at the moment of speaking.

   *Martina **is playing** tennis well these days. It's noon, and I **am sitting** in the park. It's a beautiful day, so many office workers **are eating** their lunches outside. A few people **are standing** in line in front of a park vendor. They **are waiting** for hot dogs. A little boy **is enjoying** a huge ice cream cone.*

2. The simple present is also used to express customs and habitual activity.

   *Many office workers **take** a fifteen-minute coffee break every day.*
   *I **drink** three cups of coffee every morning.*

2. The present continuous is also used to express a single activity or a series of activities happening over a given period of time, but not necessarily at the moment of speaking.

   *This quarter my roommate **is working** in the dorm cafeteria. He serves breakfast from 6:30 to 8:30 every morning. He **is taking** only two night courses this quarter, so his father agreed to let him work. His mother, however, **is trying** to convince him to quit the job.*

3. The simple present is also used to express future time with a future time word or phrase.

   A. *What time **does** the flight to Bogota **leave** tomorrow?*
   B. *It **leaves** at noon.*

3. The present continuous is also used to express future time. A future time word or phrase is necessary to distinguish between a present and future time reference. Sometimes an earlier statement makes the future time clear, and a future time word is not necessary.

   *Jim's plane **is arriving** at Denver at 6:00 tonight.*

*He and his wife **are meeting** with their lawyer tomorrow.*
*They**'re leaving** Denver next week.*
*They**'re flying** to Texas.*

4. The simple present is also used to express opinions, sense perceptions, emotions, and possession.

*My landlady **makes** excellent coffee.* (opinion)
*This coffee **tastes** bitter.* (sense perception)
*I **hate** bitter coffee.* (emotion)
*This cup **belongs** to the secretary.* (possession)

Exercise 1   *Find the ten tense mistakes in the letter from Carlo to his girlfriend, Marta. Then correct the mistakes.*

Dear Marta,

I'm missing you so much. I have no idea what I do here without you. Every day is so empty, and I dream of you every night. I wonder if you suffer as much without me.

What do you do these days? Do you study hard, or do you spend a lot of time with your friends? I hope you study hard. I want you to pass your exams so that you can come as soon as possible to be with me.

Right now I'm lying in my bed and writing to you. I try to concentrate, but it's difficult because my roommate takes a nap. He always takes a nap in the middle of the day and then stays up all night. He loves to party.

As for me, I love nothing or no one but you. I hope you are loving me too.

All my love,
Carlo

■ 1-2 NON-CONTINUOUS VERBS

■ Verbs Expressing Sense Perceptions ■

feel	hear	see	smell	taste

1. These verbs do not usually occur in the continuous tenses (present continuous, present perfect continuous, past continuous, past perfect continuous, future continuous).

2. These verbs usually refer to involuntary actions of the senses; we do these actions without consciously thinking about them.

3. Some of these verbs, however, can also express a voluntary use of the senses. When these verbs are used to express voluntary actions, they *can* be used in the continuous form. Compare:

Involuntary Actions	Voluntary Actions
I *feel* cold. Close the window.	Alicia *is feeling* the material to see if it's real silk.
I *smell* something burning.	
Your soup *tastes* great.	I'm *smelling* the meat to see if it's spoiled.
Do you *see* my keys anywhere?	Al *is tasting* the soup to see if it needs salt.
I *hear* voices. Someone is downstairs.	

4. *Feel* can also be used in the continuous form when it is used in a medical sense.
   I'm not *feeling* well today.   I have a cold.

5. *See* can be used in the continuous form when it has the following meanings:
meet by appointment:	Ali *is seeing* the director today.
visit places of interest:	Maria *is* out *seeing* the sights of Washington today.
date on a regular basis:	Sonia *is seeing* Alvaro these days.

■ Verbs of Thinking, Attitudes, or Opinion ■

appear	doubt	guess	need	remember	think
believe	feel	know	prefer	seem	understand
consider	forget	mean	realize	sound	

1. These verbs seldom occur in the continuous tenses.

2. When *feel* indicates *opinion,* it cannot be used in the continuous form.
   Correct: I *feel* we should stay home tonight.
   Incorrect: I am *feeling* we should stay home tonight.

3. *Consider* and *think* can be used in the continuous form if the speaker is *not* giving an opinion.

Not Giving an Opinion	Giving an Opinion
I'm thinking about my vacation plans.	*I think Disney World is a tourist trap.*
Linda is considering buying my old car.	*She considers it a good buy.*

▪ Verbs Expressing Possession ▪

belong	have	own	possess

1. These verbs also do not usually occur in the continuous tenses.

2. *Have* can be used in the continuous form when it does *not* express possession. Compare:

Non-Possession	Possession
We're having a test today.	*The teacher has the tests upstairs.*
Ted and Pam are having a party tomorrow.	*They have a beautiful apartment.*
The Smiths are having a good time in Paris.	*They have a lot of money.*
My sister is having a baby in June.	*She already has five children.*

▪ Verbs Expressing Emotion ▪

care	hate	refuse
desire	like	want
forgive	love	wish

1. These verbs also do not usually occur in the continuous tenses.

2. *Wish* can be used in the continuous form when the speaker expresses a desire silently to himself or herself.

Mother: *Why do you have your eyes closed and your fingers crossed?*
Little girl: *I'm wishing for a baby brother to play with.*

Exercise 2   *A mother is speaking to her sixteen-year-old son. Complete each sentence with a verb of emotion. Use* not *where necessary.*

1. Your father and I _____ about you. You are our only child.

2. We don't want to make you miserable. We only _____ the best in life for you.

3. Don't worry. Your father _____ you for wrecking the family car.

4. Remember, however, that he _____ careless drivers.

5. You realize, of course, that I _____ reckless drivers either.

6. We know teenagers _____ speed; nevertheless, we _____ to let you use the car again until you slow down.

7. We _____ to see you in the hospital.

8. I _____ you would think about this conversation carefully.

Exercise 3 ░ *Complete the dialog, using the simple present or the present continuous form of the verb* taste.

Yuko: This international party was a great idea.

Ana: It certainly was. Look at all the food!

Yuko: That dish from Libya _____ great. What are you doing?

1

Ana: I _____ the Mexican dish I cooked.

2

Yuko: What's the matter with it? Does it _____ all right?

3

Ana: No, it doesn't. It _____ terrible. I didn't put enough

4

salt in it.

Yuko: Don't worry about it. Nobody will notice it.

Ana: Look at our teacher. He's walking from table to table.

He _____ every dish.

5

Yuko: Yes. Except the one he brought.

Ana: Isn't it good?

Yuko: I didn't like it. American food _____ bland to me

6

because Americans don't use enough spices.

Ana: Look. He _____ my dish now. Don't tell him I cooked it.

7

I don't want to fail reading this quarter.

■ 1-3 PAST TIME TO PRESENT TIME

■ **Present Perfect** ■	■ **Present Perfect Continuous** ■
1. The present perfect is used to express an action or emotion that started in the past and has continued into the present.	1. The present perfect continuous is used to emphasize the continuous nature of an activity that started in the past and has continued into the present.
*I **have read** that book. It's very good.*	*I **have been reading** that book for weeks; I wonder if I'll ever finish it.*
*Dr. Jones **has lived** in New York for many years.*	*Manuel **has been living** in New York for one year.*
2. The present perfect is used more than the present perfect continuous for actions that are more long-term in nature.	2. The present perfect continuous is used more than the present perfect for actions that are more recent in nature.
*Tom **has made** a lot of money since 1980.*	*Tom **has been making** a lot of money since he began his new job seven months ago.*
3. The present perfect is used to indicate a single action that is complete.	3. The present perfect continuous is often used to indicate a single action that is incomplete.
*Mary **has washed** the dishes.* (The job is finished.)	*Mary **has been washing** the dishes.* (The job probably isn't finished.)
4. The present perfect is used to indicate the number of times an action has been done or the number of things that have been done.	4. The present perfect continuous is used to emphasize the duration of an action, *not* the number of times an action has been done.
*I **have read** this statistics problem five times.*	*I've **been reading** it for the past hour.*
*Zoe **has** already **completed** six problems.*	*I've **been trying** to understand the same problem all night.*

5. The present perfect is used to indicate an action that happened at an indefinite time in the past. The time of the action is not given.

*Ana **has finished** her composition.*
*The teacher **has corrected** it.*
*I **have received** my college acceptance letter.*

When the time is given, the simple past is used.

*Ana **finished** her composition two days ago.*
*The teacher **corrected** it last night.*
*I **received** the letter the day before yesterday.*

6. When used with *just* and *already,* the present perfect expresses an action that started in the past but finished recently or very close to the moment of speaking.

A: *Don't forget to mail the package.*
B: *I've **already** mailed it. I went to the post office this morning.* OR *It's on the way.*
*I've **just** returned home from the post office.*

Note: The present perfect and present perfect continuous are sometimes interchangeable.

*I **have flown** to Toronto a great deal this month.*
*I **have been flying** to Toronto a great deal this month.*

Native speakers of English choose between the present perfect and the present perfect continuous depending on their desire to make the listener or reader *feel* the uninterrupted nature of an activity or to make the listener or reader *feel* the speaker's attitude or emotion toward the activity.

*I **have been waiting** for you for one hour.*
*I **have waited** for you for one hour.*

While both sentences are grammatically correct, a native speaker would probably say the first, which is more effective than the second if the speaker wants to express his or her annoyance at waiting so long. Which of the following sentences seems to indicate that the speaker is tired?

*I **have been reviewing** this chapter for three hours.*
*I **have reviewed** this chapter for three hours.*

Note: The present perfect continuous is <u>not</u> used to express an action that is not continuous in nature. The present perfect <u>is</u> used.

Correct: *I **have** finally **returned** the book to the library.*
Incorrect: *I have finally been returning the book to the library.*

Also, because of their meaning, many verbs cannot be used in the present perfect continuous.

Correct: *The plane **has arrived**. It's over there. (A plane arrives only once.)*
Incorrect: *The plane has been arriving. It's over there.*

Exercise 4 ■■
■ ■ ■ ■ ■ ■ ■ ■ ■ ■ ■ ■ ■
Complete the account, using the correct form of the verbs in parentheses. Use the simple present, present continuous, or present perfect. In some sentences more than one tense may be correct.

Ali and Roberto _____ (be) graduate students in the department of
1
physics at Harvard University. They _____ (be) students at Harvard
2
for one year. This institution of higher learning _____ (be) the oldest
3
university in the United States, and it _____ (have) the distinction of
4
being a very prestigious school. This quarter, Roberto _____ (work) in
5
the library on Friday and Saturday nights. He _____ (take) only two
6
courses this quarter, so he _____ (have, not) many assignments. His
7
girlfriend _____ (try) to convince him to quit his job so that they can go
8
out on the weekends.

It's noon now, so they _____ (eat) lunch in the student union.
9
Many students _____ (stand) in line and _____ (wait) for
10   11
someone to take their orders. Ali and Roberto _____ (be) in line for
12
nearly twenty minutes, and they _____ (get) a little impatient.
13
Although they _____ (have) lunch in the union a few times a week,
14
Roberto _____ (prefer) to eat in the dorm cafeteria because the service
15
_____ (be) faster.
16

Their spring break _____ (begin) next week, and Ali
17
_____ (fly) to his country by airplane to visit his family.
18
He _____ (receive, already) a big check from his father, so he
19
_____ (plan) to fly first class. His flight _____ (depart)
20   21
at seven o'clock in the morning. Both Ali and Roberto _____ (register)
22
for a course in aerodynamics next quarter because the phenomenon of flying
_____ (fascinate) them since they were children.
23

Exercise 5 ▪▪
▪▪▪▪▪▪▪▪▪▪▪▪ *Complete the sentences, using the present perfect or the present perfect continuous form of the verbs in parentheses. If both tenses are correct, write both tenses in the blanks.*

1. Jay _____ (fail) his driving test three times because he doesn't know how to park. However, he _____ (practice) three hours every day for the past week, and I think he _____ (make) a lot of improvement.

2. My brother _____ (not pass) his driving test either.

3. He _____ (worry) about this for two months.

4. I _____ (study) the driver's manual for hours every day, but I _____ (take) my test yet.

5. My father _____ (help) me to review the questions.

6. My roommate _____ (just buy) a new CD player.

7. She _____ (play) CDs since six o'clock this morning, and she is driving me crazy.

8. The other students on our floor _____ (complain) to our resident assistant, but she _____ (not say) anything to my roommate yet.

9. Everyone is especially annoyed because we are taking final exams this week. My roommate _____ (take) two exams already, and she _____ (fail) both of them because she _____ (not study).

10. I _____ (think) about moving out of the dorm, but I _____ (not make) a definite decision yet.

11. Donna _____ (not receive) a check from her parents in two months.

12. She _____ (look) for the mail carrier every day.

13. Her friends _____ (lend) her money so that she can buy food and other necessities.

14. Donna _____ (just begin) a part-time job in the library, but she _____ (not get) her first paycheck yet.

15. She _____ (work) in the library for only one week.

Exercise 6 *With another student, decide how your teacher would answer the questions. Then check your answers by asking your teacher the questions. Use the present perfect or present perfect continuous.*

1. How long/teach?
2. How long/work at this school?
3. How many different schools/work at?
4. Which foreign countries/teach in?
5. How many hours/work today?
6. How often/attend department meetings?
7. How many students/teach this term?
8. How long/live in *(town where you live)*?
9. How many times/move in the past five years?

■ 1-4 PAST TIME

■ Simple Past ■

1. The simple past is used to describe actions of short duration in the past.

   *Alan **talked** to his boss about the problem.*

   *I **met** Dr. Dance yesterday, and we **talked** for a few minutes.*

2. The simple past is also used to describe actions that took place over a period of time in the past.

   *Dr. Dance **taught** at Michigan State for ten years.*

■ Past Continuous ■

1. With a point in time, the past continuous expresses an action that began before the time given and probably continued after it. The exact beginning and end of the action are unknown.

   *Alan **was talking** to his boss when I walked in.*

   *At 12:30 we **were eating** lunch in the park.*

2. With a period of time, the past continuous is used to express an action that continued for a rather long period. Again, we do not know exactly when the action began or ended.

   *Yesterday morning I **was jogging** through the park.*

3. The simple past is also used to describe past habitual actions.

   *When Dr. Dance was at Michigan State, he **rode** his bike to classes.*

3. During a period of time, the past continuous is used to express the beginning and ending of an action.

   *From eight to ten yesterday morning, we **were playing** soccer*

4. The past continuous is also used to express two actions that were happening at the same time in the past.

   *The children **were playing** while their mothers **were watching** them.*

5. The past continuous is also used to express an action that began *before* another action in the past and probably continued after it.

   *As I **was jogging**, a man stopped me and asked for the time.*

Note: In some sentences either the simple past or past continuous is possible. The speaker will choose the simple past to indicate that the action started and finished. If the action started and continued for a period of time, the speaker will use the past continuous. With the past continuous, the speaker wants to emphasize the duration of an action. The speaker wants the listener to feel the continuing nature of an action in progress.

Note: The choice between the simple past and the past continuous depends on the meaning of a sentence. Compare:

*When I got up this morning, my roommate **prepared** breakfast. (He waited for me to get up.)*

*When I got up this morning, my roommate **was preparing** breakfast. (He started before I got up.)*

Exercise 7   *Change the simple past to the past continuous where possible. Keep in mind the meaning of the verbs.*

Examples: I filled in the immigration form completely while I was on the plane.

   no change

   We waited for half an hour before we could get off the plane.

   We were waiting for half an hour before we could get off the plane.

1. When the plane landed at the airport, everybody got off the plane and walked to Immigration.

   _____

2. I stood in a long line for more than three-quarters of an hour.

   _____

3. Some of the passengers were very tired.

   _____

4. Other passengers stood around and talked to each other until it was their turn.

   _____

5. The immigration officer asked me a lot of questions.

   _____

6. When I began to answer the questions, she entered the information into her computer.

   _____

7. She asked me one question over and over again, but I couldn't understand her.

   _____

8. Finally, she asked if anyone in the line could translate for me.

   _____

9. When a teenager came up to help me, I felt very embarrassed.

   _____

10. Finally, the immigration officer stamped my passport and told me I could go.

    _____

11. The suitcases came out very slowly in the baggage pick-up area.

    _____

12. Some young children ran around the area and made a lot of noise.

    _____

13. Their parents didn't pay any attention to them.

    _____

14. The children gave me a headache.

    _____

15. At 5:30, an hour and a half after the plane arrived, my suitcases finally appeared.

    _____

Exercise 8 ▪▪
▪▪▪▪▪▪▪▪▪▪▪

Describe to another student a funny, unusual, or frightening experience you have had. As you listen to your partner's story, ask questions to clarify anything you do not understand. Be ready to give a summary of your partner's story to the rest of the class if your teacher asks you to.

Exercise 9 ▪▪
▪▪▪▪▪▪▪▪▪▪▪

Your teacher is going to read the following questions. Close your books. Write the numbers 1 to 24 on a piece of paper, and write down the name of the tense you hear in each question. When your teacher finishes, open your books and check to see if you wrote down the correct tense names.

Personal Information

1. Which subject did you enjoy in high school?
2. Were you studying or working before you came here?
3. What are you planning to study in the United States?
4. Have you always been interested in this field?
5. Have you been enjoying your English classes so far?

Marriage

6. At what age do people generally marry in your country?
7. Has this always been the custom?
8. Are people marrying young nowadays?
9. Did your parents marry when they were young?
10. Who in your family or among your friends has been thinking about getting married?

Sports

11. What is the most popular sport in your country?
12. Has this always been the favorite sport in your country?
13. Are people still attending the games enthusiastically?
14. Did the national team have a successful year last year?
15. Does your country usually send a team to the Olympic games?

Universities

16. Are universities crowded in your country?
17. Have they always been crowded?
18. Are many students still trying to enter a university?
19. Did you attend a university before you came here?
20. How long have you been studying in the United States?

Religion

21. What is the predominant religion in your country?
22. Has it always had the largest number of followers?
23. Are most people still attending religious services regularly?
24. Have you been attending services since you have been here?

Exercise 10 ▪▪
▪▪▪▪▪▪▪▪▪▪▪▪ *In a group of three or four, discuss the topics Personal Information, Marriage, Sports, Universities, and Religion. Use the questions in Exercise 9 as a guide for your discussion, but do not limit your discussion to merely answering these questions. Find out as much information as you can about the people in your group and life in their home countries.*

▪ 1-5 FUTURE TIME

▪ *Be Going to* + Verb ▪   ▪ *Will* + Verb ▪

1. *Be going to* is used to make predictions.

   *The class **is going to be** fun.*

   *We**'re going to eat** well tonight. Robert's a great cook.*

2. *Be going to* is used to express a feeling of certainty about the future because of present conditions.

   *Look! There's not a cloud in the sky. It's **going to be** a beautiful day.*

3. *Be going to* is used to express a future action that has been deliberately planned. The speaker has given the action previous thought and planning.

   *Ahmed bought a lot of food this morning and borrowed my CD player. He's **going to have** a party tonight.*

1. *Will* is also used to make predictions.

   *The class **will be** fun.*

   *We**'ll eat** well tonight. Robert's a great cook.*

2. *Will* is used with *sure, certain,* and *know* to express certainty about the future.

   *Look! There's not a cloud in the sky. I'm **sure** it **will be** a beautiful day.*

3. *Will* is used to express willingness to do a future action. The decision is made at the moment of speaking. There is no previous thought or planning. Therefore, *will* is used to make promises and offers of help.

   A: I haven't finished this work yet, and I have to pick the children up in ten minutes.
   *B: Don't worry. I'**ll pick** them **up**.*

4. *Will* is used to express expected future actions, actions that usually or normally happen.

   *I'**ll see** you tomorrow in class.*

5. *Will* is also used for future habitual actions that we assume will happen.

   *Mr. Ray **will give** us a test on Friday. (He always does.)*

6. *Will* is also used with verbs of the senses, emotion, thinking, and possession to express the future.

   *I'll **see** you tomorrow.*
   *She'll **forgive** you. I'm sure of it.*

Note: Sometimes it is not clear whether the speaker has given the action previous thought or planning. The speaker may only be reporting a future event or asking a question about a future event.

> My parents **are going to arrive** at 8:00 tonight.
> My parents **will arrive** at 8:00 tonight.

> Our conversation teacher is absent today. Who is **going to teach** the class?
> Our conversation teacher is absent today. Who **will teach** the class?

> **Is** the president **going to be** in Denver tomorrow?
> **Will** the president **be** in Denver tomorrow?

Note: When you are communicating an idea, you will not necessarily give all the background information on an action you want to express. The previous plans and thoughts will stay in your mind. But when you use *be going to*, the listener will understand that you have given this action previous thought and/or planning.

Note: When the verb in the main clause is in a future tense, the verb in the dependent time clause is in the present tense, not in the future tense.

> Correct: *I **will come** home after I **finish** shopping.*
> Incorrect: *I will come home after I will finish shopping.*

Exercise 11 *Complete the following dialogs, using* be going to *or* will *and the correct form of the verbs in parentheses.*

1. **A:** I left the food in the car.

   B: I _____ (get) it for you.

2. **A:** What are you doing with the soap and water?

   B: I _____ (wash) the car.

3. **A:** Daddy, look at me!

   B: Pat, come down from that tree. You _____ (fall).

4. **A:** Why _____ (we/have) pasta for dinner?

   B: Because there's nothing else in the house.

5. **A:** The phone's ringing.

   B: Don't get up. I _____ (answer) it.

6. **A:** That guy in the red car is crazy. Look how he's cutting in front of everyone.

   B: You're right. He _____ (cause) an accident.

7. **A:** Why are you putting on your raincoat?

   B: It _____ (rain). Look outside and see for yourself.

8. **A:** I'm having a lot of trouble in my writing course.

   B: Stop worrying. I _____ (help) you.

▪ Simple Present ▪   ▪ Present Continuous ▪

1. The simple present is usually used with verbs of arriving and departing (*come, go, leave, arrive, depart, return*) to express a scheduled or planned event in the future.

   *I **leave** for Texas tomorrow.*

   *My flight **leaves** Denver at 3:00 tomorrow.*

   *It **arrives** in Houston at around 5:00.*

1. The present continuous is also used with verbs of arriving, departing, starting, and finishing for a scheduled or planned event in the future.

   *I'**m leaving** for Texas tomorrow.*

   *I'm sorry. This store **is closing** in ten minutes.*

   *My flight **is arriving** in Texas at 3:00 tomorrow.*

2. The simple present is also used with verbs of starting and finishing: *begin, commence, start, finish, end, close, conclude.*

   *Final exams **begin** next week.*

   *The semester **ends** in two weeks.*

3. The simple present may also be used with other verbs to express a scheduled event in the future. A future time word or phrase is used to make the time clear.

   *I **have** a doctor's appointment next Monday.*

2. Verbs of the senses, emotion, thinking, and possession cannot be used in the present continuous to express future actions. Exceptions to this rule are *see* when it means *have an appointment with* and *have* when it does not mean possession.

   *My doctor **is seeing** me tomorrow at 9:00.*

   *I'm **having** an eye examination.*

3. To avoid confusion and make the time clear, a future time word accompanies the present continuous, unless the future time is already clear because of an earlier statement, in this case, the first sentence.

   *My parents **are arriving** this weekend, and I'm very excited because I haven't seen them in six months. I'm **picking** them up at the airport in my new car.*

3. If an earlier statement makes the future time clear, a future time word may not be necessary.

   *I won't be in class next Wednesday. Our soccer team **plays** in Michigan.*

Exercise 12

Complete the paragraphs, using the correct form of the verbs in parentheses. You will need to use a variety of future forms. When you finish, be ready to discuss the use of various forms and to explain why more than one form is correct for some sentences.

This semester _____(end) one month from now. My roommate and I

   _____ (go) to the Bahamas for our summer vacation. I

   _____ (be) happy to get away from grammar tests for a while. At the

moment, we're studying for a grammar test that we _____ (have)

tomorrow.

After the test, everyone _____ (meet) at Pedro's apartment for a party.
The party _____ (start) at 5:00. Tomorrow is Pedro's birthday; he
_____ (be) twenty-one. All our classmates _____ (help) him
to celebrate this happy occasion. He told us not to bring birthday presents, but
everyone _____ (buy) him something. I don't know what I
_____ (give) him yet, but I _____ (get) something before I go
to the party.

At the party, I _____ (not worry) about my grammar test.
It _____ (begin) at 3:00 tomorrow and _____ (end) at 4:00.
I _____ (not think) about it after 4:00.

■ 1-6 ADVERBIAL TIME EXPRESSIONS

■ Present Time ■

*I work (or am working) in a bank **now**.*
*I'm helping a customer **right now**.*
*The bank president is meeting with the tellers **at the moment**.*

■ Past Time ■

*Maria decided to quit her job **the day before yesterday**.*
*She found a new job **yesterday**.*
*She was working (or worked) in the bank with me **last week**.*

■ Future Time ■

*I leave for New York **tomorrow**.*
*Will you be in class **the day after tomorrow**?*
*We're having the test **two days from now**.*

1. It is important to pay attention to the time words and expressions that usually accompany the various tenses. In sentences expressing only one action, a time word or expression helps to make the time of the action clear. An incorrect time expression makes the sentence confusing.

   Incorrect: *I have not completed my assignment yesterday.*
   I did not complete my assignment already.

2. In writing, it is important to use the tenses consistently. If you begin writing in one tense, do not change to another tense unnecessarily or suddenly. When you change to a different tense, you must have a specific and clear reason for changing, *and* you must signal to the reader that you are going to change so that the reader will not become confused. The use of time words and expressions will help you to tell the reader that you are going to change the time of events.

3. Time words are very important because they signal the use of a particular tense. It is not necessary to use a time word in every sentence, however. The meaning of what you are talking about will make the time clear, and you will use a time word only when you change the time of the events.

4. Some words do not clearly indicate a specific time period, but they are used regularly with certain tenses.

Simple Past	Giving an Opinion
*I finished my report two days **ago**.*	***While** I was working, you were out dancing at a disco.*

Present Perfect	Present Perfect Continuous
*Ali has been sick **for** two weeks.*	*I've been working on this composition **for** two weeks.*
*He has been sick **since** last week.*	*We've been reviewing the tenses **since** the course began.*
*Deb has **already** completed her reading assignment.*	
*She hasn't finished the grammar assignment **yet**.*	
*We've written only two compositions **so far**.*	
*We've taken only one test **up to now**.*	
*Have you **ever** failed a test?*	

5. Adverbs of frequency tell *how often* an activity takes place. Most of these adverbs of frequency can be used with several tenses. With the simple present tense, the meaning of the adverbs of frequency is habitual, repeated action.

I **always complete** my homework assignments on time.

Rolando's homework **is sometimes** late.

Hans **never finishes** his assignments on time.

His **are usually** more than two days late.

I **often give** my compositions to the instructor early.

The instructor **occasionally returns** our compositions the next day.

With the simple past tense, the meaning of the adverbs of frequency is habitual, repeated action for a definite time in the past. In the following sentences, the definite time in the past is *last semester*.

I **always completed** my homework assignments on time last semester.

Rolando's homework **was sometimes** late.

Hans **never finished** his assignments on time.

His **were usually** more than two days late.

I **often gave** my compositions to the instructor early.

The instructor **occasionally returned** our compositions the next day.

With the present perfect tense, the meaning of the adverbs of frequency is to describe action from a point of time in the past to the moment of speaking.

I **have always completed** my homework assignments on time.

Rolando's homework **has sometimes been** late.

Hans **has never finished** his assignments on time.

His **have usually been** more than two days late.

I **have often given** my compositions to the instructor early.

The instructor **has occasionally returned** our compositions the next day.

Additional adverbs of frequency that may accompany these tenses are *scarcely, rarely, seldom, hardly ever.*

6. The expression *once in a while* may also be used with several tenses to indicate *how often*.

I **see** my old high school friends **once in a while**.

When I was home last year, I **saw** my chemistry teacher **once in a while**.

Next summer I **will help** my father in his store **once in a while**, not every day.

7. The word *still* is also used with several different tenses in affirmative, negative, and interrogative statements. With the simple present, it indicates an activity that has not changed over a period of time.

*My 1985 Toyota **still runs** well.*

With the present continuous, *still* indicates an activity that is happening at the moment of speaking.

*I'll be ready in a few minutes; **I'm still combing** my hair.*

With the simple past, *still* indicates an activity that did not change over a period of time.

*The teacher patiently explained my mistakes to me, but I **still didn't understand.***

With the past continuous, *still* indicates an activity that is in progress at a given point in time in the past.

*At four o'clock, the teacher **was still trying** to help me.*

With the present perfect, *still* indicates an activity that started in the past but is not yet completed at the moment of speaking.

*I **still haven't completed** last week's assignment.*

With the future, *still* indicates a situation that will not change.

*I **will still love** you after we're old and gray.*

Exercise 13 *First, underline the time expressions in the sentences. Then write the correct tense of the verb* talk *to fit the time expressions.*

1. I _____ to my parents every week.

2. I _____ to my parent every week last quarter.

3. I _____ to my parents yet.

4. I _____ to my parents for two straight hours.

5. I _____ to my parents from eight to ten yesterday evening.

6. I _____ to my parents two days from now.

7. I _____ to my parents at the moment.

8. I _____ to my parents occasionally.

9. I _____ to my parents five times since the quarter began.

10. I _____ to my parents three days ago.

Exercise 14 ▪▪▪
▪▪▪▪▪▪▪▪▪▪▪▪
First, underline the time expressions in the sentences. Then write the correct tense of the verb protest *to fit the time expressions.*

1. Some students _____ front of the dean's office now.

2. They _____ again this coming Thursday.

3. They _____ in front of his office since eight o'clock this morning.

4. They _____ while we were in class.

5. They _____ two weeks from today.

6. They _____ for the past two hours.

7. They seldom _____ in front of the dean's office last year.

8. They _____ to the president yet.

9. They _____ in a few minutes.

10. They _____ ever since this morning.

11. They _____ last Friday.

12. They _____ still _____ in front of the dean's office.

13. They _____ in two weeks.

Exercise 15 ▪▪▪
▪▪▪▪▪▪▪▪▪▪▪▪
First, read the account and underline the time expressions. Then complete the account, using the correct form of the verbs in parentheses.

I _____ (visit) quite a few cities since 1993. In June of 1993, I
_____1_____

_____ (finish) high school in Michigan. After my graduation, my
_____2_____

parents _____ (send) me to Stanford University in California. After one
_____3_____

year at Stanford, I _____ (ask) my father if I could go to the Sorbonne
_____4_____

in France. He _____ (agree) to let me go, so in June of 1994, I
_____5_____

_____ (fly) to Paris, France.
_____6_____

It's now 1996, and I _____ (be) in France for two years. At first, it
was difficult for me to understand the French language, but I _____
(study) very hard, and little by little, I _____ (learn) to speak French
very well. I _____ (like) the French language. In fact, I
_____ (like) it since I was in junior high school.

Of course, my life _____ (be) very busy since I came to Europe.
I _____ (work) hard, and I _____ (meet) many
interesting people. Last month, I _____ (go) to Italy, and next
month, I _____ (go) to Spain. While I _____ (stay)
in Italy, I _____ (see) my friend Karl, whose parents live in Germany.
He _____ (invite) me to meet them, so we _____
(hitchhike) to Berlin. He _____ (introduce) me to his mother and father,
who _____ (make) me feel very comfortable in their home. I
_____ (never, forget) their kindness.

I _____ (complete) my studies next year. Right now, I
_____ (think about) my return to Michigan, but I realize that I
_____ (miss) my friends in Europe.

Exercise 16   *First, read the account and underline the time expressions.
Then complete the account, using the correct form of the
verbs in parentheses. When you finish, be ready to discuss
the use of various tenses and to explain why more than one
tense is correct for some sentences.*

Last week, on Wednesday, we _____ (have) our first grammar test.
It _____ (be) a test on the tenses. The instructor _____
(not be) very happy with the results because not enough students _____
(receive) high grades. As a result, on Thursday, she _____ (review)

the test with the class. While we _____ (talk) about the test and

₆

the correct use of the tenses, I _____ (think) about how difficult it

₇

_____ (be) to learn to use the tenses spontaneously. I

₈

_____ (be) a little disappointed with my grade because this test

₉

_____ (be) the first grammar exam that we _____ (have)

₁₀ ₁₁

so far, and I really _____ (want) to get a good grade.

₁₂

Since we _____ (be) in class, we _____ (discuss) how

₁₃ ₁₄

the tenses show meaning, but I have to say that I _____ (still, have) a

₁₅

little trouble with this. I _____ (have) trouble with meaning since I first

₁₆

_____ (begin) to study English.

₁₇

At the moment, I _____ (see) that every student _____

₁₈ ₁₉

(concentrate on) this exercise. Our instructor _____ (stand) in front of

₂₀

the class now, but a few minutes ago she _____ (walk) around the room

₂₁

looking at our papers. After our review, last Thursday, I _____ (feel)

₂₂

better about the tenses, so today I _____ (feel) confident, and I

₂₃

_____ (believe) that I _____ (do) well on this exercise.

₂₄ ₂₅

As I _____ (mention) earlier, changing from one tense to another

₂₆

_____ (be, never) easy for me; however, I _____ (know)

₂₇ ₂₈

I _____ (continue) to improve until the end of the quarter.

₂₉

Exercise 17 *Write a composition, using the questions as a guide. Do not merely answer the questions; add additional information where appropriate. Use the simple present, simple past, present continuous, past continuous, present perfect, and present perfect continuous tenses. Your composition should be at least two and a half pages long.*

Paragraph 1

1. Where were you living when you received your acceptance letter to the intensive English program?
2. When did you arrive here?
3. How long have you been here?
4. In which level are you studying this quarter?

Paragraph 2

1. Generally speaking, do you enjoy traveling by plane?
2. How was your plane ride to the United States?
3. What were you thinking about when the plane took off?

Paragraph 3

1. What do you like about this city?
2. What do you not like about it?
3. What have you seen since you have been here?
4. Where have you gone since you have been here?
5. What have you been doing since classes started?

Paragraph 4

1. What are you planning to do during the next vacation period?
2. What do you plan to do after you finish studying English?

LESSON TWO

■ 2-1 PAST PERFECT

By the time the package arrived,
$\left\{\begin{array}{l}\text{I}\\\text{he}\\\text{she}\\\text{we}\\\text{you}\\\text{they}\end{array}\right\}$
had (not) left.

Had $\left\{\begin{array}{l}\text{you}\\\text{he}\\\text{she}\\\text{they}\end{array}\right\}$ **left** by the time the package arrived?

Yes, $\left\{\begin{array}{l}\text{I}\\\text{we}\\\text{he}\end{array}\right\}$ **had.**

No, $\left\{\begin{array}{l}\text{she}\\\text{they}\end{array}\right\}$ **hadn't.**

1. The past perfect is formed with *had (not)* + the past participle. The contraction for the past perfect is *'d (I'd left, he'd left, she'd left, we'd left, you'd left, they'd left).*

2. The past perfect is used in English to talk about an action in the past that happened before another action in the past. The first past action is in the past perfect. The second past action is in the simple past.

PAST		*PRESENT* *(now)*	*FUTURE*
had left	**arrived**		
✕	✕		
past perfect **(first action)**	simple past **(second action)**		

The past perfect indicates that the first action had finished completely before the second action started.

3. The past perfect usually occurs with the simple past, but the past perfect can be the only tense in a sentence if a specific past time is given. The past perfect is often used with *by* + a time.

By three o'clock *Professor Larson's lecture* **had ended.**

4. The past perfect is often used with the words *already, just, never, ever,* and *yet* to emphasize the event that happened first.

   When I got home, my roommate **had already cleaned** *the apartment.*

   I was surprised because he **had never cleaned** *the apartment before.*

   I **had just started** *to tell my roommate how nice the apartment looked when the phone rang.*

5. If it is clear which action happened first, the simple past can be used for both actions. In these sentences, the words *after* and *before* make the relationship between two actions clear.

   After *I finished reading the book, I lent it to Bob.*

   Before *I arrived, the library closed.*

6. If it is not clear which action happened first, it is necessary to use the past perfect. Note the difference in meaning between these sentences.

   When Professor Dance **gave** *her lecture, she* **sat** *down.* (She was speaking and sitting at the same time.)

   When Professor Dance **had given** *her lecture, she* **sat** *down.* (She stood and gave her lecture; then she sat down.)

7. Note the comma after a time clause when it appears at the beginning of the sentence. There is no comma when the time clause is not at the beginning of the sentence.

   When Professor Dance had given her lecture, she sat down.

   Professor Dance sat down when she had given her lecture.

Exercise 1 *With another student, discuss the difference in meaning between the pairs of sentences.*

1. a. When I got to the office, Andrea left.
    b. When I got to the office, Andrea had left.

2. a. We realized that someone was in your apartment.
    b. We realized that someone had been in your apartment.

3. a. I arrived at the meeting. The meeting started.
    b. I arrived at the meeting. The meeting had started.

4. a. There wasn't anything we could do about the problem. We packed our bags.
    b. There wasn't anything we could do about the problem. We had packed our bags.

5. a. Kim was happy. She wrote two letters.
    b. Kim was happy. She had written two letters.

Exercise 2   ■■   *Complete the sentences, using the past perfect.*
■ ■ ■ ■ ■ ■ ■ ■ ■ ■ ■

Example: By the time Ko came to the United States,
          he had finished two years of college.

1. He had sent in his housing application three months before he left his country, so when he arrived on campus, the housing office _____.

2. By the time he found his dormitory room, his new roommate _____.

3. He was very tired from the long plane ride, so he overslept the first morning. By the time he got to the cafeteria, _____.

4. His roommate ate breakfast without him because _____.

5. His roommate's father was in the diplomatic corps for twenty years, so Ko's roommate's family traveled all over the world. By the time Ko's roommate was eleven, he _____.

6. Ko, however, at first found living in a foreign country very unsettling because _____.

Exercise 3   ■■   *Complete the sentences, using the past perfect.*
■ ■ ■ ■ ■ ■ ■ ■ ■ ■ ■

1. Last week we had a test. Ali overslept, so when he got to class, _____.

2. By the time he began the test, the other students _____.

3. He had a lot of trouble with Part I of the test, so when the instructor asked for the papers, Ali _____.

4. As soon as Ali had given the instructor his paper, she returned it because he _____.

5. When he got home, his apartment door was open and the place was a mess. Someone _____.

6. He ran to the closet and looked for his new coat, but it was gone. He felt terrible because his parents _____.

7. He began to clean the apartment immediately, so by the time I arrived, he _____.

8. I was surprised when he told me what _____.

Exercise 4 ▪ ▪
▪ ▪ ▪ ▪ ▪ ▪ ▪ ▪ ▪ ▪ ▪ ▪

Make a list of accomplishments or important events in your life, using the past perfect. If you are older than 18, add a few more sentences up until two years ago. When you finish, compare your events with those of another student.

Example: By the time I was 12, *I had started helping out in my mother's grocery store.*

1. By the time I was 1, I _____.

2. By the time I was 2, I _____.

3. By the time I was 3, I _____.

4. By the time I was 5, I _____.

5. By the time I was 8, I _____.

6. By the time I was 11, I _____.

7. By the time I was 14, I _____.

8. By the time I was 16, I _____.

9. By the time I was 17, I _____.

10. By the time I was 18, I _____.

Exercise 5 ▪ ▪
▪ ▪ ▪ ▪ ▪ ▪ ▪ ▪ ▪ ▪ ▪ ▪

Check (✓) the severe weather conditions that have happened in your hometown (or an area near your hometown) in the past few years. Then make a list of what people can do or should do to prepare for the conditions that you have checked. Finally, tell another student the preparations you had made or hadn't made before the event. Add any severe weather conditions that are not listed below but that occur in your hometown.

flood	*snow storm*	*Other* _____
	hurricane	*typhoon*

Example: *By the time the hurricane struck, we had stocked up on bottled water*

and canned food, but we hadn't boarded up the windows of our house.

That's why the house suffered some damage.

Exercise 6 ■ ■
■ ■ ■ ■ ■ ■ ■ ■ ■ ■ ■

Read the pairs of sentences. First, decide which action happened first. Then combine the sentences, putting the first action in the past perfect. Use when *and by the time.*

1. The snow storm arrived. Mario put snow tires on his car, so he wasn't worried.
2. The first snowflake fell. Mario made a warm fire and was enjoying the view.
3. Eight feet of snow fell. The storm was over.
4. A lot of cars got stuck in the snow. The police closed some highways.
5. The police closed some highways. Nina left work. She was going to have a very difficult time getting home.
6. The snow became very deep. Many travelers found hotel rooms for the night, so they were not in danger.
7. The storm came. The television weathercasters warned everyone to expect it, but some people were not prepared.
8. Schools were shut for four days. They reopened.

Exercise 7 ■ ■
■ ■ ■ ■ ■ ■ ■ ■ ■ ■ ■

In a group of three or four, discuss things you had never done before coming to study (and/or live) in this country.

■ 2-2 PAST PERFECT CONTINUOUS

I
He
She } **had (not) been sleeping** for a long time when someone rang the doorbell.
We
They

Had { you
he
she
they } **been sleeping** for a long time when the package arrived?

Yes, { I
he
she } **had.**

No, { we
they } **hadn't.**

1. The past perfect continuous is formed with *had (not) + been +* the present participle.

2. The past perfect continuous is used in English to emphasize the continuous nature of an action that happened before another action in the past. Compare:

   Chris **had waited** *for an hour when she decided to leave.*

   Chris **had been waiting** *for an hour when she decided to leave.*

   Both sentences are correct, but in the second sentence the speaker or writer emphasizes the duration of the waiting.

3. The past perfect continuous can also be used to emphasize that the first action was recent to the second action or another time in the past.

   The class **had discussed** *the final exam when the instructor came in.* (They had started the discussion before the instructor entered and were talking about something else when the instructor came in.)

   The class **had been discussing** *the final exam when the instructor came in.* (They had started the discussion shortly before the instructor entered. Either they had just finished when the instructor walked in, or they were still discussing the final exam when the instructor walked in.)

4. The past perfect continuous is *not* used when you mention the number of times something was done.

   Correct: *I didn't go to the hospital to see Sue yesterday because I* **had** *already* **visited** *her twice this week.*

   Incorrect: *I didn't go to the hospital to see Sue yesterday because I had already been visiting her twice this week.*

5. The past perfect continuous is often used with *for +* a time.

Exercise 8   *Complete each sentence, using the past perfect or the past perfect continuous.*

1. My brother has always been a superb swimmer. By the time he was ten years old, he _____ (win) many medals.

2. When he finished high school, he _____ (be) captain of the swimming team for four years.

3. He is now training for the national championship games, so he goes jogging every morning from 5:30 to 8:00. By 7:30 this morning, he _____ (jog) for two hours.

4. When I got up at 9:00, he _____ (shower), _____ (eat), and _____ (leave) for work.

5. Our neighbor was very sick last night, and by the time he called us, his temperature _____ (reach) 102 degrees Fahrenheit.

6. We called the hospital before we left home, so when we reached the emergency room, the doctor _____ (wait) for thirty minutes.

7. The doctor gave him a shot, so by the time we returned home, he _____ (begin) to feel a little better.

8. He was glad he _____ (come) to us for help because he _____ (not feel) well for a couple of days.

Exercise 9 *Complete each sentence, using the correct form of the verbs in parentheses. Use the simple past, past perfect, or the past perfect continuous.*

1. Carla _____ (go) to the department store and _____ (return) the dress she _____ (buy).

2. She _____ (return) home happy because the clerk _____ (refund) her money.

3. She _____ (begin) to watch a movie on television when she _____ (finish) dinner.

4. She _____ (change) from Channel 7 to Channel 4 because she _____ (already see) the movie on Channel 7.

5. She _____ (watch) the movie for a while when she _____ (become) bored.

6. She _____ (just turn off) the set when the telephone
   _____ (ring).

7. By the time she _____ (answer) it, the person on the other end
   _____ (hang up).

8. It was getting late, so she _____ (decide) to take a shower and go
   to bed.

9. She _____ (just get) undressed when someone _____
   (knock) on the door.

10. After she _____ (put on) her robe, she _____ (open) the
    door and _____ (discover) that someone _____ (leave)
    her a package.

11. After she _____ (close) the door, she _____ (sit down) and
    _____ (try) to figure out who _____ (give) her the package.

12. When she _____ (open) the package, she _____ (be)
    surprised to see a birthday card and a beautiful scarf.

Exercise 10   *With another student, respond to each sentence, using the*
past perfect progressive. All the sentences are about the
Dixon family. Neal and Diana have seven children, and life is
never perfect.

1. Neal couldn't get through on the phone to his wife because the line was busy for over an hour. He was angry with his daughter Chris when he got home.

2. Diana was upset with their son Danny when he came home from school with cuts and bruises on his face and arms.

3. Neal was annoyed with their daughter Sheila. At 1:00 in the afternoon she came downstairs in her nightgown and was rubbing her eyes.

4. Diana was upset with their three-year-old son, Stevie. He came in the room just before dinner with chocolate all over his hands and face.

5. Diana was annoyed with her eight-year-old daughter, Lizzy. When Diana went into her office to do some work, she found Lizzy's dolls and other toys all over the floor.

6. When Neal and Diana came home late one Saturday night, the house was a mess. There were at least a dozen empty pizza boxes and a lot of soda cans in the living room. Also, the furniture had been moved, and there were CD boxes all over the place. They were angry with their son Kevin.

7. Larry, their oldest son, was supposed to meet his father at 5:00. He didn't show up until 6:00. Neal was angry with Larry.

8. And Diana and Neal were also angry with the family dog, Crackers. They found a large hole in their flower garden.

Exercise 11 *Complete the paragraph, using the correct form of the verbs in parentheses. You will need to use a variety of tenses.*

Last Saturday, my friend and I _____ (decide) to drive to Central
                                        1
City. This _____ (be) a small mountain town about twenty-five miles
                  2
west of Denver. In the late 1800s, Central City _____ (be) a successful
                                                          3
mining town where people _____ (find) silver and gold in large
                                    4
quantities. Today, during the summer, the town _____ (be) full of
                                                            5
tourists from all over the world, but in the autumn this small community usually

_____ (have) a peaceful atmosphere. However, this was not true last
        6
Saturday.

When we _____ (arrive), there _____ (be) hundreds of
                    7   8
people standing behind thick ropes, and huge trucks loaded with cameras and

electronic equipment filled the streets. Small groups of people dressed in the style of

the old West _____ (walk) casually along the sidewalks. As my friend
                      9
and I _____ (move) toward the crowd of people, we _____
            10   11
(stop) a local police officer and _____ (ask) him what
                                            12
_____ (happen). He _____ (tell) us that a Hollywood
        13   14
movie studio _____ (make) a movie and that the crowd
                        15
_____ (be) there since 6:30 in the morning. It was now 11:00 A.M. The
        16
police officer _____ (get up) at 5:00 A.M. to direct the traffic and keep
                        17
order. He also told us that Kevin Costner and Meg Ryan were the stars of the movie.

Both these performers _____ (be) excellent actors, so we
                                18
_____ (probably, see) the movie when it is finished.
        19

Neither my friend nor I _____ (ever, watch) a Hollywood studio
                                20
make a movie before, so we were glad we _____ (choose) to drive west
                                                        21
to Central City instead of going south to Colorado Springs.

We _____ (push) through the crowd to get closer to the camera
        22
operators, director, and actors on the other side of the rope. We were finally in a
position to see all the activity. As we _____ (stand) there waiting for the
                                                    23
action to begin, a woman _____ (point to) a man who was talking to the
                                    24
director of the movie. The man _____ (be) Kevin Costner. I really like
                                            25
him. In fact, I _____ (see) most of his movies, but I _____
                    26   27
(never, see) him in person before that day. Suddenly a man _____ (yell),
                                                                        28
"QUIET!" Everyone _____ (become) silent, and the director shouted,
                            29
"ACTION!"

LESSON THREE

■ 3-1 FUTURE CONTINUOUS

I
He
She   } **will (not)**
It

                        be working tonight.

We
You   } **are (not) going to**
They

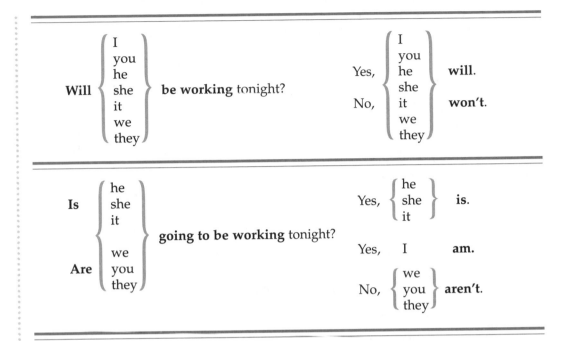

1. The future continuous is formed with *will (not)* + *be* + the present participle or with a form of *be going to* + *be* + the present participle.

2. The future continuous expresses an action that will be in progress at a specific time in the future.

   *Don't call my roommate tonight between seven and eleven. She **will be studying** for a test.*

   *This is Reza's last course in the intensive English program. This time next semester he's **going to be taking** engineering courses.*

3. The future continuous also expresses an action that will continue to happen at different times in the future.

   Instructor: *Welcome to the class. In this course, you will have a test after every chapter, a midterm exam, and a final exam.*

   Student: *Is that all?*

   Instructor: *No. **I'm going to be giving** surprise quizzes from time to time.*

   Student: *And **I'll be suffering** from headaches all semester.*

4. The future continuous also expresses an action that will happen at an unknown time in the future. This will happen as a matter of course.

   Gita: *Did you get a letter from your boyfriend?*

   Yuko: *No, not today.*

> **Gita:**   *You haven't heard from him for a month. Aren't you a little worried?*
> **Yuko:**   *No. I'**ll be getting** a letter or a phone call from him soon.*

Exercise 1

Complete the sentences, using the future continuous or the simple future (will + verb.)

1. **A:** I hope you don't mind if I drop the report off tomorrow at around 9:00.
   B: Oh, that should be fine. I _____ (not do) anything special.

2. **A:** What should we serve for dinner next Sunday?
   B: I don't know, but don't make lamb. Myra _____ (like) it.

3. **A:** How _____ (I/recognize) you?
   B: I _____ (hold) some flowers.

4. **A:** How do you know Brian _____ (sleep) when we get home?
   B: Because it's 11:30. He always goes to bed at 10:00.

5. **A:** Let's have dinner at Dillon's.
   B: No. It _____ (cost) too much.

6. **A:** It _____ (take) a long time to get to Stephanie's place by bus.
   B: Then we'd better take a taxi.

7. **A:** Will anybody be at the airport when your plane arrives?
   B: I think my sister _____ (wait) for me.

8. **A:** He doesn't understand.
   B: I _____ (explain) it to him.

9. **A:** Should I stop by in a couple of hours to see Harold?
   B: No. He _____ (attend) a meeting then. Why don't you come at 4:30?

10. **A:** Don't wait up for me. I _____ (finish) late tonight.
    B: Okay. But I _____ (leave) your dinner on the stove.

Exercise 2

Write down a time that you would like to get together with your classmates next Saturday. Then walk around the room and find out what they will be doing at that time. Talk to as many classmates as possible. Write down the names of those students who will be free and the plans of those students who will not be free. How many students will be able to get together with you?

■ 3-2 FUTURE PERFECT AND FUTURE PERFECT CONTINUOUS

■ Future Perfect ■

I He She We You They	**will (not) have finished** by next week.

Will	I he she we you they	**have finished** by next week?	Yes, No,	I he she we you they **will.** **won't.**

1. The future perfect is formed with *will (not)* + *have* + the past participle.

2. The future perfect expresses an action that will be finished at some time in the future. English speakers do not usually use this tense unless the completion time of the activity is clear.

   The next time we meet I **will have completed** *the courses for my Masters degree.*
   Rita already has her Masters, and she **will have gotten** *her Ph.D. before she's 25.*

3. The future perfect is often used with *by* + a time, *before* + a time, or *in* + a time.

   We **will have finished** *this review of tenses* **by the end of this week.**
   Before this course is finished, *my classmates and I* **will have taken** *20 quizzes.*
   Our instructor **will have gotten** *his new car* **in two weeks**.

4. Adverbs such as *already, probably,* and *certainly* are placed after the first auxiliary.

   By the end of this week, we will **certainly** *have finished this review.*
   Don't worry. Before the party begins I will **already** *have cleaned our apartment.*

Part 1

▪ **Future Perfect Continuous** ▪

I
He
She
We
You
They
} **will (not) have been studying** English for six months by the end of this course.

Will {
you
he
she
we
they
} **have been studying** English for six months by the end of this course?

Yes, {
I
you
he
she
we
they
} **will.**

No, **won't.**

1. The future perfect continuous is formed with *will (not) + have been +* the present participle.

2. The future perfect continuous emphasizes the continuous nature of an action that will be in progress at a specific time in the future before another action.

   *By the time we get to Baltimore, we **will have been driving** for six hours.*

3. The future perfect continuous cannot be used with verbs that do not usually occur in a continuous form. Only verbs that show continuous action can be used. These verbs include *study, work, travel, write, listen,* and *watch.*

   Correct: *I **will have been studying** English for three semesters by the time I take the TOEFL exam.*

   Incorrect: *I will have been finishing the review for the test by next week.* (A person can't keep on finishing something.)

Exercise 3   *With another student, discuss the difference in meaning between the pairs of sentences.*

1. a. I'll have cleaned the apartment by 2:00.

    b. I'll have been cleaning the apartment by 2:00.

2. a. I'll start cooking at 5:30.

    b. I'll have started cooking by 5:30.

3. a. When you get here, my mother will rest.

    b. By the time you get here, my mother will have been resting for awhile.

4. a. Jack will retire in June.

    b. Jack will have retired by June.

5. a. When we get there, the director will leave.

    b. By the time we get there, the director will have left.

6. a. I'll pay the rent at the end of the month.

    b. I'll have paid the rent before the end of the month.

Exercise 4   *Imagine the perfect life in the year 2015. How do you hope the world will have changed by then? How do you hope your hometown will be different? What do you hope you will have accomplished? Make a list of your hopes, using the future perfect. When you finish, compare lists with another student. How many similar hopes do you have?*

Example: I hope that by the year 2015 I will have made a lot of money.

Exercise 5   *The president of one country and the prime minister of another country are going to meet next week. With another student, use the schedule of the president's activities for Monday to ask and answer the questions that follow. Use the future continuous or the future perfect.*

MONDAY

8:00–8:50	Conference with presidential advisors
9:00–9:50	Breakfast meeting with the prime minister, the president, and their interpreters
10:00–10:50	Television speech by the president on peace relations between two countries
11:00–11:50	President and prime minister and their wives will visit automobile factory.
12:00–1:00	Private lunch with presidential advisors
1:00–3:00	Discussion of import-export needs of the two countries: president, prime minister, and ministers of trade
3:00–3:30	Signing ceremonies for new trade treaty
3:35–4:00	Meeting with television and newspaper reporters: president and prime minister
4:00–5:00	Rest in hotel
5:00	Get ready for formal dinner at 6:00.

Examples: on Monday morning at 8:00 / what / the president / do

On Monday morning at 8:00, what will the president be doing?

He'll be talking with his advisers.

what / already / happen / before 9:00

What will already have happened before 9:00?

He'll already have met with his advisers.

1. what / the president / do / at 9:00

2. whom / the president / meet with / at 9:00

3. by 10:00 / what two things / the president and prime minister / already do

4. at what time / the president / make / his speech on television

5. what / happen / at 11:00

6. what four things / the president / already do / by 1:00

7. why / these officials / meet / from 1:00 to 3:00

8. by 4:00 / what important document / they / sign

9. when / the president and prime minister / meet / with reporters

10. the president / tour / the city from 4:00 to 5:00

11. by approximately what time / the president / get / ready to go to dinner

12. before the day is over / how many meetings / the president / have

Exercise 6 *In a group of three or four, take turns asking and answering the questions. Answer in complete sentences.*

1. What will you probably be doing at eight o'clock tonight?

2. Which assignments will you be working on tonight?

3. Will you have finished today's homework assignments before eleven o'clock tonight?

4. At nine o'clock tomorrow morning, will you still be sleeping?

5. By five o'clock tomorrow, which classes will you have already had?

6. By 12:30 tomorrow, will you have finished lunch?

7. At this time next year, what will you be doing?

8. Will you have completed your university degree by the time you return to your country?

9. Will you be studying in the summer?

10. Where do you think you will be living next year?

11. By next year, how long will you have been living in the United States?

12. Do you know anyone who will be getting married this summer?

13. Who do you know who will have been married for more than two years at the end of this year?

14. By the time you finish your studies in the United States, will your parents have had a chance to visit you here?

Exercise 7 *Complete the note from a teacher to her students.*

While I _____ (sit) at my desk at home, trying to think of an interesting
                1
way to test your understanding of the tenses, I suddenly _____ (have)
                                                                      2
the idea of writing you a note.

As all of you know, class _____ (begin) eleven days ago, so we
_____ (be) together for approximately two weeks. At the start of the
quarter, our class _____ (have) only thirteen students; however, it
_____ (grow) to sixteen students on the third day. We are now in the
second full week of classes, so I _____ (know) we _____
(get, not) any additional students.

By now, all of you know that I _____ (love) to teach grammar. During
my teaching career, I _____ (teach) many subjects, but for some reason I
_____ (always, enjoy, teach) grammar. All your courses
_____ (be) important, but I _____ (believe) that grammar is
especially important because speaking, reading, and writing well depend on a good
understanding of the structure of a language.

During the time that we _____ (be) in class, some of you
_____ (complain) about doing homework. I _____ (realize)
that you _____ (take) other classes, and I _____ (understand)
that the life of a student _____ (be) not easy. However, remember that I
_____ (be) still a student, too. Last week while I _____
(study) in the library, I _____ (ask) myself why I was working so hard.
Then I _____ (remember) that one of my goals _____ (be,
always) to finish my Ph.D. You _____ (have) goals, too, so you must work
hard until you reach them. As I _____ (promise) the other day, I
_____ (give, never) you an assignment that will take hours to complete;
however, during the first half of the quarter I _____ (give) you an
assignment almost every night because I want you to improve your English as quickly
as possible.

Some of you _____ (complete, not) your assignments, and as a result
you _____ (have) trouble in class. Generally speaking, however, this is a
good class, and all of you _____ (be) very intelligent individuals. Work
hard and accomplish your own individual goals. By the time this quarter is over, you
_____ (learn) much, and you _____ (be) one step closer to
your dream.

Practice Exam

■ SECTION 1

Find the tense mistake in each sentence and correct it. In some sentences there is more than one mistake.

1. Pollution is a serious problem since 1970.

2. In the past, nobody was caring about the problem.

3. Many countries still try to solve this problem today.

4. Before everyone realized the dangers, pollution became a major threat to the environment.

5. Every day, some company has been polluting the environment.

6. In the early 1960s, the problem is unnoticed.

7. Last week, while I am listening to the news, I have heard that pollution is now a major problem in several countries.

8. I am in the United States for two months, but I have not been buying a car yet.

9. Last month, I am thinking about buying a used car.

10. My father has sent me a lot of money last month, so now I can buy a new car.

11. By this time next month, I am driving a new sports car.

12. I went to a car dealer last night, but he already closed.

■ SECTION 2

Complete the paragraphs, using the correct form of the verbs in parentheses.

One thing I _____ (notice) since I _____ (be) in the
                        1   2
United States _____ (be) the number of cars. As is true in many large
                    3
cities in the world, the streets of Denver _____ (be) filled with
                                              4
automobiles. Although the automobile _____ (become) a necessity for
                                          5

many people, it _____ (be) a dangerous necessity. For example, cars
6

_____ (pollute) the air in cities for many years. In addition to pollution,
7

the automobile _____ (increase) the problem of congestion in crowded
8

urban areas. A professor of medicine and public health from Yale University

_____ (believe) that the automobile _____ (be) responsible
9   10

for a large number of the heart attacks that Americans have because they

_____ (not, walk) much any more.
11

   While I _____ (read) a report on pollution in the United States the
12

other night, I _____ (learn) that the average American family
13

_____ (own) two cars and many _____ (have) three. It is
14   15

obvious that cars _____ (contribute) a great deal to the problem of
16

pollution that this country _____ (have). One solution, of course,
17

_____ (be) to create better systems of public transportation. If the large
18

cities do not create better systems of public transportation, by the year 2015 many

Americans _____ (buy) gas masks, and they _____ (wear)
19   20

them everywhere they go.

   However, the automobile may not be a big problem in the future because of the

cost of fuel. In this country at the moment, the big American oil companies

_____ (have) a lot of trouble. In fact, they _____ (have) a
21   22

lot of trouble since they _____ (begin) to raise the price of gasoline. In
23

the summer of 1979, the oil companies _____ (increase) the price of
24

gasoline dramatically, and the American public _____ (become)
25

extremely angry. Many people _____ (not believe) that it
26

_____ (be) necessary for the companies to ask for more money because
27

they _____ (receive) very high profits for many years. Many citizens
28

_____ (sell) their large cars, and they _____ (buy) smaller
29   30

ones. This _____ (create) another problem in this country for at least
31

one of the large automobile manufacturers, the Chrysler Corporation, located in

Detroit, Michigan. Years ago, this company _____ (not see) the future
32

need for small cars, so it _____ (manufacture) only big cars. Today,
33

however, many Americans _____ (want) small automobiles. In 1979, the
                                          34
Chrysler Corporation _____ (ask) the U.S. government for money so it
                                    35
could prepare its factories to build small cars.

   Before I _____ (come) to the United States, I _____
                        32   33
(think about) buying a big car, but since I _____ (live) here,
                                                          34
I _____ (decide) to purchase a small economy car. Tomorrow,
            35
I _____ (go) with an American friend to look at the cars at his father's
            36
automobile dealership. His father _____ (promise) to give me a
                                                  37
good deal.

■ SECTION 3

Write your own sentences, using the time words and expressions indicated.

Example: all day yesterday

         <u>*I was studying all day yesterday.*</u>

   1. still

   2. by the end of this month

   3. between seven and ten o'clock tonight

   4. ago

   5. for two semesters

   6. while

   7. by the time

   8. yet

   9. in a few minutes

   10. every week

2 Coordination

■ INTRODUCTION TO PART 2 ■ ■ ■ ■ ■ ■ ■ ■

In English several methods are used to express two or more ideas in the same sentence. In this part, you will practice coordination as a method for combining two or more complete sentences not only to produce longer sentences but also to show the proper relationship between similar or related ideas.

A sentence is formed of one or more clauses. The word *clause* refers to a group of words that has a subject and a verb. In English there are two kinds of clauses: independent and dependent. An independent or main clause has a subject and a verb and makes sense by itself. All complete sentences contain an independent clause. A dependent or subordinate clause also has a subject and a verb, but it is not a complete sentence because it does not make sense by itself. Look at the following examples.

Independent Clauses	Dependent Clauses
I saw Kayoko yesterday.	*when I saw Kayoko yesterday*
She seemed very depressed.	*why she seemed very depressed*
She was going home.	*because she was going home*

Note that there are no periods at the end of dependent clauses because they are not complete sentences.

LESSON FOUR

■ 4-1 COORDINATING CONJUNCTIONS AND PARALLEL STRUCTURE

1. Coordinating conjunctions are words that connect structures that are the same. This is called parallel structure. These are the coordinating conjunctions in English: *and, but, for, nor, or, so,* and *yet.*

2. Coordinating conjunctions are used to connect

single words:

Nouns	**A**	*Men* **and** *women are the same.*
Adjectives	**B**	*My parents were* **poor** **but** **happy**.
Verbs	**C**	*Last night I* **was sitting** **and** **thinking** *about you.*
Objects	**D**	*This typewriter is* **for the secretary** **but not** *(for) the students.*
Infinitives	**E**	*I have* **to write** **and** **(to) type** *this paper tonight.*

prepositional phrases:

F   *There is still plenty of food* **in the living room** **and** **in the kitchen.**

G   *You can lie down* **on the bed** **or** **on the sofa.**

H   *This was* **in the book** **yet not** **on the exam.**

verb phrases:

I   *I* **am sitting** *here* **and** **writing** *a letter.*

J   *Nobody* **wants to do** *homework* **or (to) listen** *to records.*

K   *She* **had left** *the room* **and (had) gone** *to bed.*

dependent clauses (incomplete sentences):

L   **Where you go** **and** **what you do** *are not my concern.*

M   *We can talk* **while you are here** **or** **when you return home**.

N   *He is a person* **whom I respect** **and** **whom I will always admire**.

independent sentences (complete sentences):

O   *Jim loves Sue,* **and** *she loves him.*

P   *He proposed,* **so** *they got married.*

Q   *They lived in her hometown,* **yet** *they were not happy.*

R   *They stayed there,* **for** *they didn't have enough money to move.*

S   *Audrey didn't have a good job,* **nor** *did Jim.*

3. Coordinating conjunctions cannot connect different structures.

$\qquad\qquad\qquad\qquad$ Adj $\qquad\qquad$ Adj

Correct: *The journalist is successful and well liked.*

$\qquad\qquad\qquad\qquad$ Noun $\qquad\qquad$ Adj

Incorrect: *The journalist is a success and well liked.*

Correct: *Sarah told her children that they should stay in the house and that they*

                                                                    Inf

   shouldn't open the door. OR *Sarah told her children to stay in the house and*

        Inf

   not to open the door.

                        Modal Verb   Inf

Incorrect: *Sarah told her children that they should stay in the house and not to open the*
   door.

4. When a coordinating conjunction connects two dependent clauses, no punctuation is necessary. (See sentences **L**, **M**, and **N**.) But when a coordinating conjunction connects two independent clauses, a comma precedes the coordinating conjunction. (See sentences **O**, **P**, **Q**, **R**, and **S**.)

5. The coordinating conjunctions *for, nor,* and *so* can only be used to connect independent clauses. Therefore, *for, nor,* and *so* cannot be used to connect single words (as in sentences **A** to **E**), prepositional phrases (as in sentences **F** to **H**), verb phrases (as in sentences **I** to **K**), or dependent clauses (as in sentences **L** to **N**).

Exercise 1   *Correct the sentences so that the structures in each sentence are parallel. There is more than one way to correct some of the sentences.*

Example: Julie is a good singer and dances beautifully.

Julie is a good singer and a beautiful dancer. OR

Julie sings well and dances beautifully.

1. In the summer we like going to the beach and to play tennis.

2. My best friend is kind and always helps.

3. Walking and to swim are both good forms of exercise.

4. When people start driving less and if manufacturers make more fuel-efficient cars, there will be less environmental damage.

5. They had gotten married and went on their honeymoon before I even heard about the wedding.

6. The game is simple yet a great way to spend a few hours.

7. You need a haircut and to get some new clothes before you go for the interview.

8. A good teacher is someone who is patient and when you ask a question always explains clearly.

Exercise 2 ▪▪ *Use a parallel structure to complete each sentence.*
▪▪▪▪▪▪▪▪▪▪▪▪

1. Most people want to find a job that is well-paying and _____.

2. Traveling to a foreign country and _____ can be a wonderful experience.

3. To learn a foreign language, you must practice speaking it and _____.

4. Smoking is a bad habit and _____.

5. The police believed that the woman knew more than she was saying but _____.

6. The old man wanted to move in with a relative but not _____.

7. Computers are easy for young people to use yet _____.

8. The company needed to hire someone who could speak Italian and _____.

■ 4-2 CONNECTING COMPLETE SENTENCES

Conjunction	Meaning	Example
and	addition	*The phone rang, **and** someone knocked on the door.*
nor	addition	*You don't have to study, **nor** do you have to stay home.*
or	alternative	*You can stay home and study for the exam, **or** you can go out and enjoy yourself.*
or (else)	condition	*I have to study, **or (else)** I will fail the course.* (If I don't study for the exam, I will fail the course.)
but	contrast	*Dr. Jones was very sick, **but** he taught the class.*
yet	contrast	*His voice was very weak, **yet** the students understood him.*
for	cause	*Dr. Jones couldn't lecture for the entire hour, **for** he had a sore throat.*
so	result	*I've been working hard all year, **so** I'm going to take a vacation during the summer.*

1. When a coordinating conjunction connects two or more sentences, the statements on both sides of the conjunction must have a subject and a verb.

   I was going to call you last night, but my roommate was on the phone for three hours.
   I was too tired to wait, so I went to bed.

2. The coordinating conjunction *nor* connects two negative ideas. As in questions, the subject and auxiliary verb must be inverted after *nor*.

   I don't speak Korean, nor do I write it. (I don't speak Korean. I don't write it.)
   I haven't done my writing assignment, nor have I done the reading one. (I haven't done my writing assignment. I haven't done my reading one.)
   Ms. Valera is not here today, nor is Mr. Adams. (Ms. Valera is not here today. Mr. Adams is not here today.)

3. The coordinating conjunction *for* is more common in formal writing. In informal speech *because* is more common.

   Formal: *Dr. Jones couldn't lecture the entire hour, for he had a sore throat.*
   Informal: *Dr. Jones couldn't lecture the entire hour because he had a sore throat.*

4. Coordinating conjunctions have different meanings, so they show different relationships between the ideas in two clauses. The relationship must always be logical.

   Incorrect: *The grammar test on tenses was very long, but it took a long time to finish.*

   The above sentence has a subject and a verb in each independent clause, and there is a comma before the coordinating conjunction *but*. Nevertheless, the sentence is not logical. The word *but* shows contrast, so after it the writer needs a statement that contrasts with the first statement. *It took a long time to finish* is not in contrast to the first statement. The writer needs to use another conjunction or a slightly different sentence. Both these sentences would be logical.

   The grammar test on tenses was very long, so it took a long time to finish.
   The grammar test on tenses was very long, but it didn't take a long time to finish.

5. Remember that when a coordinating conjunction connects two complete sentences (independent clauses), a comma precedes the coordinating conjunction. If the clauses are short, the comma is not essential, but it is always safe to add the comma.

   INDEPENDENT CLAUSE + INDEPENDENT CLAUSE
   I love you, but I can't marry you.   *I love you but can't marry you.*

Exercise 3 ⬛ ⬛
⬛ ⬛ ⬛ ⬛ ⬛ ⬛ ⬛ ⬛ ⬛ ⬛ ⬛ ⬛   *Complete the sentences. Be sure that your completed sentences are logical.*

1. The life of a foreign student is sometimes difficult, yet _____.

2. The life of a foreign student is sometimes difficult, for _____.

3. The students in this program must pass three out of five courses, and _____.

4. The students in this program must pass three out of five courses, or _____.

5. I have always enjoyed studying languages, so _____.

6. I have always enjoyed studying languages, but _____.

7. Marcel has not enjoyed living in the United States, nor _____.

8. Marcel has not enjoyed living in the United States, for _____.

Exercise 4 ⬛ ⬛
⬛ ⬛ ⬛ ⬛ ⬛ ⬛ ⬛ ⬛ ⬛ ⬛ ⬛ ⬛   *With another student, complete the statements. When you finish, compare sentences with another pair of students.*

1. This course began a few weeks ago, and _____.

2. The students in the class down the hall are all men, but _____.

3. I didn't attend class yesterday, for _____.

4. Some students have been complaining about the amount of homework, yet _____.

5. Money cannot buy love, nor _____.

6. Some people love money more than anything else, so _____.

7. I've been working hard all my life, yet _____.

8. I've never had much money, and _____.

9. I don't have a government scholarship for studying, nor _____.

10. I was a terrible student in my country, so _____.

11. The embassy of one of my classmates pays for her tuition, books, and food, but _____.

12. After I finish my studies, I will get a job, or _____.

■ 4-3 CONNECTING MORE THAN TWO SENTENCES

1. When more than two sentences are combined, it may be necessary to make changes in the sentences so that they will sound smoother. For example, these sentences need to be connected.

   My parents wanted me to have the experience of studying in a foreign country.

   My parents wanted me to have the experience of learning another language.

   My parents do not want me to remain in a foreign country too long.

   My parents do not want me to change my cultural beliefs.

   The above four sentences could be combined into one sentence.

   *My parents wanted me to have the experience of studying in a foreign country **and** learning another language, **but** they do not want me to remain here long, **nor** do they want me to change my cultural beliefs.*

   Note that the above connected sentence combines similar structures (*studying . . . learning*), connects complete sentences (*but they do not want . . . , nor do they want*), and uses pronouns to avoid repeating the same nouns (*they* instead of *parents*).

2. When writing your own sentences, it is important *not* to produce a string of sentences.

   Good style:　*You can study in the university library or in the dormitory quiet room, but you must find a quiet place to work soon.*

   Poor style:　*You can study in the university library, or you can study in the dormitory quiet room, but you must find a quiet place to study, and you must find it soon.*

Exercise 5　*Combine the groups of sentences into one sentence. Make changes where necessary, and use the correct punctuation.*

1. I haven't had an opportunity to see much of this city.
   I haven't had an opportunity to spend much time with my friends.
   The teachers have been giving us a lot of homework.
   The teachers have been giving us a lot of tests.

2. This quarter, I really like my classmates.
   This quarter, I really like the teachers.
   The teachers are very strict.
   The teachers expect us to study hard.

3. My reading instructor is very good.
   My reading instructor is extremely patient.
   Learning new vocabulary words is very difficult for me.
   I spend more time studying for my reading class than for any other.

4. We have just finished a review of the tenses.
   I'm still having a little trouble with the tenses.
   I will continue to study the tenses on my own.

5. We're going to have a test on the conjunctions next week.
   I won't be able to go anywhere this weekend.
   I want to do well on the test.
   I want to make sure that my final grammar grade is high.

6. Juan, my roommate, is very fortunate.
   Juan doesn't have to worry about tuition.
   Juan doesn't have to worry about clothes.

   I don't have a scholarship.
   My father doesn't have much money.

7. One of my classmates was very upset last week.
   His embassy told him it would not continue to pay for his wife's studies.
   This classmate will try to convince the embassy to change its mind.
   His wife is intelligent.
   His wife is interested in learning.

8. Ali will complete his English studies this quarter.
   Ali is not going to begin university work immediately.
   Ali is not planning to visit his country.
   Ali wants to travel around for a while.

LESSON FIVE

■ 5-1 CORRELATIVE CONJUNCTIONS: *Either . . . Or*

▪ **Connecting Similar Structures** ▪

A You must tell the truth. You must go to jail.

*You must **either** tell the truth **or** go to jail.* (connecting two verb phrases)

B A person is honest. A person is dishonest.

*A person is **either** honest **or** dishonest.* (connecting two adjectives)

C I will see you at home. I will see you in jail.

*I will see you **either** at home **or** in jail.* (connecting two prepositional phrases)

D I can call your father. I can call your mother.

*I can call **either** your father **or** your mother.* (connecting two noun objects)

1. The correlative conjunctions *either . . . or* mean *one or the other*. They indicate a choice or alternative and connect two affirmative ideas.

2. When two verbs or verb phrases are connected with auxiliaries, *either* follows the auxiliary verb. The auxiliary is not repeated after *or*.

   *You must **either** tell the truth **or** go to jail.*
   *He has **either** lost his watch **or** misplaced it.*
   *She is **either** crying **or** laughing very hard.*

   When there are two auxiliary verbs, *either* follows the first one.

        (1)   (2)
   *You have **either** been sleeping **or** watching television.*

3. When using *either . . . or* to connect similar structures, remember to place *either* as close as possible to the structure it is identifying.

      Correct: *I can call **either** your father **or** your mother.*
    Incorrect: *I can either call your father or your mother.*

4. Singular subjects joined by *either . . . or* take a singular verb after *or*. Plural subjects joined by *either . . . or* take a plural verb after *or*.

   Either my roommate or I am going to go to the party.

   Either my parents or my sisters are going to visit me this summer.

   If one subject is singular and the other subject is plural, the verb agrees with the subject after *or*, that is, the subject closest to the verb.

   *Either my **parents** or my **sister is** going to visit me.*

   *Either my **sister** or my **parents are** going to visit me.*

5. Note that in sentences **A** to **D**, the subjects of the two sentences are the same. It is *not* possible to connect similar structures if the subjects of the sentences are different. Therefore, the similar structures in the following sentences cannot be connected.

   ***You** will tell the truth. **I** will report you to the police.*

   Incorrect: *You will either tell the truth or report you to the police.*

■ Connecting Two Complete Sentences ■

A You must tell the truth. You must go to jail.

   Either you must tell the truth, or you must go to jail.

B A person is honest. A person is dishonest.

   Either a person is honest, or a person is dishonest.

C I will see you at home. I will see you in jail.

   Either I will see you at home, or I will see you in jail.

D I can call your father. I can call your mother.

   Either I can call your father, or I can call your mother.

E You will tell the truth. I will report you to the police.

   Either you will tell the truth, or I will report you to the police.

1. When two complete sentences are connected, a comma follows the first sentence.

   Either the baby is sick, or he is tired.

A comma is not needed when similar structures are connected.

The baby is either sick or tired.

2. Note that in sentences **A** to **D**, the subjects of the two sentences are the same, but the subjects in the **E** sentences are different. It is possible to connect two complete sentences even if the subjects of the sentences are different.

Exercise 1   *Connect the sentences, using* either . . . or *in two ways. First, connect the sentences by using similar structures. Then connect them in complete sentences.*

Example: I will study during the summer quarter. I will take a vacation.

I will either study during the summer or take a vacation.

Either I will study during the summer quarter, or I will take a vacation.

1. Jim and Bob jog every morning. They do push-ups.

   _____

   _____

2. Jim runs around the park. He runs around the block.

   _____

   _____

3. They will make the U.S. Olympic team. They will be very disappointed.

   _____

   _____

4. Bob won a gold medal. He won a silver medal four years ago. I'm not sure.

   _____

   _____

5. Jim is running. He is doing push-ups at the moment.

   _____

   _____

6. He will represent the United States this year. He will have to wait four more years.

   _____

   _____

7. Peggy Fleming was an Olympic ice skater. She was an Olympic skier.

   _____

   _____

8. My brother is going to the next Olympic games. My sisters are going.

   _____

   _____

■ 5-2 CORRELATIVE CONJUNCTIONS: *Neither . . . Nor*

■ Connecting Similar Structures ■

A Money is not important to me. Success is not important to me.

Neither money nor success is important to me. (connecting two noun subjects)

B I don't want fortune. I don't want fame.

I want neither fame nor fortune. (connecting two noun objects)

C This coffee is not good. It isn't hot.

This coffee is neither good nor hot. (connecting two adjectives)

D Your son isn't outside. He isn't inside.

Your son is neither outside nor inside. (connecting two adverbs)

E Sue has not arrived. She has not called.

Sue has neither arrived nor called. (connecting two verbs)

1. The correlative conjunctions *neither . . . nor* mean *not one or the other*. They connect two negative ideas.

2. When two verbs or verb phrases are connected with auxiliaries, *neither* follows the auxiliary verb. The auxiliary is not repeated after *nor*.

*I have **neither** finished my composition **nor** completed the reading assignments.*
*Sue is **neither** coming **nor** planning to call.*

When there are two auxiliary verbs, *neither* follows the first.

    (1)   (2)
*I have **neither** been sleeping **nor** watching television.*

3. When *neither . . . nor* connect similar structures, *neither* is placed as close as possible to the structure it is identifying.

    Correct: *I am **neither** happy **nor** sad today.*
  Incorrect: *I neither am happy nor sad today.*

4. Singular subjects joined by *neither . . . nor* take a singular verb after *nor*. Plural subjects joined by *neither . . . nor* take a plural verb after *nor*.

*Neither **Maria** nor **Jabria** is coming to the party.*
*Neither the **teachers** nor the **students want** an extra week of classes.*

If one subject is singular and the other subject is plural, the verb agrees with the subject after *nor*, that is, the subject closest to the verb.

*Neither the **director** nor the **teachers want** an extra week of classes.*
*Neither the **teachers** nor the **director wants** an extra week of classes.*

5. *Neither . . . nor* are usually used to connect words and phrases that are similar in structure. They are rarely used to connect complete sentences.

Exercise 2   *Connect the sentences, using* neither . . . nor.

    Example: Sara isn't studying this quarter. She isn't working this quarter.

                Sara is neither studying this quarter nor working. OR

                Sara is neither studying nor working this quarter.

1. Our test wasn't long. It wasn't difficult.

2. I haven't been getting very high grades. I haven't been getting very low grades.

3. I didn't review very much. I didn't study very hard.

4. Minai hasn't passed a test yet. Jose hasn't passed a test yet.

5. The next test won't cover Chapter 1. It won't cover Chapter 2.

6. The bank wouldn't cash my check. The supermarket wouldn't cash it.

7. I haven't gotten a student I.D. yet. I don't have a U.S. driver's license.

8. I don't have any food to eat. I don't have any money to buy food.

9. Nevertheless, I'm not sad about this. I'm not worried about it.

10. I won't ask my parents for money. I won't borrow any money from my friends.

■ 5-3 CORRELATIVE CONJUNCTIONS: *Not Only . . . but Also*

■ Connecting Similar Structures ■

A Tom has a car. He has a motorcycle.

*Tom has **not only** a car **but also** a motorcycle.* (connecting two noun objects)

B He is a fast driver. He is a good driver.

*He is **not only** a fast driver **but also** a good one.* (connecting two adjectives + nouns)

C He repairs motorcycles. He teaches motorcycle repair.

*He **not only** repairs motorcycles **but also** teaches motorcycle repair.* (connecting two verbs)

1. When *not only . . . but also* are used to connect similar structures, *not only* and *but also* are placed as close as possible to the structures they identify.

    Correct: *It is not only a big apartment but also an inexpensive one.*

    Incorrect: *It not only is a big apartment but also an inexpensive one.*

2. Singular subjects joined by *not only . . . but also* take a singular verb after *but also.* Plural subjects joined by *not only . . . but also* take a plural verb after *but also.*

    *Not only **Maria** but also **Jabria is** coming to the party.*
    *Not only the **teachers** but also the **students want** one week less of classes.*

    If one subject is singular and the other subject is plural, the verb agrees with the subject after *but also,* that is, the subject closest to the verb.

*Not only the **director** but also the **teachers want** one week less of classes.*
*Not only the **teachers** but also the **director wants** one week less of classes.*

▪ Connecting Complete Sentences ▪

A Tom has a car. He has a motorcycle.

Not only does Tom have a car, but also he has a motorcycle.
Not only does Tom have a car, but he also has a motorcycle.

B He is a fast driver. He is a good driver.

Not only is he a fast driver, but also he is a good one.
Not only is he a fast driver, but he also is a good one.

C He repairs motorcycles. He teaches motorcycle repair.

Not only does he repair motorcycles, but also he teaches motorcycle repair.
Not only does he repair motorcycles, but he also teaches motorcycle repair.

1. When *not only . . . but also* are used to connect two complete sentences, *but also* can be kept together.

   We need a new stove. We need a new refrigerator.

   Not only do we need a new stove, but also we need a new refrigerator.

   But also can also be separated. Either of the following patterns can be used.

           but + subject + *also*:   *Not only do we need a new stove, but we also need a new refrigerator.*

   but + subject + verb + *also*:   *Not only is our stove old, but it is also ugly.*

2. When *not only . . . but also* are used to connect two complete sentences, the subject and auxiliary verb must be inverted after *not only*.

      Correct: *Not only **do the children need** new clothes, but they also need new bookbags.*
     Incorrect: *Not only the children need new clothes, but they also need new bookbags.*

3. When two complete sentences are connected, a comma follows the first sentence.

   Not only is the baby sick, but he is also tired.

   A comma is not needed when similar structures are connected.

   The baby is not only sick but also tired.

Exercise 3 *Complete each dialog, using* not only *at the beginning of each sentence.*

Example: A: That book is boring.
B: Is it difficult too?
A: Yes. *Not only is the book boring, but it is also difficult.*

1. **A:** I enjoy living in another country.
   B: Do you enjoy learning a second language too?
   A: Yes. _____

2. **A:** Portuguese is a beautiful language to me.
   B: Is it easy for you to learn?
   A: Yes. _____

3. **A:** The customs here are different.
   B: Are they interesting?
   A: Yes. _____

4. **A:** The Brazilian people are friendly.
   B: Are they hospitable?
   A: Yes. _____

5. **A:** I love Brazilian music.
   B: Do you love Brazilian art?
   A: Yes. _____

6. **A:** I have traveled all over Brazil.
   B: Have you been to other parts of South America?
   A: Yes. _____

7. **A:** I have met many Brazilian people.
   B: Have you met many Argentinians?
   A: Yes. _____

8. **A:** I like Brazilian food.
   B: Do you like Argentinian food?
   A: Yes. _____

9. **A:** My parents are coming to Rio de Janeiro next month.
   B: Are they bringing your younger sister?
   A: Yes. _____

10. **A:** My sister wants to see me.
    B: Does she want to stay with you?
    A: Yes. _____

■ 5-4 CORRELATIVE CONJUNCTIONS: *Both . . . And*

■ **Connecting Similar Structures** ■

A Our grammar teacher is sick today. Our reading teacher is sick today.

Both our grammar teacher and our reading teacher are sick today. (connecting two noun subjects)

B I have been having trouble with grammar. I have been having trouble with reading.

I have been having trouble with both grammar and reading. (connecting two noun objects)

C Mike jogs every morning. He does push-ups every morning.

Mike both jogs and does push-ups every morning. (connecting two verbs)

D There is more food on the table. There is more food in the refrigerator.

There is more food both on the table and in the refrigerator. (connecting two prepositional phrases)

1. Subjects joined by *both . . . and* always take a plural verb.

   My mother is coming. My father is coming.
   Both my mother and my father are coming.

   My sister is coming. My brothers are coming.
   Both my sister and my brothers are coming.

   My brothers are arriving tonight. My sister is arriving tonight.
   Both my brothers and my sister are arriving tonight.

2. *Both . . . and* are usually used to connect words and phrases that are similar in structure. They are rarely used to connect complete sentences.

Exercise 4 *Complete each pair of sentences truthfully. Then use both . . . and to connect each pair of sentences.*

1. I enjoy _____.

   I enjoy _____.

2. _____ is an excellent student.

   _____ is an excellent student.

3. I go out on _____.

   I go out on _____.

4. I have always wanted to see _____.

   I have always wanted to see _____.

5. In this class we have _____.

   In this class we have _____.

6. I hope that one day I _____.

   I hope that one day I _____.

7. _____ helps (*or* help) me when I have a problem.

   _____ helps (*or* help) me when I have a problem.

8. My mother always _____.

   My mother always _____.

Exercise 5 *First, read each pair of sentences and underline the structures you will connect. Then connect the sentences, using the correlative conjunctions in parentheses.*

Example: My husband's family doesn't live near us. My family doesn't live near us. (neither . . . nor)

Neither my husband's family nor my family lives near us.

1. Dave and Nancy will have their wedding in June. They will have it in July. (either . . . or)

2. Dave's brother can't come. His sisters can't come. (neither . . . nor)

3. His brother is living in another country this year. His sisters are living in another country this year. (both . . . and)

4. They have invited the members of their family. They have invited their friends. (not only . . . but also)

5. After the ceremony, the guests can dance. They can walk around the garden. (either . . . or)

6. They do not plan to serve beer. They do not plan to serve whiskey. (neither . . . nor)

7. Dave's parents are against having liquor at the wedding. Nancy's parents are against having liquor at the wedding. (both . . . and)

8. For their honeymoon, they're planning to visit Spain. They're planning to visit Italy. (not only . . . but also)

9. In Italy, they will drive around the country. They will tour on bicycles. (either . . . or)

10. Dave says that Nancy is beautiful. He says she is intelligent. (both . . . and)

Exercise 6   *Decide if each sentence is correct or incorrect. If the sentence is incorrect, find the mistake and correct it.*

Examples: Either we leave now, or we shouldn't go at all. <u>*Correct*</u>

has
Either those pages or this page ~~have~~ the information. <u>*Incorrect*</u>

1. Not only many television programs are boring, but they also contain a lot of violence.

2. Both my roommate and I are against watching too much television.

3. Neither the movies nor TV are good for young children.

4. Parents either should check what their children watch or not allow their children to watch TV at all.

5. Not only do I rarely watch TV, but I also hardly ever go to the movies.

6. My mother can neither read or speak a foreign language.

7. Either Jan or Lee are coming.

8. The neighbors must have been either arguing or celebrating.

9. Korea produces not only cars but also electronic goods.

10. They neither eat bread nor potatoes.

Exercise 7 ▪▪ *Connect similar structures in each pair of sentences, using the appropriate correlative conjunctions. More than one correlative conjunction may be appropriate for some sentences.*

Example: I will have coffee. I will have tea.

I will have either coffee or tea.

1. Coffee is not good for some people. Tea is not good for some people.

2. Coffee contains caffeine. Tea contains caffeine.

3. Coffee keeps some people awake. It makes them nervous.

4. My father doesn't drink coffee. My mother doesn't drink it.

5. For some people, coffee keeps them awake. For these people it helps them relax.

6. I have always preferred hot chocolate. I have always preferred cold milk.

7. When I was at home, I never drank coffee. I never drank tea.

8. My friend must have several cups of coffee in the morning. His wife must have several cups of coffee in the morning.

9. They prefer black coffee, so they don't take cream. They never have sugar.

10. They drink coffee in the morning. They drink coffee throughout the day.

11. They are nervous. They are irritable.

12. Coffee has been a popular beverage for thousands of years. Tea has been a popular beverage for thousands of years.

13. Most restaurants offer coffee. Most restaurants offer decaffeinated coffee for people who can't have caffeine.

14. Coffee has risen in cost over the past few years. Tea has risen in cost over the past few years.

Exercise 8 ▪▪ *With another student, write a sentence about each topic, using correlative conjunctions. Try to use all the different correlative conjunctions you have learned in this lesson.*

1. computers
2. friendship
3. crime
4. AIDS
5. Hollywood
6. flying
7. rock music
8. finding a job
9. politics
10. English

LESSON SIX

■ 6-1 CONJUNCTIVE ADVERBS

■ Conjunctive Adverbs of Contrast ■

A Men smoke less than in the past; **however,** the number of women who smoke is increasing.

B Studies show that cigarette smoking is dangerous to one's health; **nevertheless, however, still,** millions of people continue to smoke.

C Our last exam wasn't difficult; **on the contrary**, it was easy.

D The teacher wasn't disappointed with the test scores; **on the contrary**, she was very pleased with them.

1. Conjunctive adverbs join complete sentences (independent clauses) and express a logical relationship between the ideas in the sentences. Conjunctive adverbs cannot join single words, phrases, and incomplete sentences (dependent clauses).

2. *However* indicates contrast. (See sentence **A**.)

3. In some cases *however, nevertheless,* and *still* are interchangeable. Each can show that the second sentence is going to give an unexpected result or be in contrast to the previous sentence. (See sentence **B**.)

4. The phrase *on the contrary* also indicates contrast, but it usually connects two sentences that express ideas that are clearly the opposite of one another. It is used when the second sentence contradicts the first sentence. (See sentences **C** and **D**.)

Exercise 1   *Complete each sentence, choosing the correct conjunctive adverb from the parentheses.*

1. My roommate and I ought to study during spring break; _____, we are going to take a vacation. (nevertheless, on the contrary)

2. I had planned to drive to Mexico; _____, my car is too old. (however, nevertheless)

3. My roommate doesn't like hot weather; _____, he wants to go to Mexico with me. (on the contrary, still)

4. Scuba diving isn't cheap; _____, it can be expensive. (however, on the contrary)

5. I have gone scuba diving many times; _____, I still have to be very careful. (nevertheless, on the contrary)

6. I don't speak French very well; _____, I speak Spanish beautifully. (however, on the contrary)

7. I took French for four years in high school; _____, I don't speak it very well. (nevertheless, on the contrary)

8. I enjoyed the trip very much; _____, my roommate did not. (however, still)

9. I enjoyed the trip very much; _____, I'm happy to be home. (on the contrary, still)

▪ Conjunctive Adverbs of Addition ▪

A Barbara's biology professor encouraged her to go to graduate school; **moreover, furthermore, in addition,** he nominated Barbara for a graduate scholarship.

B Barbara majored in biology because she was fascinated by the subject; **besides,** she knew it would help her get a high-paying job in the future.

C Barbara passed all her examinations; **in fact,** she graduated with honors.

1. *Moreover, furthermore,* and *in addition* show that the second sentence is going to give additional information. They add to the idea in the first sentence. (See sentence **A**.)

2. *Besides* often adds another reason for an action. (See sentence **B**.)

3. *In fact* adds emphasis to the idea in the first sentence. (See sentence **C**.)

▪ Conjunctive Adverbs of Cause/Result ▪

A I can't speak French very well; **therefore,** / **consequently,** / **as a result,** I didn't enjoy my trip to France.

B There have been fewer factory orders for new airplanes; **hence,** many employed in the building of airplanes are fearful of losing their jobs.

C Air fares are going down; **thus**, more and more people are able to afford air travel.

1. *Therefore, consequently,* and *as a result* state the result of the idea in the first clause. (See sentence **A**.)

2. *Hence* also states the result of the idea in the first sentence, but it is more formal in tone. (See sentence **B**.)

3. *Thus* often states a logical conclusion. (See sentence **C**.)

▪ Conjunctive Adverbs of Condition ▪

A We must find solutions to the problems of pollution; **otherwise**, we may all be wearing gas masks one day.

B Don't be absent from class; **otherwise**, you will miss the review.

1. If the first sentence is affirmative, *otherwise* is similar in meaning to *if one does not.* (See sentence **A**.)

2. If the first sentence is negative, *otherwise* is similar in meaning to *if one does.* (See sentence **B**.)

▪ Conjunctive Adverbs of Time Sequence ▪

A The protesters gathered a few miles from the downtown area. **Then** they marched toward City Hall.

B The police asked the marchers to stop before they reached City Hall. **Afterward** the police began to arrest some of the demonstrators.

C At first, I was going to join the demonstration; **later** I changed my mind.

Exercise 2   *Rewrite each sentence, choosing the correct conjunctive adverb from the parentheses and adding the correct punctuation before it.*

Example: The president is meeting with his closest advisers about the crisis, and he is going to meet with members of Congress later in the day.

(As a result, In addition)

The president is meeting with his closest advisers about the crisis; in addition, he is going to meet with members of Congress later in the day.

1. The president wants citizens to know what he plans to do about the situation, so he is going to speak to the nation tonight. (moreover, therefore)

2. A solution to the crisis must be found quickly, or the situation will worsen. (in fact, otherwise)

3. Everyone knew the two countries were heading for a crisis, but nothing was done to deal with the situation before now. (furthermore, still)

4. People are not unconcerned about the problem. They are very concerned about it. (on the contrary, thus)

5. Some journalists have accused the president's advisers of incompetence in the handling of the crisis. Some newspapers have suggested that these advisers should be replaced. (in fact, nevertheless)

6. The media did not spend much time reporting on the growing crisis until recently, so many people know little about what has been going on. (otherwise, thus)

7. The financial markets are very worried about the situation. The value of the dollar has gone down. (consequently, however)

8. The other side in the dispute is threatening to take tough action. It is hoped a solution satisfactory to both sides can be found. (furthermore, nevertheless)

9. The crisis could seriously affect the prices of certain products. It could also lead to a shortage of these goods. (however, moreover)

10. People have very different opinions about what should be done because the problem affects people in different regions of the country differently. People's understanding of the situation is not great. (besides, consequently)

Exercise 3   *With another student, complete the sentences.*

1. Married students may not feel as homesick as single students; however _____

2. Single foreign students do not have any of their relatives nearby; thus _____

_____

3. Single students usually have more free time than do married students; moreover,

_____

4. A single student has only himself or herself to worry about; on the contrary, ____

_____

5. During the week, a married student cannot spend too much time with his or her

   family; otherwise, _____

6. The married student may sometimes wish that his or her spouse and children were

   in their native country; still, _____

7. Some married students find it difficult to study in their apartments; consequently,

_____

8. Married students often eat food from their native countries every night; however,

_____

9. Before coming to the United States to study, the single male student has probably

   never cooked a complete meal; in fact, _____

10. The married student with a wife and children spends more money on food;

    furthermore, _____

11. The married student's wife often misses her family and friends; therefore, _____

_____

12. During the first few months, the wife might feel excited and happy about being

    in the United States; then _____

13. A married student's wife often stays at home and takes care of young children

    all day; as a result, _____

14. At first, married and single students enjoy attending classes for five hours every

    day; later on _____

■ 6-2 POSITION AND PUNCTUATION OF CONJUNCTIVE ADVERBS

1. There are four possible patterns for sentences joined by conjunctive adverbs. The conjunctive adverb can come **between** two sentences. A semicolon is used at the end of the first sentence, and a comma follows the conjunctive adverb.

   *I'm studying English in Denver; **however,** my best friend is in Houston.*

2. The conjunctive adverb can come at the **beginning** of the second sentence. A period ends the first sentence, a capital letter begins the second sentence, and a comma follows the conjunctive adverb.

   *I'm studying English in Denver. **However,** my best friend is in Houston.*

3. The conjunctive adverb can come **within** the second sentence. The conjunctive adverb usually precedes the main verb or the auxiliary verb, preceded and followed by commas.

   *I'm studying English in Denver. My best friend, **however,** is in Houston.*

4. The conjunctive adverb can come at the **end** of the second sentence, preceded by a comma.

   *I'm studying English in Denver. My best friend is in Houston, **however**.*

5. *Then, afterward,* and *later on* usually come between two sentences or at the beginning of the second sentence. These conjunctive adverbs are usually not followed by commas.

   *I got the booklist for the course; **then** I went to the bookstore to buy the books.*
   *I got the booklist for the course. **Then** I went to the bookstore to buy the books.*

Exercise 4 Punctuate the sentences. Add commas, periods, semicolons, and capital letters where necessary.

1. In some parts of the United States there is a shortage of water thus residents in these areas can water their lawns only every three days

2. Local governments urge the residents of these cities to use water conservatively otherwise there will not be enough water for everyone

3. Water is not the only kind of shortage many American cities have in fact some cities have electric power shortages during the summer

4. The governments of many industrialized nations have been worried about the rising costs of fuel for several years most private citizens on the contrary have just begun to realize the problem

5. Many cities have been studying the possibility of converting trash into fuel to produce steam then they would like to use the steam to manufacture hydrogen as a fuel for buses

6. There are many different possible sources of fuel the problem however is the time and cost of developing them

7. The price of gasoline is much higher than it used to be therefore many Americans nowadays prefer to buy compact cars rather than large ones

8. Scientists believe that heat from the sun is an important new source of energy they realize that solar technology is still in its infancy however

9. Ecologists are also concerned about new sources of energy nevertheless they want future sources that will not harm the environment

10. People in the industrialized nations must learn to conserve energy otherwise later generations will face serious environmental challenges

Exercise 5   *Complete the paragraph, using the words listed. Use each word only once and add the correct punctuation.*

as a result	consequently	however	nevertheless	then
besides	furthermore	moreover	still	therefore

At the beginning of the quarter the students in the section 3 nine o'clock grammar class were miserable They could not enjoy a cup of coffee during the break

_____ they asked the instructor if she would think of a way to solve this
       1

serious problem She told them she would buy a large coffee pot if everyone gave her

two dollars _____ she told them she would buy coffee, sugar, and cream
              2

if everyone gave her seventy-five cents a week The instructor _____
                                                                        3

didn't collect the money for many days _____ the students became more
                                                 4

miserable _____ they couldn't stay awake during the second hour of her
              5

class One student from Saudi Arabia was especially thirsty for a good cup of coffee

_____ every day for the next two weeks he reminded the teacher to get
       6

the money from the students Finally he decided to collect the money himself He

collected two dollars and seventy-five cents from everyone in the class

_____ he gave the money to the teacher Now everyone is happy The
                7

teacher _____ is worried about the mess in her office every day after the
                8

students get their coffee _____ she is happy, too, because the students
                               9

are satisfied _____ they will be awake for her class.
                    10

Exercise 6 ▪▪ *Rewrite the paragraphs so that they read more smoothly. Be*
▪▪▪▪▪▪▪▪▪▪▪▪ *careful not to overuse the connectors, and do not produce*
              strings of sentences.

The English Language Center began three years ago. It has been a part of the
university for only a short time. It has already received much respect from the entire
university. It has received much respect from its own students. The members of the
faculty are experienced teachers. The students are serious. The program began with
only thirty-seven students in the fall quarter. It grew rapidly. In the winter quarter,
there were seventy-six students. There were almost one hundred students in the
spring quarter.

During the first year of operation, the center was in a beautiful building. There
was not enough room. It was growing very quickly. It had to move to a larger
building. The second home for the center was larger than the first one. The building
was very old. The students did not like it. The teachers did not like it. The rooms were
small. The rooms were uncomfortable. There were not enough blackboards. There was
no lounge area for the students.

The university prepared a new, permanent home for the English Language Center.
It was beautiful. Finally, students were happy. Teachers were happy.

Practice Exam

■ SECTION 1

*Complete sentences 1 through 6 with the words in the first box. Complete sentences
7 through 12 with the words in the second box. Use a capital letter where necessary.*

and	for	moreover	on the contrary	therefore	yet

1. Living alone can be difficult, _____ many people choose to do so.

2. Living alone can be difficult. _____, many single people prefer to live
   with their family or with a roommate.

3. Living alone can be difficult. _____, it can be expensive.

4. Living alone isn't easy. _____, it is difficult.

5. Living alone isn't easy, _____ one has to take care of everything.

6. Living alone isn't easy, _____ it isn't popular.

besides	but	nevertheless	nor	so	thus

7. We can't afford to buy a new car, _____ can we afford a used car.

8. We can't afford to buy a new car. _____, we don't need one.

9. We can't afford to buy a new car. _____, my wife wants to continue to look for one.

10. Sales of new cars have been down the past six months, _____ car dealers are offering lower prices.

11. Sales of new cars have been down the past six months. _____, there are fears that workers in the automobile industry will be laid off.

12. Sales of new cars have been down the past six months, _____ this is expected to change soon.

■ **SECTION 2**

Complete the sentences, using coordinating conjunctions, conjunctive adverbs, and correlative conjunctions. Add the correct punctuation where necessary.

1. Many parents in America are upset. Their children are not learning good reading and math skills in school. (cause or reason)

2. Many parents in America are upset over their children's poor reading and math skills. They are worried about the problem of discipline in the schools. (addition)

3. The parents are upset over these problems. They are demanding better teachers and stricter punishment for problem children. (result)

4. In some states, school officials want permission to spank children. Many parents are against this. (contrast)

5. School officials believe that spankings are necessary for some children. They will continue to disrupt their classes. (condition)

6. When they were children, many parents had a lot of homework. Children today have very little. (contrast)

7. Children today have very little homework. They don't get a chance to review the work they have had in class. (result)

8. At the moment, most problem students are sent to the office. Most problem students are sent home. (either . . . or)

9. Parents want to improve the schools. School officials want to improve the schools. (both . . . and)

10. Problem children interrupt their classes. They prevent themselves and others from learning. (not only . . . but also)

11. Most problem children don't like school. They don't feel comfortable there. (neither . . . nor)

■ SECTION 3

Complete the sentences. Add the correct punctuation.

1. I was a quiet child in elementary school   **therefore** _____

2. I had to be quiet   **or** _____

3. I paid attention in class   **furthermore** _____

4. I studied very hard   **but** _____

5. I studied very hard   **consequently** _____

6. My father worked at my school   **in fact** _____

7. Most of my friends hated math   **on the contrary** _____

8. I usually made _____ As _____ Bs on math tests.

9. I completed elementary school in my hometown   **then** _____

10. I have always enjoyed school   **so** _____

11. Learning is _____ easy _____ exciting for me.

12. This quarter has been interesting so far   **yet** _____

13. _____ the teachers _____ the students are enjoying this quarter.

PART 3 Indirect Speech

In the English language, there are two ways of reporting what a person has said: **direct speech** and **indirect speech**. In direct speech, we report the speaker's exact words, as in this sentence:

> *He said, "It's late, so I'm going to bed."*

Notice that in writing, a comma follows the introductory verb, and the person's words are placed between quotation marks. The quotation marks indicate that we are reporting exactly what the speaker said without changing any of his or her words. Notice also that the period, question mark, or exclamation point at the end of the statement is placed within the quotation marks.

In indirect speech, we do not give the speaker's exact words, but we keep the exact meaning of a remark or a speech. Whereas direct speech is found in conversations in books, in plays, and in quotations, indirect speech is normally used in live conversations and in written reports where we tell what an author has said.

When you begin academic work, you will discover that you will use indirect speech a great deal in both speaking and writing. In seminars and other small classes, your professors will expect you to contribute to classroom discussions by expressing your own ideas on the topics you are studying. In addition, your professors will expect you to demonstrate an understanding of the information in textbooks, articles, and journals. Therefore, you will find that you will be using indirect speech to report what others have written or said about the subject you are discussing in your classroom.

In like manner, you will discover that indirect speech will also be used in your written reports, term papers, and essay exams. Your goal at the beginning of this part should be to master the rules of indirect speech so that you are able to report quickly and correctly what you have heard or read.

LESSON SEVEN

■ 7-1 BASICS OF INDIRECT SPEECH

Direct Statements	Indirect Statements
Bill said, "Gail **knows** that man."	Bill said Gail **knew** that man.
Amy said, "Mark **is leaving** today."	Amy said Mark **was leaving** today.
Joe said, " I **have seen** that movie."	Joe said he **had seen** that movie.
Lisa said, "We **saw** it too."	Lisa said they **had seen** it too.
Tom said, "I **was thinking** about it."	Tom said he **had been** thinking about it.
Sue said, "I**'m going** to see it soon."	Sue said she **was going** to see it soon.

1. When the introductory verbs (*say, tell, ask,* etc.) are in the simple past, the tense of the verbs in the direct statement usually changes. The verbs in the indirect statements are past in form but not in meaning; the verbs may indicate past, present, or future time.

2. Even so, the tense of the verb after an introductory verb in the past does not *always* change. The verb does not change when the statement reports an historical fact or general truth.

   He **said** (that) Florida **is** in the southeastern United States.

   She **said** (that) the best coffee **comes** from South America.

   The verb also does not change when the indirect statement is given soon after the original statement.

   Ann: *I'm tired.*
   Ray: *What did you say?*
   Ann: *I **said** I'm tired.*

3. When the introductory verb is in the present tense, there is no tense change in the indirect statement.

Direct Statements	Indirect Statements
Bill says, "Gail **knows** that man."	Bill says Gail **knows** that man.
Amy says, "Mark **is leaving** today."	Amy says Mark **is leaving** today.
Joe says, " I **have seen** that movie."	Joe says he **has seen** that movie.

4. The word *that* is optional after most introductory verbs. Either sentence is correct.

   They said that they were going to come.
   They said they were going to come.

5. Do not change the infinitive after the verb.

   Instructor: *I **want to see** you after class.*
   Student: *She said she **wanted to see** me after class.*

6. Change *all* the verbs in a statement.

   *She said, "When I **see** Tony, I**'m going to tell** him the truth."*
   *She said (that) when she **saw** Tony she **was going to tell** him the truth.*

7. Pronouns and possessives change to the second or third person **except** when the speaker is reporting his or her own words.

   Mike said, "I like my new car."
   *Mike said **he** liked **his** new car.* (Another speaker is reporting Mike's words.)
   *I said I liked **my** new car.* (Mike is reporting his own words.)

   Sometimes a noun is used to avoid confusion and pinpoint the speaker.

   *Mike said, "**He** was very nice."*
   *Mike said **the car salesman** had been very nice.*

8. If the indirect report is made very soon after the direct statement or on the same day, it is not necessary to change the time word. This conversation occurred on Monday morning.

   Pete: *Hi, Fran. What are you doing?*
   Fran: *Hi, Pete. I'm packing. My vacation begins **today**, and I'm leaving for Mexico **tomorrow**.*

   On Monday afternoon Pete reported his conversation with Fran.

   Pete: *Hello, Lori. I talked to Fran this morning, and she told me that she was packing because her vacation began **today**, and she was leaving for Mexico **tomorrow**.*

   Look at Pete's report on Friday of his conversation with Fran. Note the change of time words.

   Bill: *Hi, Pete. Have you spoken to Fran this week?*
   Pete: *Sure. I talked to her **four days ago** (or **on Monday**). She told me she was packing because her vacation began **on that day** (or **on Monday**), and she was leaving for Mexico **on the following day** (or **on Tuesday**).*

9. In indirect speech, the demonstrative pronouns *(this, that, these, those)* usually change to *the.*

   *He said, "I bought **this** diamond ring for my wife."*
   *He said he had bought **the** diamond ring for his wife.*

   *She heard the sound of breaking glass, so she went into the living room. She returned with two large rocks and said, "I found **these** on the floor under the window."*
   *She told me she had found **the rocks** on the floor under the window.*

10. In indirect speech, a place expression usually replaces the word *here.*

    She said, "You can sit here."
    *She said that I could sit **on the floor** (or **beside her**).*

Exercise 1   *The conversation contains five mistakes. First, underline the examples of indirect speech. Then find the mistakes and correct them.*

Rena: Here's a post card from Miriam in London.

Fred: What does your lovely sister have to say?

Rena: She says she was having a great time on this tour because it's well-organized and very educational.

Fred: Only your sister would want to go on a vacation to be educated.

Rena: She also says that she met a guy who told her he is a friend of yours in high school.

Fred: What's his name?

Rena: She doesn't say. But he told her he remembers you being one of the funniest guys in the school. She told him that that is hard to believe because she had never heard you say anything funny.

Fred: That's because when I'm around your sister, I want to cry, not laugh.

Rena: Oh, Fred. Please don't start complaining about Miriam. I don't want to hear it.

■ Past Time Changes ■

Direct Statements	Indirect Statements
*Mel said, "Carol **arrived** last week."*	*Mel said Carol **arrived** last week.*
	*Mel said Carol **had arrived** last week.*

1. The simple past usually changes to the past perfect in indirect speech. However, sometimes in informal conversational English there is no tense change if the meaning does not change.

2. The tense must change if the meaning changes.

   *Phil said, "I **love** her."* (He still loves her.)

   *Phil said he **loved** her.* (He still loved her.)

   *Phil said, "I **loved** her."* (He doesn't love her anymore.)

   *Phil said he **had loved** her.* (He doesn't love her anymore.)

   In the last sentence, the tense change from simple past to past perfect indicates that Phil no longer loved her.

3. In spoken English, the simple past does not usually change to the past perfect if the report is made soon after the person has spoken.

   Larry: *Hi, Steve. **Did** your check **come** this morning?*

   Steve: *Larry just asked me if my check **came** this morning.*

   BUT

   Steve: *Larry asked me two days ago if my check **had come**.*

4. In written English, the simple past and past continuous usually change to the past perfect and past perfect continuous. In quoted dependent time clauses, however, the simple past and the past continuous do not usually change.

   *Barbara said, "**When I saw the police**, I stopped."*
   *Barbara said that when she **saw** the police, she stopped.*

   *She said, "**When I was driving home**, I saw Marie."*
   *She said that when she **was driving** home, she saw Marie.*

   Note that the verbs in the quoted independent clause can change or stay the same.

   *Marie said that when she was driving home, she **saw** Marie.*
   *Marie said that when she was driving home, she **had seen** Marie.*

■ Modals ■

Direct Statements	Indirect Statements
*Roy said, "Joan **will go** with us."*	*Roy said Joan **would go** with them.*
*Pat said, "I **can drive** us there."*	*Pat said she **could drive** them there.*

The mechanic said, "I **may have** time later."   The mechanic said he **might have** time later.

She said, "You **must** finish by 2:30."   She said we **must finish** by 2:30.
She said we **had to finish** by 2:30.

"**Could** I **use** your phone?" he said.   He asked if he **could use** my phone.

She said, "I **would help** you, but I **don't**   She said she **would help** me, but she **didn't**
have time today."   **have** time today.

Jeff said, "I **might go** to the party tomorrow."   Jeff said he **might go** to the party tomorrow.

Penny said, "You **should work** harder."   Penny told me I **should work** harder.

1. In indirect speech, *can* changes to *could*, *will* changes to *would*, *may* changes to *might*.

2. In indirect speech, *must* (meaning *necessity*) remains the same or changes to *had to*.

3. Note that the main verb after the modal does not change.

4. In indirect speech, *could*, *would*, *might*, and *should* do not normally change.

Exercise 2   *Read each dialog. Then complete the statement about each dialog in indirect speech, changing the tense where necessary.*

1. He said, "The police know who committed the crime."

2. The police say, "We will catch the guilty persons."

3. Mrs. Jones says, "I'm going to tell the police everything I know."

4. The police captain said, "Our investigation has already begun."

5. The reporter said, "My paper will cover the trial in court."

6. Mr. Jones said, "I did not see the men."

7. One old man said, "I was sleeping when everything happened."

8. The lawyer said, "I told the witnesses to tell the truth."

9. The witnesses said, "We can identify the men who are guilty."

10. One female witness says, "I'm not afraid to tell the truth."

11. Then she said, "I have always obeyed the law."

12. The judge said, "It is difficult to find honest and brave citizens."

13. The judge says, "My court will punish the guilty."

14. Then the judge said, "The crime rate in this city has increased 50 percent."

15. The jury said, "We found the defendants guilty."

16. The judge said, "The defendants are going to jail."

17. The defendants' lawyer said, "We are going to appeal the court's decision."

18. The reporter says, "This trial was an unusual one."

19. He also said, "The jury deliberated for only twenty minutes."

20. The defendants said, "We will never change our plea of innocent."

■ 7-2 REPORTING STATEMENTS

1. In indirect speech, *say* and *said* are usually used when the person spoken to *is not* mentioned.

   Jennifer said (that) the movie was excellent.

   When the person spoken to *is* mentioned, *tell* or *told* is used and is followed by an indirect object.

   Jennifer told Sharon that the movie was excellent.
   Jennifer told her that the movie was excellent.

   It is possible to use *said to her*, but it is less common.

2. *Say* and *tell* are usually used to introduce indirect statements. However, you may add variety to your speaking and writing by using other introductory verbs that fit the sentence and the speaker. The following verbs are often used to introduce indirect statements.

announce	declare	remark	reply	predict	deny
complain	state	mention	answer	promise	explain

   The only one of these verbs to be followed immediately by an indirect object is *promise.*

   Correct: *She answered that there were a lot of problems in the area.*
   Incorrect: *She answered me that there were a lot of problems in the area.*

   Correct: *She promised that she would come.*
   She promised me that she would come.

Exercise 3   *Replace* said *in each sentence with one of the verbs in the box. Then report the sentences in indirect speech. Choose the verb that best fits the sentence and the speaker. If you are not sure of the meaning of any of these verbs, look them up in your dictionary. You may use some verbs more than once.*

announce	complain	deny	mention	promise	reply
answer	declare	explain	predict	remark	state

Example: While we were standing in line, the man behind us said, "I have already seen this movie three times."

While we were standing in line, the man behind us remarked that he had already seen the movie three times.

1. The speaker on the radio said, "The concert in the park will begin at 8:00."
2. The angry customer said, "My new radio doesn't work."
3. The weathercaster said, "We will not get any rain tonight."
4. After the instructor's explanation, she asked Jim a question, but he said,"I don't know the answer."
5. I didn't know the answer either, so the instructor said, "The answer and explanations are in Chapter 4 of your text."
6. In his televised speech, the president said, "My administration will cut taxes in this country."
7. The children were crying, so their mother said, "I will take you to the movies after dinner."
8. The little boy said, "I didn't eat all the cookies."
9. After he had told us about our quiz, the instructor said, "The midterm exam is going to be in two weeks."
10. The T.V. news commentator said, "This station will present a special report on the president's speech."

■ 7-3 REPORTING QUESTIONS AND ANSWERS

■ *Yes/No* **Questions** ■

Direct Question	Indirect Questions
*The president asked, "**Did you vote** for me?"*	*He asked **if** I **had voted** for him.*
	*He asked **whether** I **had voted** for him.*
	*He asked **whether** I **had voted** for him **or not**.*

1. *Yes/No* questions are reported with *if* or *whether (or not)*.

2. Instead of *ask* as an introductory verb, the expression *want to know* may be used.

   The president **wanted to know** *if I had voted for him.*

Exercise 4   *Complete the statement about each dialog, using* wanted to know *and* whether *or* whether or not.

Example: **Mr. Nolan:**   Is the next sales meeting in January?
          Secretary: Yes, it is.

          Mr. Nolan *wanted to know if/whether the next sales meeting was in January.*

1. **Manager:**   Has everyone finished his or her report for the meeting?
   Secretary: I don't know.
   The manager _____.

2. **Secretary:**   Do I have to attend the meeting?
   Manager: I think it would be a good idea.
   The secretary _____.

3. **Receptionist:** Did I get a raise?
   Supervisor: I'm afraid not.
   The receptionist _____.

4. **Manager:**   Have you been working late every night?
   Secretary: Yes, I have.
   The manager _____.

5. **Secretary:**   Has the receptionist been answering the phone correctly?
   Supervisor: I think so.
   The secretary _____.

6. **Clerk:**   Do we get two hours for lunch?
   Supervisor: No, you get only an hour and a half.
   The clerk _____.

7. **Manager:**   Is the repairman for the photocopier coming today?
   Secretary: I think so.
   The manager _____.

8. **Clerk:**   Is the repairman going to fix the photocopiers after lunch?
   Secretary: I hope so.
   The clerk _____.

9. **Repairman:**   Are the broken photocopiers in the manager's office?

   Secretary: No, they're in the storeroom.

   The repairman _____.

10. **Repairman:**   Was anyone using this machine a few minutes ago?

    Secretary: No, it hasn't been used for a few days.

    The repairman _____.

11. **Repairman:**   Can I use this desk for my work area?

    Secretary: Sure.

    The repairman _____.

12. **Manager:**   Will the company replace these machines at no charge?

    Repairman: I'll have to check with my supervisor.

    The manager _____.

▪ *Yes/No* **Answers** ▪

Direct Questions and Answers	Indirect Questions and Answers
*He asked, "**Can** you **swim**?" and I said, "No."*	*He asked me **if** I **could swim**, and I said (that) I **couldn't**.*
*She asked, "**Will** you **have** time to help me?" and I said, "Yes."*	*She asked me **if** I **would have** time to help her, and I said I **would**.*

1. *Yes/No* questions are expressed in indirect speech by subject + appropriate auxiliary verb.

2. The words *yes* and *no* do not appear in the reported (indirect) statement.

Exercise 5   ▪▪   *Report the questions and answers in indirect speech.*

1. He asked, "Do you like parties?" and I said, "Yes."

2. He asked, "Will you be at Mohammed and Carlos's party on Friday night?" and I said, "Yes."

3. She said, "Are you bringing any CDs?" and I said, "No."

4. She asked, "Did Mohammed and Carlos send out invitations to their party?" and I said, "No."

5. He asked, "Will their landlord get angry if the guests make a lot of noise?" and I said, "Yes."

6. He asked, "Have they had many parties this semester?" and I said, "No."

7. She asked, "Were they shopping for food last night?" and I said, "Yes."

8. She asked, "Are they going to fix food from their countries?" and I said, "No."

9. He asked, "Are our instructors going to the party?" and I said, "Yes."

10. She asked, "Do you plan to take a date with you?" and I said, "Yes."

11. He asked, "Can I ride with you and your date?" and I said, "No."

12. She asked, "Is Fidel bringing his girlfriend to the party?" and I said, "Yes."

13. He asked, "Has she arrived in town yet?" and I said, "No."

14. She asked, "Have you met his girlfriend before?" and I said, "No."

■ Information Questions ■

Direct Questions	Indirect Questions
He asked, "Where *do you live* in Ohio?"	He asked *where* I *lived* in Ohio.
I asked Choi, "How many years *will you be living* abroad?"	I wanted to know *how many years* Choi *would be living* abroad.

When reporting information questions, the word order in the indirect statement is as follows:

question word	+	subject	+	verb	+	remainder of sentence
where		*I*		*lived*		*in Ohio*
how many years		*Choi*		*would be living*		*abroad*

Exercise 6 *Report the questions in indirect speech, using* She asked *or* She wanted to know.

1. What area of linguistics are you planning to study after you finish your English language courses?

2. Why has Marcella decided to study the child's use of language?

3. When does a human baby usually speak his or her first word?

4. Which word does a baby usually utter first, *mama* or *papa*?

5. How many vocabulary words has a child learned by the time he or she is one year old?

6. What kinds of words does a child use first, nouns or verbs?

7. When did you speak your first word?

8. How long will a child continue to produce only single-word sentences?

9. How old is your little boy?

10. Why hasn't he formed any sentences yet?

11. Where was Rafael living when his first child began to speak?

12. How long had he lived there?

13. Why do children seem to learn a second language faster than adults?

14. Whose child speaks both his native language and English?

15. How long has Ali's little girl been attending an American school?

Exercise 7   *This paragraph is a report of a conversation between Kathy and a store clerk. Change the report to direct speech. Write it in dialog form.*

Example: When I walked in the store, I asked where I could find ski jackets.
"Where can I find ski jackets?"

The store clerk asked if she could help me. I told her I was interested in seeing the red jacket in the window. She asked me what size I wore. When I told her 14, she said she was afraid they didn't have any more red jackets in a size 14. The only color they had was black. I asked if they had any red ones in a size 12. She said she would go and find out. She came back and said that she was sorry they didn't, but that the manager had told her that they would be getting in a new order soon. She told me that if I left my name, they would give me a call when the jacket came in. I wanted to know how long it would be before the order came in, but she explained that the manager wasn't sure because the computer was down and she couldn't check. However, she expected the order to arrive the following week. I replied that that would be too late and explained that I was going on a skiing vacation in five days and I had wanted to have the jacket by then. She asked if I was sure I didn't want to try on one of the black jackets, but I told her that I didn't think so because I hated black. I had had my heart set on that red jacket, so I was very disappointed as I left the store.

Store clerk: _____

_____

Kathy: _____

_____

Store clerk: _____

_____

Kathy: _____

_____

Store clerk: _____

_____

Kathy: _____

_____

Store clerk: _____

_____

Kathy: _____

_____

Store clerk: _____

_____

Kathy: _____

_____

Store clerk: _____

_____

Kathy: _____

_____

■ 7-4 REPORTING COMMANDS AND REQUESTS

■ Reporting Commands ■

Direct Commands	Indirect Commands
"Sit down!" she said.	*She told me* **to sit** *down.*
"Don't sit down!" she said.	*She told me* **not to sit** *down.*

1. A command is an order given by someone who is in authority. To report a command, the following pattern is used.

	tell	+	indirect object	+	(not)	+	infinitive	
I	told		you		not		to do	that.

2. In addition to *tell*, the verbs *order, command, warn,* and *direct* are often used to introduce commands.

   The finance company said, "Pay immediately!"
   The finance company **ordered** *him* **to pay** *immediately.*

   The police officer said, "Move back!"
   The police officer **commanded** *us* **to move** *back.*

   The thief said, "Don't try anything funny!"
   The thief **warned** *Mr. Jones and Mrs. Jones* **not to try** *anything funny.*

   The parking attendant said, "Park your car over there on the left."
   The parking attendant **directed** *us* **to park** *our car on the left.*

■

Exercise 8 ■■   *Report each command in indirect speech, using* tell, order,
■■■■■■■■■■■■   command, warn, *or* direct. *Add an appropriate indirect*
                 object after each introductory verb.

1. The army captain said, "Don't shoot until I give the order."

2. The lifeguard said, "Stop pushing people into the pool."

3. Gail's mother said, "Don't swim in the deep end of the pool."

4. The president said, "Be more careful about conserving energy."

5. Dr. Hurst said, "Hurry and give the patient more blood."

6. The teacher said, "Boys, sit in the front of the bus."

7. The old man said, "Don't go near the house because there is a gas leak."

8. The police officer said, "Put your hands over your head!"

9. The flight attendant said, "Fasten your seat belts quickly because we have to make an emergency landing."

10. The teacher said, "Stop fighting immediately!"

Exercise 9 *These statements, questions, and commands were taken from a composition written by a student. Report each sentence in indirect speech, using* said, asked, advised, mentioned, *and so on.*

Example: For me, there's no place in the world like Venice.

The student said that for her there was no place in the world like Venice.

1. Venice is my beloved city.

2. I am thinking of it at this moment.

3. I can see its beautiful streets and architecture.

4. I will visit Venice next summer.

5. I have always been in love with Venice.

6. At night the city is like magic.

7. Go there.

8. Enjoy yourself.

9. Take a gondola ride down the Grand Canal.

10. Do not spend all your time with all the tourists in Piazza San Marco.

11. Wander around the city.

12. Visit the parts where tourists rarely go.

13. You won't see any cars anywhere.

14. Have you ever been there?

15. Are you planning to go in the near future?

16. How long are you planning to stay?

17. When can you visit?

18. I know you will love Venice as much as I do.

■ Reporting Requests ■

Direct Requests	Indirect Requests
She said, "**Will** you **hold** my packages for me?"	She asked me **to hold** her packages for her.
He asked me, "**Could** you **tell** me the time, please?"	He asked me **to tell** him the time.

1. A request is something asked for, usually in a polite manner.

2. The phrases *will you, would you,* and *could you* are often used to introduce requests. These phrases are used to make a request in indirect speech with the following pattern:

	ask +	indirect object +	*(not)* +	infinitive	
My roommate	*asked*	*me*	*not*	*to make*	*so much noise.*

Exercise 10 ▪▪

Report each request in indirect speech.

1. **Passenger:**   Could you direct me to the airlines ticket desk?
   Skycap: It's to your left, beyond the escalator.
   The passenger _____.

2. **Passenger:**   Will you please change my ticket for me?
   Ticket agent: Let me see your ticket, please.
   The passenger _____.

3. **Passenger:**   Would you please watch my little boy for a minute?
   Flight attendant: Sure.
   The passenger _____.

4. **Passenger:**   Could you give me a seat near the window?
   Flight attendant: I'll see if we have one available.
   The passenger _____.

5. **Flight attendant:** All passengers, please put your small bags under your seat.
   The flight attendant _____.

6. **Captain:**   Would you please observe the FASTEN SEAT BELT sign until we are in the air?
   The captain _____.

7. **Little boy:**   Daddy, can you take me to the bathroom?
   Father: In a minute.
   The little boy _____.

8. **Little girl:**   I want some water.
   Mother: Could you please wait a few minutes?
   The mother _____.

9. **Passenger:**   Could you get me an extra blanket, please?
   Flight attendant: Certainly, sir.
   The passenger _____.

10. **Passenger:**   I'd like to change my seat.
    Flight attendant: Would you please wait until all the passengers have boarded?
    The flight attendant _____.

Exercise 11 ▪▪▪
▪▪▪▪▪▪▪▪▪▪▪
With another student, decide who said each sentence and why the person said it. Use indirect speech.

Example: "Please keep quiet!"

A student who was studying in the library told two other students who were talking loudly to keep quiet because he couldn't concentrate and because people shouldn't make noise in the library.

1. "Why are you driving so fast?"
2. "I don't want to die."
3. "Why are you raising your voice?"
4. "I'm trying to watch television."
5. "Don't give it to me today."
6. "I've been sick for three days."
7. "Have you always smoked so much?"
8. "Will you please stop blowing smoke in my face?"
9. "Could I have your math notes?"
10. "Who asked about Chapter 4?"
11. "Are you almost finished?"
12. "Buy some new clothes."
13. "Read it carefully."
14. "Use your calculator."
15. "Do you have a nice pair of slacks?"

Exercise 12 ▪▪▪
▪▪▪▪▪▪▪▪▪▪▪
In a group of three or four, explain what different people have said to you in the past few days. Give as many details as possible.

1. Who made you angry? What did the person say?
2. Who made you laugh? What did the person say?
3. Who made you feel happy? What did the person say?
4. Who made you feel worried? What did the person say?
5. Who didn't tell you the truth? What did the person say?
6. Who made an excuse for doing something wrong? What did the person say?
7. Who made you a promise?
8. Who told you to do something?

■ 7-5 REPORTING EXCLAMATIONS

Direct Exclamations	Indirect Exclamations
*"**What** a terrible day!" she said.*	*She said **it was** a terrible day.*
*"**Ugh**! This soup tastes terrible!" he said.*	*He **exclaimed with disgust** that the soup tasted terrible.*

1. Exclamations become statements in indirect speech.

   "What a beautiful car!" he said.

   *He **said I had** a beautiful car.*

2. Exclamations such as *Oh, no!* and *Ugh!* are usually expressed by a sentence that explains the person's feelings.

   "Oh no! I have a flat tire," she said.

   *She **exclaimed with disgust that** she **had** a flat tire.*

Exercise 13 *Match each expression in column A with its reported form in column B.*

A	B
1. He said, "Thank you."	a. He congratulated me.
2. She said, "Good morning."	b. He was surprised.
3. He said, "Congratulations!"	c. He didn't believe me.
4. She said, "Okay."	d. He thanked me.
5. He said, "Aw, come on."	e. She didn't believe me.
6. She said, "You're kidding!"	f. She greeted me.
7. He said, "Really?"	g. She agreed with me.

Exercise 14 *Report the mixed sentences, using connecting words from Part 2 to combine the sentences. Use the expressions first, second, then, after that, and next to move from one idea to the next. Note in the example that each statement is either introduced by an appropriate introductory verb or connected to the following statement.*

Example: **Instructor:** Why is everyone so upset? Don't worry about the exam. Everybody will do well. I haven't included any questions on the chapter we've just finished.

The instructor wanted to know why everyone was so upset, and he told them not to worry about the exam because everybody would do well. After that, he added that he had not included any questions on the chapter they had just finished.

1. **Bob:** Are you deaf? Turn the music down. I'm trying to concentrate on my notes for a test tomorrow.

   Roommate: Okay. Remember this when I have a test.

2. **Police officer:** Give me your driver's license.

   Foreign student: I'm sorry. I left it at home.

   Officer: Where's your home?

   Foreign student: It's in Germany.

   Officer: Follow me to the station.

3. **Student:** Did the Spanish give California its name?

   Teacher: Yes.

   Student: What does the name mean in Spanish?

   Teacher: It means "heat of the ovens."

4. **Radio announcer:** The pollution in the city is becoming a major health problem for people with respiratory ailments? Don't drive to work alone. Car pool and drive with a friend.

5. **T.V. news reporter:** The state legislature has agreed on 55 miles per hour as the lawful speed limit. The police department urges motorists to observe the limit or pay expensive fines.

6. **Sergeant to Captain:** Don't order the men to attack tonight. They are too weak from lack of food. When do you expect our supplies to arrive?

7. **Mother:** What are you going to build?

   Little girl: I'm not going to build anything.

   Mother: What are you doing with the screwdriver and hammer?

   Little girl: I have to fix my television set.

   Mother: Don't you touch that television!

8. **Flight Attendant:** Can I get you anything, sir?

    Passenger: Would you bring me a blanket? The cabin temperature is extremely cold.

    Attendant: I'll be happy to provide you with a blanket. I have reported the problem to the captain. There isn't much we can do until we land.

9. **Jason:** What have you been doing all afternoon?

    Reza: I've been trying to get my driver's license.

    Jason: Did you take the test today?

    Reza: Yes.

    Jason: What happened?

    Reza: I failed it again.

    Jason: You're kidding! This is the fourth time.

10. **Janet:** Why were you standing at the bus stop last night?

    Jean: I was waiting for the bus.

    Janet: Is your car in the shop?

    Jean: No. I sold it.

    Janet: Why?

    Jean: I can't afford to buy gas anymore.

11. **Store clerk:** Who's next?

    Customer: I am. I've been standing here for ten minutes while you were talking to your friend.

    Clerk: Can I help you with something?

    Customer: Yes. You can give me the name of your supervisor.

12. **Travel agent:** When are you planning to visit Disneyland?

    Customer: I intend to go in two months.

    Agent: Will you be traveling with children?

    Customer: Yes.

    Agent: Have you made hotel reservations?

    Customer: No, not yet.

    Agent: Make them now. This is a busy time of year.

    Customer: Is it too late to get rooms in the hotel across the street from Disneyland?

    Agent: I don't think so.

    Customer: Thank you for your help.

Practice Exam

Before Mary registered for the fall quarter, she met with her advisor, Dr. Tucker, and had this conversation. Report the conversation in indirect speech in the form of a paragraph. Use the connecting words from Part 2 (see pages 48–74). Use the expressions first, second, after that, *and* finally *to move through the paragraph.*

Before Mary registered for the fall quarter, she met with her advisor, Dr. Tucker.

Dr. Tucker: Have you decided which courses you're going to take?

Mary: I want to take Economics 102, Statistics 203, German 101, and Speech Communication 212.

Dr. Tucker: You're planning to take too many courses. Do you think you will be able to do all the work?

Mary: Yes. I plan to study diligently this quarter.

Dr. Tucker: I believe you. But when will you have time to sleep?

Mary: Do you really think it's too much work?

Dr. Tucker: I certainly do. Don't take so many courses the first quarter. I've seen many discouraged freshmen students who could not keep up with their assignments.

Mary: Okay. I'll drop the statistics course.

Dr. Tucker: That's a good idea.

Mary: Thanks for your time.

Dr. Tucker: Where is your schedule of classes?

Mary: I left it in the dorm.

Dr. Tucker: Take it with you to registration. It contains all the courses, their times, and their locations.

Mary: Could you give me a map of the campus?

Dr. Tucker: Certainly.

Subordination

INTRODUCTION TO PART 4 ■ ■ ■ ■ ■ ■ ■ ■

In Part 2 you studied coordination as a means of connecting two or more independent clauses (complete sentences). In Part 4, you will study how to join an independent clause with a dependent clause. This is called subordination.

DEPENDENT CLAUSE   INDEPENDENT CLAUSE

Although I had a wonderful vacation, it was too short.

This method of subordination allows the speaker or writer to express a larger variety of relationships between ideas. It also allows the speaker or writer to show the relationships between facts or ideas more clearly and specifically. Compare:

A. *I opened the medicine cabinet, and a bottle fell out.*
B. *When I opened the medicine cabinet, a bottle fell out.*

In sentence **A**, the coordinating conjunction *and* simply adds one fact to another. In sentence **B**, by changing one of the independent clauses to a dependent adverb clause of time, we are able to bring out the relationship between the two facts.

LESSON EIGHT

■ Introduction to Adverb Clauses ■

1. Adverb clauses have the same function as single-word adverbs or adverbial expressions. They modify a verb by answering questions such as *when?*, *where?*, *how?* and so on about the verb.

    *Yousef bought a new car **recently**.* (single-word adverb)
    *Yousef bought a new car **last week**.* (adverbial expression)
    *Yousef bought a new car **after he had wrecked his Jeep**.* (adverb clause)

All the sentences answer the question *when?* about the verb. The last sentence is an adverb **clause** because, like all dependent clauses, it contains a subject *(he)* and a verb *(had wrecked)*, but it does not make sense by itself.

2. The following words introduce adverb clauses. These words are called **subordinating conjunctions**.

Time	Place	Manner	Condition
after	where	as	as long as
as	wherever	as if	if
as long as		as though	in case
as soon as	**Reason**		provided that
before	because	**Contrast**	unless
since	since	although	whether or not
until		though	
when	**Purpose**	even though	**Result**
whenever	so that	while	so . . . that
while	in order that	in spite of the fact that	such . . . that

3. It is important to remember the punctuation rules about adverb clauses. If the adverb clause precedes an independent clause, a comma must follow the adverb clause.

When I was a child, I loved Dracula movies.

If the adverb clause is within an independent clause, a comma precedes and follows the adverb clause.

Once, after I had seen a Dracula movie, I had a nightmare.

If the adverb clause follows an independent clause, a comma is not needed.

My mother would not let me watch any more Dracula movies because they gave me nightmares.

Exception: A comma is sometimes used when the adverb clause comes after the independent clause to indicate a pause in speaking.

■ 8-1 ADVERB CLAUSES

■ Subordinating Conjunctions of Time ■

After it had stopped snowing, I went outside.
As I was walking to the store, it began to snow again.
I will never like the snow as long as I live.
As soon as I returned home, I made some hot tea.

*My roommate had decided to go skiing **before** I returned.*
*I had never seen snow **until** my family moved from Florida to Boston.*
***When** I was a young child, I thought snow was only in Alaska.*
*In Boston, my father tried to get me outside **whenever** it snowed.*
***While** he was putting on his boots, I was hiding in my room.*

1. *When* indicates a specific point in time or a period in time.

   When I met my roommate, I liked her immediately.
   When we were roommates, we had a great time doing all sorts of crazy things.

2. *Just* is often used before the words *as* and *when*.

   *He arrived **just as** we were getting ready to leave.*
   *He arrived **just when** we were getting ready to leave.*

3. *While* indicates a period of time during which another simultaneous action takes place.

   While we were waiting inside, our friend was waiting outside.

4. *Whenever* means *any time*.

   Whenever I think of the time when we were roommates, the memories are always good.

5. *Until* indicates from an unknown point in the past up to the time that something happens.

   My roommate and I continued to live together until she got married.

6. When the verb in the independent clause is a future tense, the verb in the time clause is in the present tense.

   *After I **leave** the library, I **will return** home.*
   *I **will finish** before you **return** home.*

7. When the adverb clause starts with since, its verb is in the simple past tense if the verb refers to an action that started and finished in the past. The present perfect, present perfect continuous, or past perfect is used in the independent clause.

   *My roommate **has been** in the cafeteria since it **opened** this morning.*
   *He **has been eating** since the servers **put** out the food.*

   When the adverb clause starts with *since*, its verb is in the present perfect if the verb refers to an action that started in the past and continues into the present.

   *My roommate **hasn't missed** breakfast since he **has lived** in the dorm.*

Exercise 1 ▪▪ *Make complete sentences with adverb clauses by matching items in column A with items in column B.*

A	**B**
1. John F. Kennedy became president of the United States	a. whenever he spoke.
2. He had been a naval officer	b. as long as I live.
3. As soon as he became president,	c. when he was forty-three years old.
4. While he was in office,	d. since this country began.
5. The American people listened carefully	e. as I was watching the news of his death.
6. Two American presidents have been assassinated	f. he pledged to help people everywhere.
	g. before he was elected president.
7. Until an assassin's bullet killed him,	h. he created the Peace Corps.
8. I cried bitterly	i. Lyndon B. Johnson became president.
9. After he had died,	j. he was one of the most beloved American presidents.
10. I will remember President Kennedy	

Exercise 2 ▪▪ *Complete the sentences.*

1. Most politicians smile a lot when _____.
2. Many people approved of Kennedy's decisions while _____.
3. I vote in an election whenever _____.
4. My brother wants to enter politics as soon as _____.
5. I had thought that all politicians were dishonest before _____.
6. A large investigation into Kennedy's death was carried out after _____.
7. My brother has wanted to be in politics since _____.
8. I really didn't have much respect for politicians until _____.
9. I learned about Kennedy's death as _____.
10. Kennedy was a member of Congress before _____.

11. Whenever he made a speech, _____.

12. While I was watching the news about his assassination on television, _____.

■ Subordinating Conjunctions of Place ■

1. *Where* means a *definite place*.

   I prefer to live where the sun shines all year.

2. *Wherever* means *any place*.

   Wherever it's sunny and warm, I'm happy.

Exercise 3   *Complete the sentences with* where *or* wherever.

1. Put the packages _____ you want.

2. Did you find the packages _____ I had put them?

3. I don't know _____ he went.

4. I'll go _____ you want; it doesn't matter to me.

5. My parents are staying _____ we stayed when we visited San Francisco.

6. Every village was noisy. _____ we stayed, we couldn't get away from the noise.

■ Subordinating Conjunctions of Reason and Purpose ■

1. The subordinating conjunctions *because* and *since* introduce the reason for the situation expressed in the independent clause.

   *My brothers are studying in California **because** they don't like snow.*
   ***Since** it is so beautiful there, my parents are going to move.*

2. The subordinating conjunction *since* can mean both *reason* and *time*.

   Reason: *He took another course in English **since his TOEFL score was so low**.*
   Time: *He has been studying very hard **since the new course began**.*

3. The subordinating conjunctions *so that* and *in order that* are similar in meaning to *in order to* and show the purpose for the action in the independent clause.

   *My parents are going to move to California **so that** they can be closer to my brothers.*
   *A lawyer has advised my parents about selling their business **in order that** they might avoid legal problems.*

4. The subordinating conjunction *so that* is usually followed by the modal auxiliaries *can, could, may, might, will,* or *would*. Use *can, may,* or *will* when the verb in the independent clause is in a present, present perfect, or future tense.

   *We make our airline reservations early **so that** we **can be** sure of a seat.*

   Use *could, might,* or *would* when the verb in the independent clause is in a past tense.

   *We made our airline reservations early **so that** we **could be** sure of a seat.*

5. The subordinating conjunction *in order that* has the same meaning as *so that*, but it is more formal and is usually followed by *may* or *might*.

   *We made our reservations early **in order that** we **might be** assured of seats on that flight.*

6. In informal English *so* by itself can also introduce a clause of purpose.

   *We made airline reservations early **so we would be sure of a seat**.*

   No comma precedes *so* when it introduces a clause of purpose. (Compare *so* as a coordinating conjunction that introduces a result. See Lesson Four, pages 51–52.)

Exercise 4 *Restate each sentence, using the subordinating conjunction in parentheses.*

Example: We bought the tickets early in order to get good seats. (so that)
   We bought the tickets early so that we could get good seats.

1. This manual should be read carefully in order for you to be able to operate the device correctly. (in order that)

2. Please keep this number handy in order for us to help you if a problem arises. (in order that)

3. The meeting was held late in the day in order for students from the other campus to attend. (in order that)

4. All students were asked to submit their questions in advance in order for the university president to answer those questions at the meeting. (in order that)

5. I'm going to use a computer in order to do the assignment quickly. (so that)

6. You'd better go to the library early in order to use a computer terminal there. (so that)

7. Please read this report in order to see if there are any problems. (so that)

8. I've made some changes in order for it to be clearer. (so that)

Exercise 5 *Complete the sentences with adverb clauses, according to the meaning in parentheses.*

Examples: I have been searching for a good lawyer since _____. (time)
I have been searching for a good lawyer since *I found out about the problem.*
I need the name of a good lawyer since _____. (reason)
I need the name of a good lawyer since *I have to appear in court next week.*

1. Amy has wanted to be a teacher since _____. (time)
2. Amy will probably be a good teacher since _____. (reason)
3. My roommate has not received one letter since _____. (time)
4. I don't read my letters in front of my roommate since _____. (reason)
5. Ray has wanted to marry Sylvia since _____. (time)
6. Ray hasn't asked Sylvia to marry him since _____. (reason)
7. Louisa hasn't had a car since _____. (time)
8. Louisa's going to get a car since _____. (purpose)

Subordinating Conjunctions of Manner

1. The subordinating conjunction *as* means *the way* (that is, manner).

In California, we can enjoy the beach *as we used to in Florida.*
You didn't do the report *as I had showed you to.*

2. The subordinating conjunction *as* can also mean *time*.

   *They arrived **as I was leaving**.*

3. The subordinating conjunctions *as if* and *as though* refer to how something appears, not how it is.

   *My brothers swim **as if** they were fish.*
   *In California, I would feel **as though** I were alive again.*
   *You look **as though** you know each other.* (Maybe you do, and maybe you don't.)

4. The idea that follows *as if* or *as though* may be possible, or it may be untrue. Compare:

   *It looks **as if it is going to rain**.* (It might rain.)
   *She looks **as if she had seen a ghost**.* (She didn't see a ghost. She was just very shocked.)

5. When the idea that follows *as if* or *as though* is untrue, a past tense is often used for a present meaning. In such sentences *were* is used for all persons.

   *I feel **as if I were** on top of the world.* (I'm not on top of the world.)
   *I felt **as though I had been hit** by a car.* (I wasn't hit by a car.)

   The choice of verb tense is similar to the choice of tenses used in conditional sentences. (See Lesson Thirteen for an explanation of the verb tenses used in conditional sentences.)

Exercise 6

Make complete sentences by matching items in column A with items in column B.

A	B
1. She backed into the driving space as	a. he knows a lot about computers.
2. The man is tired and looks as if	b. she had been driving all her life.
3. He writes as	c. she's going to fall.
4. The thirteen-year-old drove as though	d. she were thirteen.
5. My thirty-year-old sister sometimes acts as if	e. he talks.
6. The mechanic thinks he's smart and acts as if	f. he's been running.
7. She looks as if	g. her mother did when she was alive.
8. She cooked as	h. her driving instructor had taught her.

Exercise 7 ▪▪▪ *Complete the dialogs with* as if *or* as though.

Example: **A:** Has Joanne been studying all night?

　　　　　 B: No, but I agree she looks <u>*as if she's been studying all night.*</u>

1. **A:** Ria is nicer to her cats than some people are to their own children.

　 B: I know. She treats her cats _____.

2. **A:** Has Joe been playing the piano since he was a child?

　 B: No, but he plays _____.

3. **A:** Does Anthony really know everything?

　 B: No. He just talks _____.

4. **A:** Is John's father rich?

　 B: No, but he spends money _____.

5. **A:** Did Brenda know about the accident?

　 B: I'm not sure, but when I told her she acted _____.

6. **A:** Hasn't Sheila met you before?

　 B: Yes, she has. I don't know why she acted _____.

7. **A:** Have you been running?

　 B: No. Why? Do I look _____?

8. **A:** Is Andy the boss?

　 B: No, but he likes to act _____.

▪ Subordinating Conjunctions of Condition ▪

*I will enjoy living with my brothers **as long as** they keep the apartment clean.*

If *they keep it clean, I will stay with them.*

In case *they become too messy, I'm going to save enough money to get my own apartment.*

*I will become a good water skier **provided that** I can find a good teacher.*

Unless *the lessons are very cheap, I won't be able to take any.*

*I'm definitely planning to take surfing lessons **whether** they are cheap **or not**.*

　　　　　　　　　　　　　　　　　 whether or not *they are cheap.*

1. The subordinating conjunction *as long as* means that the situation in the dependent clause must be true for the situation in the independent clause to be true. In this sentence, in order for you to avoid a fine, your check must arrive on time.

   As long as we get your check on time, you won't have to pay a fine.

2. The subordinating conjunction *whether or not* means that neither this situation nor that situation matters. Note that it is possible to separate *whether* and *or not*.

   *They're going to get married **whether or not** their parents approve.*
   *They're going to get married **whether** their parents approve **or not**.*

3. The subordinating conjunction *whether or not* can also mean that there is a choice between two alternatives.

   *I'm not sure **whether or not** I want to go.*

   (See Lesson Thirteen, page 236, for an explanation of *in case, provided that*, and *unless*.)

Exercise 8   *Complete the sentences.*

1. As long as the tickets are not expensive, I'll _____.
2. As long as you're not busy, could you _____?
3. As long as the weather is good, why don't we _____?
4. As long as you don't make noise, you can _____.
5. As long as you're careful, you shouldn't _____.
6. I'll go whether _____.
7. Whether or not I have the money, _____.
8. The president will not be re-elected whether _____.
9. I wake up early whether _____.
10. You should apply for the scholarship whether _____.

■ Subordinating Conjunctions of Result ■

1. When the conjunctions *so . . . that* or *such . . . that* are used, the word *that* introduces the result.

   *California is **so** beautiful **that** I can't imagine staying in Boston.*
   *California is **such** a beautiful state **that** I can't imagine staying in Boston.*

2. *So . . . that* can be used in the following patterns.

so + adjective + *that*	It was **so hot that** we couldn't sleep.
so + adverb + *that*	The air conditioner was humming **so loudly that** I couldn't sleep.
so + *many* + plural noun + *that*	There were **so many students** in the small room **that** I couldn't breathe.
so + *few* + plural noun + *that*	There were **so few windows that** the air circulation was poor.
so + *much* + uncountable noun + *that*	There was **so much noise that** I couldn't hear the professor.
so + *little* + uncountable noun + *that*	There was **so little time** to finish the exam **that** I gave up.

3. *Such (a/an) . . . that* can be used in the following patterns.

such + *a* (or *an*) + adjective + noun + *that*	He had **such a low grade that** he hid his exam paper. This is **such an interesting book that** I can't stop reading it.
such + adjective + uncountable noun + *that*	She makes **such good coffee that** I always have more than one cup.
such + adjective + plural noun + *that*	She wears **such beautiful dresses that** everyone always compliments her.

Exercise 9 *Combine the sentences. First, use* so . . . that. *Then, if possible, use* such . . . that.

Example: The line at the movie theater was long. We had to wait an hour.

The line at the movie theater was so long that we had to wait an hour.
The movie theater had such a long line that we had to wait an hour.

1. The theater was crowded. We couldn't breathe.

2. The people sitting behind us talked loudly. We couldn't hear.

3. The movie was exciting. We saw it twice.

4. The popcorn tasted salty. We got our money back.

5. I was thirsty. I had to get a drink in the middle of the movie.

6. The seats were comfortable. We didn't want to get up.

7. The movie was good. We've been telling all our friends to see it.

8. The end of the movie was happy. Everyone left the theater smiling.

9. There were cars in the parking lot. We couldn't find our car.

10. There was traffic on the way home. We got home late.

Exercise 10 With another student, take turns asking each other the questions. In your answers use *so . . . that* or *such . . . that.*

Example: How homesick were you when you first came to the United States?

I was so homesick that I called home every day.

How difficult was the test?

It was such a difficult test that I couldn't answer ten of the questions.

1. How bad did you feel the last time you were sick?

2. How nervous were you on the first day of class?

3. How cold (or hot) is the weather in your hometown?

4. How good a time did you have at the last party you went to?

5. How tired are you?

6. How hungry are you?

7. How much time did you spend studying for the last test?

8. How much money do you spend every week?

▪ Subordinating Conjunctions of Contrast ▪

Although Boston is a beautiful city, I just don't like cold weather.

Though my father likes mountains and snow, I'm sure he will learn to like beaches and sand.

*He'll probably enjoy water skiing, **even though** he prefers to ski in snow.*

While I will never miss the cold weather, I will miss my friends in Boston.

*I'll probably visit Boston from time to time, **in spite of the fact that** I will never live there again.*

1. The subordinating conjunction *while* can mean both contrast and time. When *while* shows contrast, it is usually placed at the beginning of a sentence.

   Contrast: While I don't like studying English grammar, I know I have to.

   Time: *I heard a strange noise **while I was studying the other night**.*

2. A comma can be used before the subordinating conjunctions *though, although, even though, while, and in spite of the fact that* when the dependent clause follows the independent clause. This happens when the dependent clause introduces ideas that are unnecessary or connected only loosely with the ideas in the independent clause.

I sometimes eat at the restaurant down the street, **even though** *the food and the service are not very good.*

The restaurant does a good business, **in spite of the fact that** *nobody I know likes it.*

Exercise 11 *Rewrite each sentence, using the subordinating conjunction in parentheses.*

1. There are many people in the world who are afraid to fly, but air travel is very popular. (even though)

2. Airline companies offer courses to help people overcome their fear of flying. However, few people know about these courses. (although)

3. One of my friends is very afraid of flying, yet she still flies when she has to. (though)

4. More people are afraid of flying than of driving; traveling by airplane is much less risky than traveling by car. (in spite of the fact that)

5. Passengers are not required to keep their seat belts fastened during an entire flight, but pilots recommend that they do. (despite the fact that)

6. My children love to fly. Nevertheless, they rarely do. (even though)

7. When I am on a plane during a thunderstorm, I worry a bit. I am generally not afraid to fly. (even though)

8. I prefer to travel by train. Traveling by plane is fast and safe. (in spite of the fact that)

Exercise 12 *Complete the sentences.*

1. While I believe our grammar instructor is a good teacher, _____.

2. Although I know it's necessary to take tests, _____.

3. In spite of the fact that I believe this is a good English program, _____.

4. While I think it's necessary to practice speaking in class, _____.

5. Even though I dislike memorizing words, _____.

6. _____, in spite of the fact that I have been happy here.

7. _____, though I believe that it's a good experience to study in a foreign country.

8. While my English has gotten better since I've been in this country, _____.

Exercise 13 *In a group of three or four, make up a story by using the phrases in sentences with adverb clauses. You can use the phrases in any order, and you will need to add other details.*

go there	*receive a note*
see somebody I know	*be very crowded*
have a good time	*know everything*
get some information	*make plans*
not have enough money	*not want to leave*

■ 8-2 SEQUENCE OF TENSES

1. In sentences that contain independent and dependent clauses, it is important to be careful of the choice of tense in each clause. Two or more actions must be put into the correct relationship with each other. Remember that meaning also plays an important part in the decision how to combine various tenses.

2. The simple present tense in the independent clause can be followed by any tense in the dependent clause.

   I *feel* calm although I*'m waiting* for the dentist.

   I *feel* calm whenever I *go* to the dentist.

   I *feel* calm because I *had* a good night's sleep.

   I *feel* calm even though I *was shaking* earlier.

3. When the verb in the independent clause is in a past tense, the verb in the subordinate clause must also be in a past tense.

   I *ate* Chinese food every night because I *liked* it.

   I *ate* Chinese food every night because I *was working* in a Chinese restaurant.

   At that time, I *was eating* Chinese food every night because I *was working* in a Chinese restaurant.

Exercise 14 ▪▪ *Read the sentences and underline the verbs in the two clauses. Then identify the verb tense in each clause.*

	Independent Clause	Dependent Clause
Examples:		
She <u>is</u> angry because he <u>will be leaving</u> ahead of time.	*Simple present*	*Future continuous*
Before the instructor <u>asked</u> for the exam, Ann <u>had finished</u> it.	*Past perfect*	*Simple past*

1. I eat Italian food every night because I like it. _____ _____

2. I eat Italian food every night because I have always liked it. _____ _____

3. They are disappointed because the plane will have left by then. _____ _____

4. Even though I was shaking earlier, I feel calm now. _____ _____

5. I'll see you before you leave. _____ _____

6. Because my girlfriend will be visiting me soon, I haven't written her for a few weeks. _____ _____

7. Although I needed only three courses to graduate, I was taking five. _____ _____

8. Lou was trying to get a taxi because he had been waiting for his cousin to pick him up at the airport for two hours. _____ _____

9. The little girl is doing her homework carefully since her father has promised her a reward. _____ _____

10. While I'm studying in this country, my parents are coming to visit me. _____ _____

Exercise 15 ▪▪ *Find and correct the tense mistake in each sentence.*

1. We can have the party in my apartment next Saturday unless my parents came a day early.

2. I didn't want to have the last party at my place because my roommate is sick.

3. The party last week was so good that many people have stayed very late.

4. Our landlord never minds parties as long as the guests were quiet.

5. Our next-door neighbor had a very loud party two months ago, and at 1:00 in the morning the landlord was knocking on his door as though he will tear it down.

6. As soon as he leaves, our neighbor's party became less noisy.

7. As the guests are leaving, I noticed that they were speaking in low voices.

8. My roommate and I finally got to sleep after everyone has gone home.

9. At our party next Saturday we will tell our guests not to get too loud so that we didn't disturb the other people in the building.

10. The landlord probably won't bother us provided that everyone paid attention to our request.

11. Since we were living in this apartment for two years and we like it, we really don't want any trouble.

12. Although everyone is having the right to entertain his personal friends, we must respect the rights of the other people in the building.

Exercise 16 ▪▪   *Complete the sentences, using the correct tenses.*
▪▪▪▪▪▪▪▪▪▪▪▪

1. The instructor told us to sit wherever _____.

2. Before the instructor handed out the history exams, _____.

3. While I was taking the exam, _____.

4. Even though I had studied for two weeks, _____.

5. I answered the questions in Part 2 quickly so that _____.

6. Part 3 of the exam was so difficult that _____.

7. Since I didn't answer all the questions, _____.

8. So that the instructor could read my answers, _____.

9. Since I have been in this class, _____.

10. In spite of the fact that I had really studied, _____.

11. Although I did the best I could, _____.

12. Provided that the instructor agrees with my answers, _____.

13. If he grades the papers strictly, _____.

14. As soon as I see my grade, _____.

15. Until I get my grade, _____.

16. While I usually don't worry about grades, _____.

17. When the exam was finished, _____.

18. I may get a passing grade on the exam unless _____.

19. I'm studying for a make-up test in case _____.

20. I will never take another history class as long as _____.

Exercise 17 ▪ ▪
▪ ▪ ▪ ▪ ▪ ▪ ▪ ▪ ▪ ▪ ▪ ▪

You are going to read part of a text about Albert Einstein. Then you are going to summarize what you read to a partner. Your partner will use your summary to complete some sentences. If your partner cannot complete the sentences, he or she will need to ask you some questions to get more specific information.

Student A should look at the story. Student B should look at the incomplete sentences on the next page.

Student A: Read the two paragraphs about Albert Einstein. Then summarize what you read for your partner. If he or she asks you a question, look again at the text; then summarize the answer in your own words.

Albert Einstein (1879–1955)

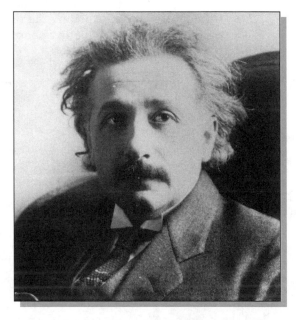

In his early years, Einstein showed no obvious sign of genius. He did not even talk until the age of three. In high school, in Germany, he hated the system of rote* learning and the drill sergeant* attitude of his teachers; as a result, he annoyed them with his rebellious* attitude. One of his teachers remarked, "You will never amount to anything."

Yet there were also some hints* of the man to be. At five, when he was given a compass,* he was fascinated by the mysterious force that made the needle move. Before adolescence* Einstein went through a very religious period, and he frequently argued violently with his freethinking father because his father strayed* from the path of Jewish orthodoxy* that Einstein believed in. Einstein calmed down after he began studying science, math, and philosophy on his own. He especially loved math. At age sixteen he devised one of his first "thought experiments." These are experiments that an individual must do in the mind; they cannot be done in a laboratory.

rote:	Learning by rote is memorizing without thought or understanding.
drill sergeant:	An army officer whose job it is to train new soldiers.
rebellious:	Someone who refuses to do what others tell him or her to do.
hints:	Small signs of something that will happen.
compass:	An instrument used for finding directions.
adolescence:	The period of a person's life when he or she develops from a child to an adult.
strayed:	To have gone away from where he or she is supposed to be.
orthodoxy:	The traditional and accepted beliefs of a particular religion.

Student B: Listen to your partner's summary. Then complete the sentences. If you need to, ask your partner questions about specific sentences.

1. Until he was three years old, _____.

2. When Einstein was in high school, _____.

3. His high school teachers in Germany didn't like him because _____.

4. In spite of the fact that his high school teachers said he would never amount to anything, _____.

5. Before he became a teenager, _____.

6. In school, he annoyed his teachers whenever _____.

7. He treated his teachers as if _____.

Student B: Read the next two paragraphs about Albert Einstein. Then summarize what you read for your partner. If he or she asks you a question, look back at the text; then summarize the answer in your own words.

Albert Einstein (1879–1955)

Within a year after Einstein's father's business failed and he moved his family to northern Italy to start a new business, Einstein dropped out* of school and renounced* his German citizenship. He spent a year hiking in the Apennine Mountains of Italy, where he visited relatives and toured museums so that he could forget the bitter memories of his high school days in Germany. He then decided to enroll in the famous Swiss Federal Institute of Technology in Zurich. It is interesting to note that he failed the entrance exam because of deficiencies* in botany and zoology as well as in languages. After a year's study at a Swiss high school, however, the institute admitted him. Eventually, Einstein became a Swiss citizen.

Even at the Institute of Technology, Einstein's rebellious attitude continued. He cut* lectures, read what he wanted to read, used the school's lab illegally, and made his teachers hate him. One of the teachers, mathematician Hermann Minkowski, who later made valuable contributions to Einstein's new physics, called him a "lazy dog." Einstein was able to pass his two major exams and graduate in 1900 only because he borrowed scrupulous* notes from one of his classmates, Marcel Grossman, and crammed* for the exams.

*dropped out: Stopped going to school without finishing the program.
　renounced: Gave up his citizenship formally.
deficiencies: Weaknesses or imperfections.
　　　　cut: Stayed out of class deliberately.
scrupulous: Careful attention to details.
　crammed: Learned as much as possible in a short time just before an exam.

Student A: Listen to your partner's summary. Then complete the sentences. If you need to, ask your partner questions about specific sentences.

1. His father's business in Germany failed, so the family moved in order that _____.

2. Even though he failed the entrance exam to the Institute of Technology, _____.

3. Einstein had to take courses in botany, zoology and languages before _____.

4. After he had studied for one year in the Swiss high school, _____.

5. Although he cut most of his classes at the institute, _____.

6. His attendance at the Institute of Technology was so poor that _____.

7. He borrowed his friend's lecture notes so that _____.

Exercise 18 ▪▪   *Complete the sentences, using the correct tenses.*
▪▪▪▪▪▪▪▪▪▪▪

1. When Yolanda was living in her country, her father always let her drive the family car provided that _____.

2. Before she left the house, he often gave her money so that _____.

3. Her father is a generous man, but he would never let her use the car unless _____.

4. Because she came home past her curfew one night, _____.

5. Even though she was always a careful driver, _____.

6. One night she had an accident, in spite of the fact that _____.

7. Another time the police stopped her as soon as _____.

8. Nevertheless, her father usually agreed to let her use the car since _____.

9. One night, however, something happened to her, and she began driving as though _____.

10. Until she gets a driver's license for the state she's studying in now, _____.

11. She has been thinking about buying a used car since _____.

12. She had thought about getting a Volkswagen until _____.

13. Wherever she goes in the United States, _____.

14. People in her country drive safely, but the people here drive so recklessly that _____.

15. Before she tries to take the driver's test, _____.

16. While her mother knows that she is a good driver, _____.

■ 8-3 BUILDING SENTENCES WITH ADVERB CLAUSES

Now that your ability in English has reached an advanced level, your spoken and written sentences should contain enough information to express clearly the ideas you wish to state. The use of one or more adverb clauses in a sentence enables you to add necessary information.

When I walked in the room, *the secretary looked at me* **as if I had done something terribly wrong**.

Since I don't have all the papers I need, *I will have to make another appointment as soon* **as I get them all together.**

Exercise 19 *Rewrite the sentences so that some of the ideas are expressed in adverb clauses.*

Example: I enjoy fall. I prefer summer. The trees and flowers are in bloom.

Although I enjoy fall, I prefer summer because the trees and flowers are in bloom.

1. Yesterday, John went to the bank after class. He had to cash a check. He would have enough money for the weekend.

2. He has an account at City Bank. They would not let him cash a check. He could present them with the proper identification.

3. John was protesting their refusal to cash his check. The other customers looked at him. He was crazy.

4. John reached in his pocket for his wallet. He discovered he had left it at home.

5. His apartment is near the bank. He decided to go home. He could get his wallet.

6. John was angry with the teller. John couldn't think clearly.

7. John had gotten angry with the teller. He knew that the teller was only doing his job. His supervisor had instructed him.

8. Nevertheless, the experience was an unpleasant one. He couldn't concentrate on his assignments. He returned home.

9. John knew that he would not have that experience again. He remembered to put his wallet in his pocket. He left for classes in the morning.

10. That night, John left his wallet. He could find it easily in the morning.

Exercise 20 *Complete the sentences with adverb clauses, according to the meaning in parentheses. Use the correct punctuation. Some sentences require two adverb clauses.*

Example: _____ I wanted to order

_____. (reason + time + purpose)

Since we had to wait in line a long time, I wanted to order
as soon as we sat down so that we could get our food quickly.

1. _____ the waitress told us to sit

_____. (time + place)

2. _____ the food was terrible. (contrast) _____

3. The food was _____ salty

_____. (reason + result)

4. _____ I had to write a check

_____. (time + reason)

5. We didn't leave the waitress a tip, and she looked at us _____

_____ (manner) _____

6. _____ we will never go

to that restaurant again. (reason)

Exercise 21 *Write five sentences with adverb clauses about one of the topics. Make sure each of your sentences is about the same topic.*

1. A current issue in the news

2. Your English program

3. Family life

4. American customs

5. Weekend activities when you were in your country

6. Studying and living in a foreign country

Exercise 22

This paragraph has no grammar mistakes, but the writing style is poor. Combine sentences whenever you think doing so will improve the style, but be careful not to overconnect. You can choose from the following words, but try not to use any word more than once. Punctuate correctly.

Coordinating Conjunctions	Conjunctive Adverbs	Subordinating Conjunctions	
and	however	when	where
but	moreover	while	wherever
so	otherwise	whenever	because
for	nevertheless	as soon as	so that
nor	furthermore	before	as if
or	therefore	after	if
yet	then	since	unless
	still	so . . . that	although
	also	as	even though
	on the other hand	until	in spite of
	besides		the fact that
	thus		
	in fact		
	as a result		

Not every culture in the world eats every kind of meat. Nearly everybody enjoys chicken. One of the most famous names in chicken is Kentucky Fried Chicken. The man who started this business was not always a wealthy man. At one time, he owned a small gas station next to a main highway. Many truck drivers stopped at his gas station. They wanted to get gas and rest. Many of the drivers had been driving for many hours. They were hungry. Mr. Sanders realized they were hungry. He began serving sandwiches and coffee. He served only sandwiches and coffee. The sandwiches were good. The sandwiches didn't cost too much. More and more drivers began to eat at his place. Mr. Sanders began serving fried chicken.

The drivers had eaten it. They told their friends. His new business grew rapidly. It did not last long. The highway department built a new main highway. Much of the traffic bypassed Mr. Sanders' station and restaurant. He had to close the restaurant. This happened. He was sixty-five years old. He knew his recipe for fried chicken was good. He went around the country trying to sell his idea of opening small restaurants that would specialize in fried chicken. By 1967, there were almost five thousand Kentucky Fried Chicken restaurants. You go anywhere in the United States. You will see one. You like fried chicken. You will enjoy eating the colonel's chicken. Colonel Sanders died in 1980. His name will live on.

■ 8-4 REDUCTION OF ADVERB CLAUSES

■ Adverb Clauses of Time ■	■ Reduced Adverb Phrases ■
I fell while I was running down the stairs.	*I fell while running down the stairs.*
While I was walking to the library, I saw my psychology professor.	*While walking to the library, I saw my psychology professor.*
Before I left the class, I asked about about the exam.	*Before leaving the class, I asked the exam.*
Since I began this class, I have learned a lot.	*Since beginning this class, I have learned a lot.*
After I had taken the class, I understood more about human nature.	*After taking the class, I understood more about human nature.*

1. Sometimes it is possible to reduce a long, complicated word group to a shorter, simpler word group. This is called **reduction**. To reduce a word group means to simplify it without changing the meaning of the statement.

2. An adverb clause can be reduced to an adverb phrase if the clause begins with *after, before, since, when,* or *while.*

3. An adverb clause cannot be changed to a phrase if the subjects of the dependent and independent clauses are different. This sentence cannot be reduced because the subject in the dependent clause *(I)* is different from the subject in the independent clause *(the student).*

    While I was taking the exam, the student beside me was looking at his notes.

4. To reduce an adverb clause to a phrase, omit the subject and the *be* form of the verb in the adverb clause.

    Adverb clause: *I was very sad **while I was packing my suitcases.***
    Reduced phrase: *I was very sad **while packing my suitcases.***

5. When there is no *be* form of the verb in the adverb clause, omit the subject and change the verb to its *-ing* form.

    Adverb clause: ***Before I left** my country, I had a lot of things to do.*
    Reduced phrase: ***Before leaving** my country, I had a lot of things to do.*

    Adverb clause: ***Since I came** here, I have been very happy.*
    Reduced phrase: ***Since coming** here, I have been very happy.*

Exercise 23

In each sentence, change the adverb clause to a reduced phrase.

1. While Sandy and I were camping in the mountains, we had many wonderful experiences.

2. Before we left for the mountains, we checked all our equipment.

3. After we had found the perfect place for our camp, we put up our tent.

4. When Sandy looked around at the beautiful scenery, she was breathless.

5. We saw many beautiful birds while we were fishing in a beautiful little lake.

6. When Sandy saw me catch fish after fish, she began using the same bait.

7. I had told her before we left to use that bait if she wanted to catch a lot of fish.

8. After we had caught six fish, we returned to our camp.

9. We talked about the beautiful day while we were eating our dinner.

10. Before we went to bed, we put out our campfire completely.

■ Adverb Clauses ■   ■ Reduced Adverb Phrases■

When my mother saw me board the plane, my mother began to cry.	*Seeing me board the plane, my mother began to cry.*
While I was waiting to board the plane, I couldn't help but think about what the future would be like.	*Waiting to board the plane, I couldn't help but think about what the future would be like.*
Because I wanted to be brave, I simply smiled.	*Wanting to be brave, I simply smiled.*

1. If the adverb clause begins with *when, while,* and *because,* it is sometimes possible to omit both subordinating conjunction and subject and change the verb to *-ing.*

2. An adverb clause beginning with *when, while,* and *because* cannot be reduced to a phrase if the subjects of the two clauses are different, as in this sentence.

   Because I put on a brave face, my mother felt better.

Exercise 24 *First, check (✓) the sentences in which it is possible to reduce the adverb clause to a phrase. Then rewrite those sentences, changing the adverb clause to a reduced phrase. Remember to omit the subordinating conjunction.*

1. Because I didn't know how to use the public transportation system when I first arrived in the city, I took a taxi.

2. When I got in the taxi, the taxi driver asked me where I wanted to go.

3. While I was riding though the city streets for the first time, I was amazed by the silence.

4. Because it was pretty late in the evening, there weren't many people around.

5. When I arrived at the dorm, I had to pay the taxi driver.

6. Because I had no change, I gave the taxi driver a $100 bill.

7. When I gave him the change, he told me he couldn't change a $100 bill.

8. While we were talking about what to do, we saw a police officer coming down the street.

9. Because the police officer couldn't change the $100 bill either, he advised us to go to the nearby police station.

10. When I finally entered my room at 1:00 A.M., I couldn't believe that I had spent my first couple of hours in this country in a police station.

Exercise 25 ▪▪   *With another student, complete the sentences.*
▪▪▪▪▪▪▪▪▪▪▪

1. Since coming to _____.
2. Before leaving _____.
3. While going _____.
4. Wanting to _____.
5. Believing that _____.
6. After receiving _____.
7. When not knowing _____.
8. Being very tired _____.
9. While talking _____.
10. Since starting this course _____.

Practice Exam

▪ SECTION 1

First, underline the adverb clauses. Then identify the meaning of the subordinating conjunction—for example, time, place, or contrast.

Although the institution of marriage has suffered in many countries, in the past few years, there has been an unusually large number of divorces in the United States. In the past, when two people married each other, they did so with the idea of staying together for life; but today many individuals seem to enter marriage with the feeling that they can always get a divorce, provided that the marriage does not work out. In the past, a large majority of Americans frowned at the idea of divorce. Furthermore, many people believed that getting a divorce was a luxury that only the rich could afford. Indeed, getting a divorce was very expensive. However, since so many people have begun to take a more casual view of marriage, it is interesting to note that the costs of getting a divorce are lower. In fact, wherever you go in the Untied States today, it is not unusual to see newspaper ads that provide information on how and where to go to get a "cheap divorce."

In spite of the fact that Hollywood has always been known as the divorce capital of the world, today the divorce rate among the movie stars is so high that it is difficult to know who is married to whom, if you are interested in this kind of information. Today, many movie stars change husbands and wives as though they were changing clothes. Until the institution of marriage again becomes a serious and important part of many people's lives, we will probably continue to see a high rate of divorce.

Subordinating Conjunction	Meaning
1. although	contrast
2. _____	_____
3. _____	_____
4. _____	_____
5. _____	_____
6. _____	_____
7. _____	_____
8. _____	_____
9. _____	_____
10. _____	_____

■ SECTION 2

Combine the groups of sentences, using adverb clauses.

1. The last test was difficult. I received a high grade on it. I had studied for it.
2. Part 3 of the test was long. I almost didn't finish it.
3. Ms. Golden is very nice. She permitted some of her students to finish Part 3 in her office at noon. She was eating lunch.
4. A few students start studying. They will not pass the class.
5. Some students in the class stay up late at night. They manage to get to class on time.

■ SECTION 3

Complete the sentences with adverb clauses, according to the meaning in parentheses. In some sentences two adverb clauses are required.

1. _____, both Ms. Berriman and Ms. Pearson give too much

   homework. (contrast)

2. During a test, they usually let their students sit _____

   _____. (place + condition)

3. _____, Ms. Berriman was checking

   our writing assignments. (time)

4. During the last test, Ms. Pearson looked at one of her students _____

   _____. (manner + reason)

5. _____, Ms. Pearson told us there was no homework

   for the next class _____. (time + reason)

■ SECTION 4

Change the reduced phrase in each sentence to a full adverb clause.

1. We ran out of gas while driving home from the mountains.
2. Before leaving, we had forgotten to check the gas gauge.
3. Seeing us standing beside the car, a friendly motorist offered us a ride to the nearest gas station.
4. Being cold and tired, we didn't talk very much in the car.
5. After getting some gas, the woman drove us back to our car.
6. Wanting to thank the woman for all her help, we offered to give her some money.

LESSON NINE

■ 9-1 ADJECTIVE CLAUSES

*The woman **who is standing over there** is from Puerto Rico.*

*Did you know that the man **to whom you were speaking** is Shirley's husband?*

*Shirley attended the meeting **that was held yesterday afternoon**.*

*Are you going to apply for the job **that was advertised in the paper**?*

*Do you know the name of the guy **whose car is parked outside**?*

*The day **when my daughter was born** was the happiest day of my life.*

*The place **where they live** is very dangerous.*

*I don't know the reason **why we can't pay by credit card**.*

1. Adjective clauses are subordinate (dependent) clauses that have the same function as single-word adjectives. They describe and modify nouns.

2. These words, called **relative pronouns**, introduce adjective clauses.

who	which	whose
whom	that	

These subordinators also introduce adjective clauses.

when	where	why

3. *Who* refers only to people.

   [The man is a police officer. He lives next door.]
   *The man **who lives next door** is a police officer.*

4. *Whom* is the objective form of *who* and refers only to people.

   [He is a police officer. I respect him very much.]
   *He is a police officer **whom I respect very much**.*

   In informal spoken English, *who* is often used instead of *whom*. In formal speech or writing, *whom* is preferred.

5. *Which* refers to animals, things, and groups of people (*the audience, crowd, class*).

   [Last week someone hit Ed's dog. The dog was only a puppy.]
   *Last week someone hit Ed's dog, **which was only a puppy**.*

   [The driver ran through a stop sign. The stop sign is on the corner.]
   *The driver ran through a stop sign, **which is on the corner**.*

   [Officer Smith often gives lectures to high school classes. These classes are learning safe-driving principles.]
   *Officer Smith often gives lectures to high school classes **which (or who) are learning safe-driving principles**.*

6. *That* refers to people, animals, and things.

   [The police officers respect him, too. Officer Smith works with them.]
   *The police officers **that Officer Smith works with** respect him, too.*

   [He was very happy with the new puppy. I gave him the puppy last night.]
   *He was very happy with the new puppy **that I gave him last night**.*

   [I also gave his son a book. The book tells about caring for pets.]
   *I also gave his son a book **that tells about caring for pets**.*

7. *Whose* indicates possession and is used for animals, people, groups of people, and things.

   [The first puppy was six weeks old. His coat was really beautiful.]
   *The first puppy, **whose coat was really beautiful**, was six weeks old.*

   [He is a little boy. His love for animals is very strong.]
   *He is a little boy **whose love for animals is very strong**.*

   [We should report pet owners. Their animals are mistreated.]
   *We should report pet owners **whose animals are mistreated**.*

   [This dog house is very old. Its roof has holes in it.]
   *This dog house, **whose roof has holes in it**, is very old.*

   Although *whose* may express a possessive relationship for things, speakers of English often use a *with* phrase.

   The old house with the old roof needs a lot of repair work.
   The old house whose roof is very old needs a lot of repair work.

8. The subordinator *when* introduces adjective clauses describing nouns referring to time.

[This is the time of year. There are good sales now.]
This is the time of year when there are good sales.

The subordinator *where* introduces adjective clauses referring to location.

[This is the music store. My friend works here.]
This is the music store where my friend works.

The subordinator *why* introduces adjective clauses that modify such words as *reason* and *explanation*.

[My friend didn't tell me the reason. He quit his job.]
My friend didn't tell me the reason why he quit his job.

Be careful not to confuse adjective clauses beginning with *when* and *where* and adverb clauses beginning with *when* and *where*. Remember that adjective clauses modify nouns; adverb clauses modify verbs.

Adjective clause: My parents called on a day when I was out.
Adverb clause: They called when I was out.

Adjective clause: I eat at the restaurant where I work.
Adverb clause: I eat where I work.

9. It is important to place the adjective clause immediately after or as close as possible to the noun it describes.

Correct: *The senator who is from Arizona hopes to run for president.*
Incorrect: *The senator hopes to run for president who is from Arizona.*

However, sometimes a short prepositional phrase occurs next to a noun and also modifies it. It is best to keep the prepositional phrase after the noun.

Correct: *He lives in an area of Colorado that is a famous ski resort.*
Incorrect: *He lives in an area that is a famous ski resort of Colorado.*

Correct: *I'm waiting for the ski instructor in red, who will be my teacher.*
Incorrect: *I'm waiting for the ski instructor, who will be my teacher in red.*

Correct: *The book about Olympic skiers, which you will enjoy reading, is great.*
Incorrect: *The book which you'll enjoy reading about Olympic skiers is great.*

10. The noun before the verb *be* and the noun after the verb *be* often refer to the same person.

My brother is a doctor.

Brother and *doctor* refer to the same person; *brother* is the noun subject, and *doctor* is the subjective complement, that is, additional information about the subject. If you want to add an adjective clause to the sentence, the adjective clause should follow the noun subject.

   Correct: *My brother **who lives in Texas** is a doctor.*

   Incorrect: *My brother is a doctor who lives in Texas.*

Exercise 1

Look back at the texts about Albert Einstein on pages 116 and 117. Underline the adjective clauses in the texts.

Exercise 2

Combine the sentences, using whose.

1. The Red Cross is helping the families. The families' homes were damaged by the storm.

2. One house was almost destroyed. The roof of the house was blown off.

3. A little girl has been crying for a week. Her dog was killed.

4. The families lost everything in the storm. Their homes and cars were completely destroyed.

5. A few stores were heavily damaged. The windows of the stores were shattered.

6. The store owners will not be able to start new businesses. Their properties were demolished.

7. A woman is helping another store owner to clean up. Her store was not damaged.

8. Public agencies will have to find temporary homes for all children. These children's parents were seriously injured.

Exercise 3   *In a group of three or four, discuss how you would complete the sentences. Use adjective clauses.*

1. I would not live in a place _____.

2. I can't stand spending time with people _____.

3. I'll never forget the time _____.

4. I can't understand the reason _____.

5. I don't like to eat food _____.

6. I rarely watch T.V. programs _____.

7. In my country people _____ are highly respected.

8. In my country the New Year holiday is the time of year _____.

9. I like traveling to places _____.

10. I dream of a time _____.

■ 9-2 NECESSARY VS. UNNECESSARY ADJECTIVE CLAUSES

1. Sometimes an adjective clause is needed to identify a noun and to make the meaning of the sentence clear. A necessary adjective clause is called a "restrictive" adjective clause. These are restrictive adjective clauses.

   A *All students **who do not study** will fail this course.* (Will *all* students fail the course? No. Only those students *who do not study*.)

   B *The bathrooms **that are on the second floor** are for women only.* (Are all the bathrooms for women only? No. Only those bathrooms *that are on the second floor*.)

   Without the adjective clause in sentence **A**, it is not clear which students will fail; without the adjective clause in sentence **B**, it is not clear which bathrooms are for women only.

2. Sometimes the information in an adjective clause is interesting, but it is not needed to identify the noun or to make the meaning of the sentence clear.

   C *My brother who lives in Chicago got married yesterday.*

   D *My brother, who lives in Chicago, got married yesterday.*

In sentence **C**, the speaker has two or more brothers. (*Which* brother got married? The adjective clause tells you it is the brother in Chicago, not the brother in Texas.) In sentence **D**, the speaker has only one brother. (The adjective clause gives additional information, but because the speaker has only one brother, the clause is *not* needed to identify *which* brother.)

3. An unnecessary adjective clause is separated by commas from the rest of the sentence.

   *My father, **who is very tall**, played tennis in college.*

   *I learned how to play tennis from my father, **who is an excellent player**.*

4. The relative pronoun *that* is used to introduce necessary (restrictive) adjective clauses. It is not used to introduce unnecessary adjective clauses.

   Correct: *Chicago, which is in the state of Illinois, is the third largest city in the United States.*

   Incorrect: *Chicago, that is in the state of Illinois, is the third largest city in the United States.*

5. Sometimes it is difficult to distinguish between necessary and unnecessary adjective clauses. The following guidelines may help.

   a. If a noun is preceded by modifiers, these modifiers are usually enough to identify the noun; therefore, the following adjective clause is not necessary.

      *My grammar book, **which is at home**, was not very expensive.* (The modifier *grammar* identifies which book the speaker is talking about, so the adjective clause provides additional, unnecessary information.)

   The modifiers in these sentences also make the adjective clauses unnecessary:

      *The first grammar test, **which was on the tenses**, was difficult for me.*

      *When the teacher returned my test, she gave me a disappointed look, **which made me feel very uncomfortable**.*

   b. The names of specific places, persons, and geographical locations usually do not require a necessary adjective clause.

      *Denver, **which is a beautiful city**, has two universities.*

      *Nelson Mandela, **who spent many years in prison**, became the first black president of South Africa.*

      *If you are looking for a new doctor, I can recommend Dr. Parker, **who is associated with City Hospital**.*

      *The Arctic Ocean, **which is a polar ocean**, occupies about 5,440,000 square miles between North America and Greenland.*

6. In compositions and free writing exercises, the decision to use commas to indicate that a clause is unnecessary depends not only on the points mentioned above but also on the context and the information previously given. A noun in the tenth sentence of a composition may not need a necessary adjective clause because of information in the second sentence.

Exercise 4 *First, underline the adjective clauses in the sentences. Second, circle the noun that each clause identifies. Third, punctuate the unnecessary clauses. Finally, be prepared to explain why a clause is necessary or unnecessary.*

1. Our grammar class which meets at nine in the morning is very interesting.

2. In the class, we don't have any students who are from China.

3. My best friend Carlos whose ability to speak English is very good is from Mexico.

4. The students who entered the class late are having a little trouble.

5. The grammar teacher dislikes students who are intelligent but lazy.

6. Sedig Kenous who is an excellent student is from Libya.

7. His parents live in Tripoli whose ancient name was Tripolis.

8. His father who is very tall is an engineer in Libya.

9. His parents whom he spoke to last night are going to visit him during the next break.

10. They are planning to spend a week in Puerto Rico which is a beautiful island.

11. Sedig's birthday which is in February is only two weeks away.

12. We are planning to give him a surprise birthday party which will be at my apartment.

13. The party that we had last week was for another student who has to return home.

14. The place where we had the party last week was too small.

15. I don't enjoy parties where everyone is crowded into one small room.

Exercise 5   *Read the sentences about the singer Elvis Presley. Each sentence contains a necessary or an unnecessary adjective clause. Circle the explanation that best describes each sentence.*

1. Elvis Presley, whose records made him a millionaire, was a legendary singer.
   a. There was only one Elvis Presley.
   b. There was more than one Elvis Presley.

2. His fans, who still have wonderful memories of his performances, continue to buy his records.
   a. All of his fans have wonderful memories of his performances.
   b. Only some fans have wonderful memories of his performances.

3. His fans who still have wonderful memories of his performances continue to buy his records.
   a. All of his fans have wonderful memories of his performances.
   b. Only some of his fans have wonderful memories of his performances.

4. Elvis Presley was like many other popular singers, who began their careers singing in church choirs.
   a. Popular singers in general began their careers singing in church choirs.
   b. Only some popular singers began their careers singing in church choirs.

5. Elvis Presley was like many other popular singers who began their careers singing in church choirs.
   a. Popular singers in general began their careers singing in church choirs.
   b. Only some popular singers began their careers singing in church choirs.

6. Elvis Presley also made many movies whose success was tremendous.
   a. All of his movies had tremendous success.
   b. Some of his movies had tremendous success.

7. Elvis Presley also made many movies, whose success was tremendous.
   a. All of his movies had tremendous success.
   b. Some of his movies had tremendous success.

8. At the beginning of his acting career, movie critics who gave his movies poor reviews said he didn't have any talent.
   a. All movie critics gave his movies poor reviews.
   b. Some movie critics gave his movies poor reviews.

9. At the beginning of his acting career, movie critics, who gave his movies poor reviews, said he didn't have any talent.
   a. All movie critics gave his movies poor reviews.
   b. Some movie critics gave his movies poor reviews.

10. After Elvis Presley died, his fans who suffered tremendous grief over his death visited the Presley mansion in Nashville, Tennessee.
    a. All of his fans suffered tremendous grief over his death.
    b. Some of his fans suffered tremendous grief over his death.

11. After Elvis Presley died, his fans, who suffered tremendous grief over his death, visited the Presley mansion in Nashville, Tennessee.
    a. All of his fans suffered tremendous grief over his death.
    b. Some of his fans suffered tremendous grief over his death.

12. His career, which was magical and successful, was cut short.
    a. All of his career was magical and successful.
    b. Some of his career was magical and successful.

Exercise 6 *Combine the sentences, using who, which, or that. Add commas where necessary.*

1. The author was a Frenchman. He wrote this book.

2. He came from an area in France. This area is famous for its white wine.

3. He married a beautiful woman. This woman was also an author.

4. Do you remember the name of his novel? The novel won the Pulitzer Prize.

5. They had only one son. He became an artist in the style of impressionism.

6. That is the editor. He publishes most of their works.

7. The apartment is now a famous tourist attraction. The apartment is used as an art studio by their son.

8. The painting is one of my favorites. The painting is hanging over the fireplace.

9. A friend purchased the painting for me last year. This friend is a successful art dealer in New York.

10. The painting depicts a café scene. The scene was very common during the nineteenth century.

Exercise 7 *Combine the sentences, using when, where, or why. Add commas where necessary.*

1. Sue met Dick during the summer quarter. She was studying in New York then.

2. They got married a year later. He finished his degree in marketing at that time.

3. Dick didn't give an explanation. He changed from psychology to marketing.

4. They are now living in Houston, Texas. Dick's company is located there.

5. They didn't give a reason. Dick wanted to leave Texas.

6. Next year, they will move to Boston. Dick will become the executive in charge of marketing for his company's new East Coast office there.

7. They will not move until June. The weather is nice for driving long distances at that time of year.

8. Sue has not given an explanation. They decided to drive instead of fly.

Exercise 8   *With another student, write sentences containing these adjective clauses. When you finish, compare sentences with another pair of students.*

1. , who's been in a lot of movies lately,

2. , which was invented in the nineteenth century,

3. , whose name has been in the news a lot lately,

4. , where we're studying English

5. , when people gather together with their families,

6. , which was popular a few years ago,

7. , whose work is known all over the world,

8. , who died not too long ago,

■ 9-3 GRAMMATICAL FUNCTIONS OF RELATIVE PRONOUNS

■ Relative Pronouns as Subjects of Adjective Clauses ■

1. The relative pronouns *who, which,* and *that* can be the subject of an adjective clause. In sentence **A**, *who* replaces the subject *he*. In sentence **B**, *which* replaces the subject *the symphony*. In sentence **C**, *that* replaces the subject *it*.

   [I have a friend. **He** has many classical records.]
   A *I have a friend **who** has many classical records.*

   [I really enjoy the symphony. **The symphony** is by Beethoven.]
   B *I really the enjoy the symphony **which** is by Beethoven.*

   [Here is a beautiful recording. **It** was made by the Boston Pops Orchestra.]
   C *Here is a beautiful recording **that** was made by the Boston Pops Orchestra.*

2. As subject of a clause, *that* may replace *who* or *which*, although *who* is preferable for a person.

I have a friend **who** *has many beautiful classical records.*
I have a friend **that** *has many beautiful classical records.*

I really the enjoy the symphony **which** *is by Beethoven.*
I really the enjoy the symphony **that** *is by Beethoven.*

Note: Remember, *that* can be used only in necessary (restrictive) adjective clauses. *That* cannot be used in unnecessary adjective clauses.

Exercise 9 Combine the sentences, using who, which, or that. *Add commas where necessary.*

1. The professor is a famous chemist. He wrote the book on synthetic fuels.

   _____

2. His book is in the library. The book is for graduate students.

   _____

3. Chemistry can be enjoyable. Chemistry is a difficult subject.

   _____

4. The chemistry students have worked hard this quarter. The students have Dr. Smith.

   _____

   _____

5. Dr. Smith is going to go to Spain next semester. Dr. Smith has already taught in several European countries.

   _____

   _____

6. He will lecture at the University of Madrid. The University of Madrid is a well-known university in Spain.

   _____

   _____

7. My roommate has been accepted by Harvard for next year. He received a scholarship.

   _____

   _____

8. Harvard is a prestigious American university. It is in Massachusetts.

   _____

9. Many politicians are high government officials. They graduated from Harvard.

   _____

10. John F. Kennedy was a graduate of Harvard. He was the thirty-fifth president of the United States.

    _____

    _____

■ Relative Pronouns as Objects of Adjective Clauses ■

1. The relative pronouns *whom, which,* and *that* can be the object of an adjective clause. In sentence **A**, *whom* replaces the object *her*. In sentence **B**, *which* replaces the object *the records*. In sentence **C**, *that* replaces the object *it*.

   [She is the friend. I visited **her** last week.]
   A *She is the friend **whom** I visited last week.*

   [She has many classical records. She bought **the records** in Vienna.]
   B *You will like the classical records **which** she bought in Vienna.*

   [I am looking for the symphony. She bought **it** last week.]
   C *I am looking for the symphony **that** she bought last week.*

2. As object of the clause, *that* may replace *whom* or *which*, although *whom* is preferable.

   *She is the friend **whom** I visited last week.*
   *She is the friend **that** I visited last week.*

   *You will like the classical records **which** she bought in Vienna.*
   *You will like the classical records **that** she bought in Vienna.*

3. Notice that when a relative pronoun is used as the object of the clause, the relative pronoun *whom* is placed in front of the subject-verb combination.

   *The man **whom I met** was a famous conductor.*

   Compare this with *who* as subject of the clause.

   *He is a man **who enjoys** classical music.*

4. In spoken and written English, when the pronoun functions as the object of the adjective clause, the relative pronoun that introduces the clause is often omitted.

   She is the friend whom I visited last week.
   She is the friend I visited last week. (omitted)

   Again, the relative pronoun can be omitted only in necessary adjective clauses.

   You will like the classical records which she bought in Vienna.
   You will like the classical records she bought in Vienna.

   I am looking for the symphony that she bought last week.
   I am looking for the symphony she bought last week.

   It is easy to determine when the relative pronoun can be left out. Just look for a subject-verb combination that follows right after the noun.

Exercise 10  *Write* who, whom, which, *or that* only in the sentences that need a pronoun.

1. John Wayne, _____ was a famous American cowboy actor, died in 1979.

2. Most of his movies, _____ have been seen all over the world, were westerns.

3. Westerns were the movies _____ he loved most of all.

4. The Hollywood director with _____ John Wayne enjoyed working was John Ford.

5. The ranch _____ the Wayne family owns is in California.

6. John Wayne lived in California, but the state _____ he was born in was Iowa.

7. His father was a druggist _____ moved his family to California early in John Wayne's life.

8. The film _____ we saw last week was his last movie.

9. John Wayne also produced several of the movies _____ he starred in.

10. *The Alamo* is the name of one of the films _____ he produced.

11. The film for _____ he received an Academy Award was *True Grit*.

12. Many movie critics _____ constantly gave his movies bad reviews didn't believe he was a good actor.

13. However, it was the ordinary moviegoer to _____ John Wayne owed his success.

14. Isn't that the movie studio in _____ he made many of his films?

15. John Wayne had three wives by _____ he had a total of seven children.

16. Cowboy fans, _____ are all over the world, will miss him greatly.

Exercise 11 *First, underline the adjective clause in each sentence. Then decide if the sentence is correct or incorrect. If the sentence is incorrect, find the mistake and correct it.*

1. I have just spoken with a friend I met in Michigan last year.

2. He is currently finishing a Ph.D. degree which I haven't even started yet.

3. He is really a very intelligent student who all his professors respect.

4. Last semester he wrote a paper that his economics professor urged him to send to a business journal for publication.

5. Another professor he had for a marketing course often used him as an assistant.

6. He recently scored 95 on an economics test the other students failed.

7. Here is the score that I received it on the test.

8. I failed parts 1 and 2 which I didn't understand very well of the test.

9. The final grade will probably be very low that I get in economics.

10. In addition to being a very good student, my friend is a nice person who all his classmates like.

Exercise 12 *With another student, improve the following text. First, decide where in the text to insert each sentence **a** through **k**. Then rewrite the text, using adjective clauses. Add commas where necessary.*

> a. *The stations show these commercials when children's programs are on.*
> b. *I know him.*
> c. *We will let these programs into our homes every night.*
> d. *Most Americans own a T.V. set.*
> e. *The networks put these shows on early in the evening.*
> f. *The networks offer these programs night after night.*
> g. *We watch these programs.*
> h. *I watched these shows last night.*
> i. *Their children believe the commercials.*
> j. *A newscaster was interviewing this executive.*
> k. *I have heard these critics express negative opinions about most of the programs on television.*

A T.V. set may be more dangerous than the kitchen stove because not all the programs are desirable. There are many television critics. The chief objections are that television has raised the crime rate among young people and has caused students' test scores to go down. In addition, many parents believe there is too much sex and violence on the shows. Indeed, the majority of the shows are full of fighting and killing.

Many people also criticize T.V. commercials. Some parents feel that these commercials do not teach the children good eating habits. My neighbor, Sandy Waller, said that her young son refused to eat anything but candy and sugar-coated cereals.

Recently a top network executive was trying to defend the network's choice of children's programs, but what he said wasn't good enough. In fact, all programs broadcast must represent a higher quality of entertainment than sex and violence. We, as viewers, must learn to choose the programs.

Exercise 13 ■■ *Combine the sentences. Omit the relative pronouns where*
■■■■■■■■■■■ *possible, and add commas where necessary.*

1. The adverb clause test was easy. The test was last Friday.

___

2. I enjoy taking grammar tests. The tests are easy for me.

___

3. Our grammar teacher didn't tell us the test would take two hours. She surprised everyone.

___

4. I had reviewed the practice exam. I understand it very well.

___

5. The test will be on adjective clauses. We will take this test next.

___

6. This quarter is almost over. It started approximately six weeks ago.

___

7. The students in this class will be studying in a partial academic program next quarter. The students receive an average of 70 in their classes this quarter.

___

8. When I enter the university, I'll study economics. I have always liked this subject.

___

9. Before I begin my academic work, I'm going to take a short vacation. I need a vacation.

___

10. My parents are planning to visit the United States at this time. I really want to see them.

___

11. My sister isn't coming with them. I haven't seen her in two years.

___

12. My sister is going to have a baby soon, so I'll be an uncle. She was married last year.

___

13. When I talked to her on the phone last week, she told me that her husband was really a nice person, so I'm anxious to meet him. I have never seen her husband.

___

14. Her husband has a good job with the government. He has a master's degree in economics.

___

■ Relative Pronouns as Objects of Prepositions ■

1. Sometimes a preposition is used with a relative pronoun, for example, *with which, for which, to whom*. The preposition is a part of the adjective clause, and it is determined by the verb and the meaning you want to communicate.

   [The man had just arrived in the United States. We spoke to *(or* with*) (or* for*)* him.]
   *The man **to whom we spoke** had just arrived in the United States.*
   *The man **with whom we spoke** had just arrived in the United States.*
   *The man **for whom we spoke** had just arrived in the United States.*

   The relative pronouns *whom, which,* and *that* can be the object of the preposition.

2. In formal English the prepositions precede the relative pronouns.

   *The composer **to whom** I am listening is Brahms.*
   *The country **in which** Brahms was born is Germany.*

3. Prepositions may also be separated from the relative pronoun and placed at the end of the adjective clause.

   *The composer **whom** I am listening **to** is Brahms.*
   *The country **which** he was born **in** is Germany.*
   *Ms. Parks is the music teacher **whom** I studied **with** for many years.*

4. When *that* is used as object of the preposition, the preposition can *never* be placed in front of the relative pronoun.

   Correct: *The concert **that** I told you **about** was last night.*
   Incorrect: *The concert about that I told you was last night.*

5. If the adjective clause is long, it is best to keep the preposition and relative pronoun together.

   Correct: *Ms. Parks is the music teacher **with whom** I studied in Denver two years ago.*
   Incorrect: *Ms. Parks is the music teacher whom I studied in Denver two years ago with.*

6. In spoken and written English, when the pronoun functions as the object of the preposition and when the preposition is at the end of the adjective clause, the relative pronoun that introduces the adjective clause is often omitted.

   This is the book that I am interested in.
   This is the book I am interested in. (omitted)

Here is a copy of the first test which I told you about.
Here is a copy of the first test I told you about.

In the following sentence, the preposition *for* is not at the end of the adjective clause, so the relative pronoun cannot be left out.

Correct: *She is the teacher **for whom** I worked so hard.*

Incorrect: *She is the teacher for I worked so hard.*

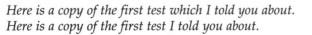

Exercise 14 *Combine the sentences, using adjective clauses in two ways. Remember to use* that *only in necessary clauses.*

Example: Professor Ray is the woman. So much has been written about her.

Professor Ray is the woman about whom so much has been written.

Professor Ray is the woman whom so much has been written about.

1. Dr. Jones is the man. I have talked about him many times.

   _____

   _____

2. This is the hospital. He has worked in this hospital for several years.

   _____

   _____

3. He has performed many difficult operations. He has received much acclaim for them.

   _____

   _____

4. Many people are grateful to him. He performed successful operations on them.

   _____

   _____

5. The surgeon is still alive. Dr. Jones studied with this surgeon.

   _____

   _____

6. Dr. Jones is a very modest man. The Nobel Prize in medicine was awarded to him.

   _____

   _____

7. This award is greatly valued by people around the world. He worked hard for it.

_____

_____

8. Alfred Bernhard Nobel was a Swedish chemist and inventor. The Nobel Prize was named after him.

_____

_____

9. Medicine is one of six fields. The Nobel Foundation presents awards in these fields.

_____

_____

10. Dr. Jones is undoubtedly a great man. I have much respect for him.

_____

_____

11. He is the physician. My doctor studied under him when he was in medical school.

_____

_____

12. His hospital staff is planning a celebration. Dr. Jones will be the guest of honor at this celebration.

_____

_____

■ 9-4 UNNECESSARY ADJECTIVE CLAUSES THAT REFER TO COMPLETE SENTENCES

1. Sometimes an adjective clause comes after the entire sentence and refers to the entire sentence instead of to a single noun. In this sentence, John's parents were not happy because of the *exams*; they were happy because *John made high grades on his exams*.

   John made high grades on his exams, **which made his parents happy.**

2. When the adjective clause refers to the entire sentence, only the relative pronoun *which* can begin the clause.

3. This type of adjective clause is common in spoken English. In written English, the comma must be included. If it is left out, the adjective clause becomes a necessary clause and will modify only the noun in front of it.

   Incorrect: *Jim tried to sing at the party which made everyone laugh.*

   The party didn't make everyone laugh. *Jim's singing at the party* made everyone laugh.

Exercise 15 ▪▪   *Restate the sentences so that an adjective clause modifies the entire statement.*

1. The little girl brought her pet frog to class. This surprised the teacher.

2. The frog escaped from its basket, and this caused all the other children to scream.

3. The frog jumped on top of a bookcase. This made it difficult to reach.

4. The students finally recaptured the frog, but it wasn't an easy job.

5. While the children were trying to catch the frog, they were screaming and yelling. All this disturbed the class next door.

6. The principal of the school sent the little girl home. This action made her parents punish her.

7. The little girl had to stay in her room, and this punishment made her sad.

8. She promised never to take the frog to school again. Her parents were thankful for this.

Exercise 16 ▪▪   *In a group of three or four, discuss your experience of learning English. Complete the sentences with adjective clauses. All sentences must relate to the topic of the discussion. Be careful of prepositions, which will determine the verbs that can be used after them.*

1. English is a language _____.

2. I first started learning English in the year _____ _____.

3. I think teachers _____ are the best teachers.

4. Teachers shouldn't get annoyed with students _____.

5. Students _____ learn to speak English the fastest.

6. I think it's best to use books _____.

7. I find it a waste of time to do homework _____.

8. I like to be in a class with students _____.

9. I have (or haven't) spoken to my last English teacher _____.

10. My last English teacher is an individual for _____.

11. I decided to study English in this school because I wanted a place _____.

12. The first time _____ I was very nervous.

13. I have a hard time using English grammar correctly _____.

14. I like learning vocabulary _____.

15. I don't understand the reason _____.

16. This book has lots of grammar exercises _____.

17. I enjoy class _____.

18. Our teacher is an individual about _____.

19. It is good to study English in a country in _____.

20. Studying English abroad has been an experience _____.

Exercise 17 ▪▪ *Rewrite the paragraph, using adjective clauses to connect the sentences.*

Coffee is a rich, aromatic drink. Coffee has been a popular beverage for more than a thousand years. Although many people drink coffee, it contains a stimulant. This stimulant affects the nervous system. The effect it has depends on each person's individual system, the amount of caffeine a person consumes, and the amount of coffee an individual usually drinks every day. One or two cups of brewed coffee contains only mild doses of caffeine. These mild doses make you more alert and less tired. The person may experience headaches, nervousness, and irritability. This person habitually drinks three to six cups of brewed coffee. This amount contains heavy doses of caffeine. It is interesting to note that large doses of caffeine affect heavy coffee drinkers differently than light coffee drinkers. The person becomes less nervous and has fewer headaches with large doses of caffeine. This person is a heavy drinker. On the other hand, the people feel nervous and have upset stomachs with increased doses of caffeine. These people are light coffee drinkers. Morning is the time. At this time, the heavy drinker must have a cup of coffee to wake up and begin the day's activities. Because this drink is a stimulant, it is not good for children. These children are normally overactive.

9-5 REDUCTION OF ADJECTIVE CLAUSES

■ Full Adjective Clauses ■	■ Reduced Adjective Clauses ■
*The student **who is talking to the teacher** is from China.*	*The student **talking to the teacher** is from China.*
*Last night she gave a lecture **which was on technological developments in her country**.*	*Last night she gave a lecture **on technological developments in her country**.*
*Anyone **who is interested in this country** should plan to attend the lecture tonight.*	*Anyone **interested in this country** should plan to attend the lecture tonight.*

1. Adjective clauses can often be reduced to adjective phrases with no change in meaning.

2. An adjective clause can be reduced to an adjective phrase only if the clause (a) begins with *who, which,* or *that* as the subject of the clause and (b) contains a *be* form of the verb.

3. To reduce an adjective clause to a phrase, omit the relative pronoun and the *be* form of the verb.

   Adjective clause: *The man **who is** wearing the gray suit is my uncle.*
   Adjective phrase: *The man wearing the gray suit is my uncle.*

   Adjective clause: *He is the person **who is** most concerned about my success.*
   Adjective phrase: *He is the person most concerned about my success.*

   Adjective clause: *The essays **that are** written in this book are very interesting.*
   Adjective phrase: *The essays written in this book are very interesting.*

Adjective clause: *The book **which is** on my desk also contains many interesting essays.*

Adjective phrase: *The book **on my desk** also contains many interesting essays.*

4. If there is no *be* form of the verb, it is often possible to omit the relative pronoun and change the verb to its *-ing* form.

Adjective clause: *Anyone **who has** a library card may check out books.*

Adjective phrase: *Anyone **having** a library card may check out books.*

Adjective clause: *The library does not contain any studies **which deal** with the psychological effects of the Civil War.*

Adjective phrase: *The library does not contain any studies **dealing** with the psychological effects of the Civil War.*

5. If the adjective clause needs commas, the adjective phrase also needs commas.

Adjective clause: *You can get your passport renewed at the Kennedy Building, **which is** located near the train station.*

Adjective phrase: *You can get your passport renewed at the Kennedy Building, **located** near the train station.*

6. Some adjective clauses can be reduced to appositive phrases. An appositive phrase is a noun or pronoun with modifiers that is placed after another noun or pronoun to explain it.

Adjective clause: *History, **which is** my favorite subject, has always fascinated me.*

Appositive phrase: *History, **my favorite subject**, has always fascinated me.*

Adjective clause: *Ms. Bryson, **who is** the head librarian, has a degree in history.*

Appositive phrase: *Ms. Bryson, **the head librarian**, has a degree in history.*

Adjective clause: *Boston, **which is** an interesting city, has many historical points of interest.*

Appositive phrase: *Boston, **an interesting city**, has many historical points of interest.*

Because an appositive phrase adds only extra, unnecessary information, it is always set off from the rest of the sentence by commas.

7. Using adjective and appositive phrases and adjective clauses in written work adds variety to sentence structure and makes the writing more interesting.

Exercise 18 ⚏⚌ *Change the adjective clause in each sentence to an adjective* ⚌⚌⚌⚌⚌⚌⚌⚌⚌⚌⚌⚌ *phrase or an appositive phrase.*

Example: Dr. Chu is the professor who is teaching Chemistry 101 this semester.

Dr. Chu is the professor teaching Chemistry 101 this semester.

1. Chemistry, which is a difficult subject, can be enjoyable.

2. Nevertheless, the students who are taking Dr. Chu's class this semester are enjoying it.

3. Dr. Chu has written several chemistry books, which are used in universities around the world.

4. He has just completed an important government report, which is on reserve in the library.

5. Jessica Gelman, who was the top graduate student in Dr. Chu's advanced chemistry course last semester, helped with the research for this report.

6. The students who have been in his classes consider it a privilege to study with him.

7. He has also written several articles that comment on the effects of chemicals in our food.

8. These articles, which were written several years ago, have been published in several popular magazines.

9. He believes that we should avoid all foods which contain chemical preservatives.

10. I heard that his wife, who is a very nice person, is writing a book which is on cooking with only natural ingredients.

11. By the way, the girl who is behind you is his daughter.

12. You are fortunate to be in a class which is taught by such a respected scholar.

Exercise 19 *First, check (✓) the sentences in which it is possible to reduce the adjective clauses to phrases. Then rewrite the checked sentences, making the changes. Some sentences contain more than one adjective clause.*

1. Dr. William Fry, whose lecture I attended last Friday, has appeared on numerous talk shows recently to talk about his new book.

2. Dr. William F. Fry Jr., who is a Stanford University professor of psychiatry, is an authority on laughter.

3. He notes that of all the major psychological studies which were done on human emotions between 1877 and 1962, only 31 percent were concerned with pleasant reactions such as laughter.

4. Many members of the medical profession now believe that laughter, which everyone agrees is a common element of everyday life, has therapeutic effects on the human body.

5. Patients who suffer from heart disease, which is one of the major illnesses that exists in the Western world today, can benefit from laughter.

6. Science has demonstrated that the healthy effects that laughter provides are the activation of the muscles, the increase in heart rate, and the amplification of respiration.

7. Sudden and intense anger is an emotion which is often responsible for starting a heart attack in people who have heart trouble.

8. Dr. Fry, who is a respected authority on this subject, believes that laughter can save many lives.

9. He also believes that for individuals who lean toward aggressive behavior, laughter and humor may offer alternatives to violence.

10. If you are interested in learning more about the subject which Dr. Fry spoke about last week, you should read his most recent book.

Exercise 20 ▪▪
▪▪▪▪▪▪▪▪▪▪▪

These paragraphs on the American author Alex Haley contain short and sometimes awkward sentences. Rewrite the paragraphs, connecting the sentences with adjective clauses, adjective phrases, and appositive phrases where possible.

Alex Haley became a famous author. Alex Haley wrote the book *Roots: The Saga of an American Family*. *Roots* is the history of one African-American family. Alex Haley was born in Ithaca, New York, but spent most of his early life in Henning, Tennessee. In Henning, Tennessee, he first heard stories about the African slaves in his family's history. These stories had been passed from generation to generation. His grandmother told him these stories. Mr Haley first became interested in his family's history at a time. During this time he was in London. In London he was on a writing assignment. Mr. Haley's research eventually took him to Gambia in Africa. There he was able to learn about a young African boy. The young African boy's name was Kunta Kinte. As a child, Mr. Haley had often heard this name, and he was happy to learn that Kunta Kinte was a real person. Slave traders had stolen Kunta Kinte from his family and brought him to the United States.

The book *Roots* is more than a book about one African-American family. *Roots* was the number one nonfiction bestseller in 1977. *Roots* is an important book. It tells much about the early history of the United States. A television miniseries was broadcast in 1977. The miniseries was based on the book. The miniseries attracted some 130 million viewers.

In all of his work, Alex Haley was a writer. His works of historical fiction and reportage depicted the struggles of the African-American community. Before Alex Haley became famous for *Roots*, he was best known as the writer. He helped Malcolm X to write *The Autobiography of Malcolm X*. Malcolm X was the Black Muslim spokesman. After the publication of *Roots*, Mr. Haley wrote another book. This book was published in the spring of 1980. The title of this book is *Search*. This book is about how he wrote *Roots*. Alex Haley died in Seattle, Washington, in 1992.

Practice Exam

Rewrite the paragraphs and connect the sentences, using adjective clauses, adjective phrases, and appositive phrases where possible.

When we hear the word pollution, most people think of air pollution. However, there is another kind of pollution. It is called noise pollution. We are constantly surrounded by sounds. These sounds awake us, put us to sleep, entertain us, and annoy us. Most people have become accustomed to the noise. These individuals live in big cities. This noise surrounds them night and day. The fact is that their ears are immune to the racket around them. This fact surprises me. Indeed, I am always surprised when I see teenagers. They are wearing radio earphones. Loud rock music bombards their eardrums from these radio earphones.

I remember the time. I was visiting my friend, Reza, in New York at this time. Reza was a student at New York University. His apartment was on Fifth Avenue. Fifth Avenue is one of the busiest streets in Manhattan. Nevertheless, he slept like a baby every night in spite of the ambulance and police sirens at 3:00 in the morning. Even his dog never woke up. His dog slept beside his bed.

I enjoyed visiting New York City. New York City is a fascinating place. However, I prefer a small town. In a small town at night, only the soft sounds of crickets can be heard.

LESSON TEN

■ 10-1 NOUN CLAUSES

1. A noun clause has the same function as a single-word noun.

   His **house** is beautiful. (single-word noun)
   Where he lives is beautiful. (noun clause)

   Single-word nouns have many different functions in sentences; therefore, noun clauses have many different functions. In this lesson, you will concentrate on the four most common functions:

   - subject of a sentence: ***Whenever we start*** *will be fine with me.*
   - object of a sentence: *Did you know* ***that they weren't going to help us****?*
   - object of the preposition: *Aren't you concerned about* ***how long it will take****?*
   - complement of the adjective: *I'm not sure* ***how much time we'll need****.*

2. These words, called **subordinating conjunctions** or **subordinators,** introduce noun clauses.

who	which	how	how much
whoever	whichever	however	how many
whom	where	whose	how long
whomever	wherever	why	how often
what	when	whether (or not)	how soon
whatever	whenever	that	

3. Note the word order of noun clauses.

NOUN CLAUSE

	Subordinator	Subject	Verb	Remainder of sentence
I don't know	*where*	*Bob*	*went*	*last night.*
I can't understand	*why*	*she*	*has left*	*the children alone.*
I don't believe	*what*	*they*	*said*	*about you yesterday.*

4. Sometimes the subordinator introduces a noun clause that has its own subject and verb.

   *Nobody knows **why she went**.*

   At other times the subordinator is used as the subject of the verb in the noun clause. Only the subordinators *who, whoever, what, whatever, which,* and *whichever* can be used as the subject of the verb in noun clauses. Look at these noun clauses.

	Subordinator subject	Verb	Remainder of sentence
I can't tell you	*who*	*borrowed*	*my book.*
She understands	*what*	*happened.*	
Nobody knows	*which*	*came*	*first, the chicken or the egg.*

5. In informal spoken English, *who* and *whoever,* although incorrect, appear occasionally instead of *whom* and *whomever.* In speech and writing, *whom* and *whomever* are preferred.

   Correct: *Whomever the company hires should be willing to travel.*

   Incorrect: *Whoever he knows should be invited.*

   Whom <u>is</u> used if the verb in the noun clause already has a subject. Compare:

   *I never pay attention **to whom** my roommate telephones.*
   *I never pay attention **to who** telephones my roommate.*

6. Be careful not to confuse noun clauses beginning with *that* and *who* and adjective clauses beginning with *that* and *who.*

   Noun clause: *I heard **that you passed the test**.*
   Adjective clause: *Are you the one **that passed the test**?*

   Remember that noun clauses follow verbs or indirect objects; adjective clauses follow nouns.

7. Speakers of English often reply to a question with a sentence that contains more than one noun clause in different functions.

   A: *Is Maria dating Jose?*
   B: *I don't know **if she's dating him**, but **whether or not she is** is none of our business.*

   Note the repetition of *is* after *but. Is* occurs as the verb of the noun clause (*whether or not she is*) and as the main verb of the statement (*is none of our business*).

   A: *Why was Nopporn in the director's office all day?*
   B: *He didn't tell me **why he had been there all day**; besides, **why he was** is a private matter.*

Note the repetition of different forms of *be* after *besides*. *Was* occurs as the verb of the noun clause (*why he was*), and *is* occurs as the main verb of the statement (*is a private matter*).

Exercise 1 *Underline the noun clauses in the paragraph.*

Why some very good students often fail exams was recently studied by a professor of psychology at New York University. Professor Iris Fodor conducted research on the anxiety of some students before taking exams. Professor Fodor stated that many students fail exams because they become extremely nervous and cannot think logically. Furthermore, although they have studied, they are afraid of whatever is on the exam. Extremely nervous students forget everything they have studied, and some even become sick before a test. Dr. Fodor says how a student feels before a test is very important. She worked with fifty students and taught them how they could reduce their test anxiety and perform well on their exams. She reported that the students in the program felt better able to cope with their anxieties. What she told them to do before a test was the following:

1. Breathe deeply and slowly to relax.
2. Speak to yourself about positive and happy subjects and get rid of any negative thinking.
3. Be realistic. Don't think your life will end if you fail.
4. Don't be too hard on yourself. If you know you have studied, do your best.

If they follow these simple suggestions, Professor Fodor is certain that many unusually nervous students can perform better in test situations.

Exercise 2 *Underline the clauses in the conversation. Write **N** above the sentences that contain noun clauses. Write **A** above the sentences that contain adjective clauses.*

Lee: Nobody in the office knows whose car that is outside. Do you know who it belongs to?

Ned: Which one?

Lee: Didn't you notice that a car's been double-parked outside the building for more than an hour? Look out the window.

Ned: Oh, I think that it belongs to the woman who came for the job interview, but I'm not absolutely sure.

Lee: Well, whoever it belongs to should remove it because if the police pass by, the car will be towed. Maybe you should find out whether the car is hers.

Ned: I'll knock on the door, but I'm sure that Mr. Sullivan won't like our interrupting him during an interview.

Lee: I don't think that he'll mind. After all, the car the police had towed the last time was his, and for weeks he didn't stop complaining about how much it cost him to get his car back.

Ned: That's all right. He can afford it. It's the workers whom he doesn't pay well who can't.

■ Noun Clause as Subject of a Sentence ■

1. When a noun clause is the subject of the sentence, the main verb of the completed sentence is singular in form.

   *What they do in their free time **is** none of my business.*

   *Whether or not they stay **makes** no difference to me.*

   *The fact that fewer than 20 percent of the population voted **proves** my point.*

2. The tense of the verb in the noun clause must show a logical relationship to the main verb of the completed sentence. Compare:

   *When Sue **is going to get** married is a secret.* (Sue hasn't gotten married yet, and the date is a secret.)

   *When Sue **got** married is a secret.* (Sue got married, but the date is still a secret.)

   The tense of the verb in the noun clause also depends on the meaning of the verb. This sentence does not make sense.

   Incorrect: *When Sue has been married is a secret.*

3. These phrases are often used to complete sentences with noun clauses as subjects.

. . . does not concern [me]	. . . is up to [them]
. . . is none of [our] business	. . . is a private matter
. . . depends on several things	. . . has not worried [me]

Exercise 3   *Underline the subject of each sentence. Write **NC** next to those sentences that contain a noun clause rather than a single-word noun.*

1. Our discussion was private.

2. Her reasons for being angry surprised me.

3. What she said was rude.

4. Who you are dating is none of my business.

5. Their decision doesn't concern you.

6. Why she quit her job is a mystery.

7. How they choose to live is up to them.

8. Whether or not she takes that class is her decision.

Exercise 4   *With another student, take turns asking and answering the questions. Use a noun clause as the subject of each sentence.*

Example: **A:** What did the instructor tell John about cheating?

   B: *What she told him* is none of my business.

1. **A:** Who reported John's activities?

   B: _____ does not concern me.

2. **A:** Where is John now?

   B: _____ is none of my business.

3. **A:** When is he going to talk to the director?

   B: _____ is not my concern.

4. **A:** Why was he copying from Alison?

   B: _____ is a mystery to me.

5. **A:** Has be been cheating throughout the course?

   B: _____ doesn't really matter at this point.

6. **A:** What will happen to him?

   B: _____ depends on the director.

7. **A:** How many times has he met with the director since the course began?

   B: _____ is none of our business.

8. **A:** What did the director tell him during their last meeting?

   B: _____ is not our concern.

9. **A:** Will the director notify his parents?

   B: _____ probably depends on John's attitude.

10. **A:** John's very intelligent. Why does he get into so much trouble?

    B: _____ has always puzzled me.

Exercise 5 *Restate each sentence, using a noun clause as the subject. The underlined words will help you to choose the appropriate subordinator to use.*

Example: The president's <u>destination</u> was a secret.

Where the president was going was a secret.

OR

Where the president went was a secret.

1. <u>The time</u> of his departure was also a secret.

   _____

2. <u>His ignorance of world affairs</u> has surprised everyone in Washington.

   _____

3. <u>His reason for taking this trip</u> has been worrying his advisors.

   _____

4. The president decided not to take his wife with him. <u>This</u> surprised everyone.

   _____

5. <u>The number of days</u> he will stay is confidential.

   _____

6. <u>The leaders</u> he will meet with makes everyone nervous.

   _____

7. <u>His decision to go alone</u> concerns the members of his cabinet.

   _____

8. He did not tell anyone about this sudden trip. <u>This</u> made everyone curious.

   _____

9. <u>His strange behavior</u> has upset many people.

   _____

10. <u>His future actions</u> will certainly be of interest to everyone.

    _____

Exercise 6 ■■
■■■■■■■■■■■ ■
With another student, decide on two different ways to complete each sentence. Use noun clauses as subjects.

1. _____ doesn't concern us.
2. _____ is none of our business.
3. _____ is a private matter.
4. _____ hasn't worried me.
5. _____ was excellent.

■ **Noun Clause as Object of a Sentence** ■

1. In a reply to a question, the tense of the verb in the noun clause does not change if the main verb of the completed sentence is in the simple present.

   A: *How long **was** she there?*
   B: *__I don't know__ how long she **was** there.*

   If the main verb of the completed sentence is in the simple past, the tense of the verb in the noun clause changes.

   A: *When will they arrive?*
   B: *Nobody **told** me when they **would arrive**.*

2. To introduce the noun clause as object of the sentence, these expressions are often used.

[I] don't know . . .	I have no idea [why] . . .
[He] didn't say . . .	I can't tell you [if] . . .
[I] didn't ask [her] . . .	[She] didn't tell me . . .
[They] didn't explain . . .	[We] haven't told anyone . . .

   *I don't remember **who he is**.*
   *We didn't hear **what they were talking about**.*
   *Nobody knows **whether they passed**.*

Exercise 7   *Underline the object of each sentence. Write **NC** next to those sentences that contain a noun clause rather than a single-word noun.*

1. I don't know the answer.

2. I like where she lives.

3. I can't tell you what the answer is.

4. I don't know him.

5. I don't understand why they feel this way.

6. I love their apartment.

7. Do you remember what her name is?

8. She hasn't decided when she will tell her boss.

Exercise 8   *With another student, take turns asking and answering the questions. Use a noun clause as the object of each sentence.*

Examples: **A:** How cold was it last night?

   B: I don't know *how cold it was.*

   A: Where is your roommate going?

   B: I don't know. He didn't tell me *where he was going.*

1. **A:** Who had a party last night?

   B: I don't know _____.

2. **A:** Where was it?

   B: I have no idea _____.

3. **A:** When did it start?

   B: I can't tell you _____.

4. **A:** When was it over?

   B: I can't say _____.

5. **A:** How did Reza get home?

   B: I don't know _____.

6. **A:** Whose car did he borrow?

   B: He didn't say _____.

7. **A:** Do you know whether or not he enjoyed the party?

   B: He didn't tell me _____.

8. **A:** Did he know about the party before last night?

   B: I really don't know _____.

9. **A:** Where is he now?

   B: I have no idea _____.

10. **A:** How long will he be gone?

    B: He didn't tell me _____.

Exercise 9 *Complete each sentence, using a noun clause as object. Be careful of meaning and tense changes.*

1. Three weeks ago, a police officer stopped me and my roommate and wanted to know where _____.

2. Since I was driving, he asked me why _____.

3. I was so nervous that I began speaking in my native language, so he asked if _____.

4. I began to speak English and explained that _____.

5. He wanted to know how long _____.

6. He also wanted to know what _____.

7. Then the officer asked to see my driver's license, but I didn't know where _____.

8. My roommate, who was sitting quietly, couldn't believe what _____.

9. The officer wanted to know whether _____ or not.

10. Finally, he gave me a ticket and said that _____.

11. As we drove away, my roommate promised me that _____.

Noun Clause as Object of a Preposition

*Everyone believes in **whatever Tony says**.*
*I never think about **how I will pay my bills**.*
*I can't rely on **what you tell me**.*

Exercise 10 *Restate each sentence, using a noun clause as object of the preposition.*

Example: You can never rely on the bus schedule.

You can never rely on when the bus will come.

1. She was looking at my painting.

2. I was worried about his health.

3. The teacher wasn't interested in his excuses.

4. Nobody can depend on Jim's promises.

5. Her parents didn't approve of her decision.

6. Stacey's parents were not pleased with her behavior in the store.

▪ Noun Clause as Adjective Complement ▪

1. A noun clause as an adjective complement completes the meaning started by the adjective.

   *I'm sure **that he'll succeed**.* (He will succeed. I'm sure of it.)

   *I'm convinced **that she's unhappy**.* (She's unhappy. I'm convinced of that.)

2. *That* is the most commonly used subordinator in this pattern. It can be omitted from the sentence.

   *I'm sure **he'll succeed**.*

   *I'm convinced **she's unhappy**.*

Exercise 11 *Combine the sentences. Make the first sentence into a noun clause used after the adjective in the second sentence. Omit* that *from some of the sentences.*

Example: John cheats on every exam. I'm convinced.

I'm convinced that John cheats on every exam.

1. He always denies it. We are aware.

2. He doesn't think anybody sees him. I'm sure.

3. He has never studied for an exam. His roommate is certain.

4. Cheating doesn't bother John. We are all convinced.

5. He doesn't have a conscience. I'm positive.

6. The instructor will never find out. John is confident.

7. He thinks cheating is acceptable. I'm sure.

8. He'll get caught one day. Everyone is certain.

9. He is going to be very surprised. I'm afraid.

10. He will never stop cheating. I'm not certain.

Exercise 12 *Complete the sentences, using a noun clause as an adjective complement. Be careful of tense and meaning.*

Example: Muna has been a good student all quarter, so she is confident
that she will pass the course.

1. The final exam in grammar will cover every lesson, so I am sure _____

_____

2. Because our grammar teacher has emphasized the tenses all quarter, I am
positive _____

3. However, she may not give us a long exam; in fact, we are convinced

_____

4. I am really not worried about the exam; on the contrary, I am certain _____

_____

5. The clauses are important; therefore, I am sure _____

_____

6. For some reason, Ryoji believes that our teacher doesn't like him, so he is
convinced _____

7. Concerning the conversation final, I am positive _____

_____

8. When I talked with the conversation teacher, he seemed certain _____

_____

9. All of the students are confident _____

_____

10. We are all sure _____

_____

■ 10-2 -*Ever* WORDS IN NOUN CLAUSES

I'll invite **whoever** (*or* **whomever**) *you like.*
Whoever shows up for dinner *is welcome.*
The dog follows us **wherever we go.**
The dog will eat **whatever you give her.**
Whichever way we go *is fine with me.*
However we go *makes no difference to me.*
I'll leave **whenever you want.**

1. *Whoever* and *whomever* mean *any person.* *Wherever* means *any place.* *Whatever* means *any thing.* *Whichever* means *any possibility.* *However* means *any manner.* *Whenever* means *any time.*

2. In informal spoken English, *whoever* is often used instead of *whomever.* In formal speech or writing, *whomever* is preferred.

3. Be careful not to confuse *however* when it is used to introduce a noun clause and *however* when it is used as a conjunctive adverb. Compare:

    However *you cook the meat is all right with me.*
    I'll help you to cook it; **however,** *I don't like rare meat.*

Exercise 13 ▪▪
▪▪▪▪▪▪▪▪▪▪▪▪ *With another student, take turns asking and answering the questions. Use an -ever word in your answer.*

Examples: **A:** What should I do about my problem?

   B: Do *whatever* seems best.

   A: Can I leave now?

   B: *Whenever* you want to leave is okay with me.

1. **A:** I'm getting tired of this party. Are you ready to go?
   B: I'm having a good time, but _____ you are ready is fine with me.

2. **A:** What should I tell our hostess?
   B: Tell her _____ you think is best.

3. **A:** I'm hungry. Do you want a hamburger or some chicken?
   B: I don't care. We can get _____ you prefer.

4. **A:** Tell me. Should we go to Burger King or to Kentucky Fried Chicken?
   B: It really doesn't matter to me. Let's go to _____ you like best.

5. **A:** What's the matter with you tonight? Can't you make a decision?
   B: Nothing is the matter. _____ you want to go is all right with me.

6. **A:** How do you want your hamburger, with or without onions?
   B: _____ she prepares it is all right with me.

7. **A:** Whom should we invite to our party next week?
   B: I don't know. _____ you invite will have fun.

8. **A:** By the way, who called at 12:00 last night?
   B: I don't know because _____ called hung up before I reached the phone.

9. **A:** It's really late, and I'm getting tired. Let's not get any dessert.
   B: O.K. _____ you say.

10. **A:** Are you angry because I wanted to leave the party early?
    B: Angry? Of course not. It's your car, so you can do _____ you like. Just don't ask me to go anywhere with you again.

Exercise 14 ▪▪
▪▪▪▪▪▪▪▪▪▪▪▪ *Look back at Exercise 1 on page 157. Identify the function of the noun clauses that you underlined:* subject of the sentence, object of the sentence, object of a preposition, adjective complement.

Exercise 15 ▪▪ *With another student, take turns asking and answering the questions. Use more than one noun clause in your answer.*

Example: Is Jamal leaving the United States?

Whether he's leaving is a mystery to me because he's never home when I call, but Franco told me that he was planning a party for Jamal. Maybe it's a goodbye party.

1. Why is Jamal returning to his country?
2. Did his parents tell him to go home?
3. Is he going to return to finish his studies?
4. How long will he stay?
5. Has he received an acceptance letter to a university yet?
6. Is his family having financial problems?
7. Was he packing last night?
8. What is he going to do with his new car?
9. Will he work or continue to study at home?
10. When does he have to leave?
11. Had he been expecting this to happen?
12. Are his cousins going home, too?
13. Why haven't they been to class?
14. What was Jamal telling the director about this situation?
15. What did the director say to him?
16. Is he going to pay his phone bill before he leaves?

Exercise 16 ▪▪ *In a group of three or four, discuss how to complete the sentences.*

1. What I miss most about my country _____.
2. I don't understand why Americans _____.
3. _____ most surprised me when I first came to the United States.
4. When I go back to live in my country, I'm confident _____.
5. What bothers me most about life in this country _____.
6. _____ worried me when I first came to the United States.
7. What I most hoped for when I came to the United States _____.
8. When I leave the United States for good, I'm sure _____.

■ 10-3 NOUN CLAUSES BEGINNING WITH *That*

1. *That* can often be omitted when it introduces a noun clause used as object of the verb.

   *We assumed **our son was sick**.*

   *I could not believe **he had lied to us**.*

   *I hope **he will tell the truth soon**.*

   *Do you imagine **he knows our feelings**?*

2. *That* cannot be omitted when it introduces a noun clause used as subject of the sentence. *That* as subject of the sentence emphasizes the information in the noun clause.

   ***That he had lied to us** was unbelievable.*

   ***That we accepted his apology** made him feel better.*

   ***That small boys sometimes lie** should not surprise anyone.*

3. *That* as subject of the sentence is very formal. It rarely occurs in informal spoken English. Instead, in conversation, speakers of English often use the word *it* as subject of the sentence and place the noun clause at the end of the sentence. In this pattern, a noun clause may follow a noun, pronoun, or an adjective.

   ***It** is a fact **that the world is facing a food shortage**. (That the world is facing a food shortage is a fact.)*

   ***It** is true **that many people are starving**. (That many people are starving is true.)*

4. People also often use a noun clause beginning with *the fact that* as subject of the sentence in place of a noun clause beginning with *that*.

   ***The fact that everyone refused to attend the meeting** took us by surprise. (That everyone refused to attend the meeting took us by surprise.)*

■

Exercise 17 ▪▪ *Combine the sentences, using a noun clause beginning with that as subject of the sentence.*

Examples: He told us the truth. This made us happy.

That he told us the truth made us happy.

John failed the course. This surprised me.

That John failed the course surprised me.

1. Michael Jordan has become a millionaire. This doesn't surprise anyone.

2. He is known all over the world. This is a fact.

3. He retired from basketball for a year in order to play baseball. This upset some people.

4. Michael Jordan has done some TV commercials. This is not strange.

5. Many companies use famous people to sell their products on TV. This is not unusual.

6. He is one of the greatest basketball players in the history of the game. This is common knowledge.

7. He has been a hero to many young boys. This is true.

8. He earned a reputation for being a gambler. This cannot be denied.

9. He often scored 35 points in a game. This is on record.

10. Games in which Michael Jordan played attracted thousand of spectators. This is a well-known fact.

Exercise 18 *Restate the sentences in Exercise 17, using* it *at the beginning of each sentence.*

Example: Michael Jordan has become a millionaire. This doesn't surprise anyone.

It doesn't surprise anyone that Michael Jordan has become a millionaire.

■ 10-4 SUBJUNCTIVE FORM OF THE VERB IN NOUN CLAUSES

1. When the following verbs have a noun clause as direct object, they require the base form of the verb (the infinitive without *to*). The use of the base form stresses the urgency or importance of the statement.

advise	desire	prefer	request	urge
command	insist	propose	require	
demand	order	recommend	suggest	

The doctor advised **that Sheila remain in the hospital.**

The nurse had insisted **that Sheila's husband leave the room.**

She recommended **that he return in the morning.**

2. The base form of the verb is used regardless of the tense of the main verb or the subject in the noun clause.

   *She **recommends** that **he be** at the store as early as possible.*
   *She **recommended** that **he be** at the store as early as possible.*

3. The negative is formed by putting *not* before the verb in the noun clause.

   *The doctor **advised** that Sheila **not remain** in the hospital.*
   *The nurse recommended that her husband **not stay** too long.*

4. In informal English, the auxiliary *should* sometimes precedes the verb in the noun clause.

   *The doctor **advised** that Sheila **should remain** in the hospital.*
   *The nurse **recommended** that Sheila's husband **should return** in the morning.*

   The auxiliary *should* is not used with the verbs *command* and *demand*.

5. The base form of the verb is also used in noun clauses as adjective complements after these expressions: *it is important that, it is necessary that, it is essential that,* and *it is vital that.*

   ***It is important that** either your mother or your father **sign** these papers.*
   ***It was necessary that** you **be** here at 8:30.*

Exercise 19 *Use the verbs in the box to introduce noun clauses containing the following information. Provide an appropriate subject—for example, the teacher, my father, my mother.*

advise	desire	prefer	request	urge
command	insist	propose	require	
demand	order	recommend	suggest	

Examples: speak to the director
   The teacher advised that I speak to the director.

   move to another city
   Since my roommate can't stand the cold weather here,
   I recommended that she move to another city.

1. buy a new car

2. learn to type

3. take only three courses

4. get married

5. study in my own country

6. be on time

7. wear a suit

8. not come to class late

9. not write in pencil

10. not smoke in the hospital

11. drive carefully

12. not talk so loudly in the restaurant

Exercise 20 *In a group of three or four, prepare a list of advice for students who are planning to come to the United States to study. Use expressions like* We suggest that, It is important that, *and* Language schools require that. *When your group finishes, compare lists with another group. Which group came up with the longer list? Which group came up with the better advice?*

Exercise 21 *Underline the clauses in the sentences. Write **N** next to the sentences that contain noun clauses, **Adj** next to the sentences that contain adjective clauses, or **Adv** next to the sentences that contain adverb clauses.*

1. Yesterday, many students didn't understand what we were talking about.

2. Yesterday, many students didn't understand the lesson that was on clauses.

3. Yesterday, many students didn't understand the lesson because it was on subordination.

4. Dr. Larson, who is our director, visited our class.

5. When he came in, Behrooz looked at him.

6. What Dr. Larson said about the class was very complimentary.

7. Although Behrooz had eaten a big breakfast, he was still hungry during the class.

8. Ahmed enjoyed what he had eaten for breakfast.

9. He had had a breakfast that was good and nutritious.

10. This class understood what the instructor had said about the past perfect.

11. When the instructor explained the past perfect, everyone understood.

12. The past perfect was one of the tenses that everyone understood.

13. Ali went to the library and asked for the book that was on reserve.

14. The librarian, however, didn't know which book he wanted.

15. Before he could get the book, he had to show her the title of it.

Exercise 22 *Combine the sentences, using the type of clauses indicated in parentheses. In some sentences two types of clauses are required.*

1. Yesterday we had a review of clauses. Everyone understood the review. (adjective clause)

2. We had had the review. Everyone told the teacher this. They felt much better about the clauses. (adverb clause + noun clause as object)

3. Some students went into the lounge. They relaxed or did homework there. (adjective clause)

4. The grammar teacher gave Miwako copies of an additional exercise. She had forgotten to give the exercises to the students. They left the grammar class. (adjective clause + adverb clause)

5. Miwako had given everybody a copy of the exercise. They went to their reading class. (adverb clause)

6. The students felt more secure in using the clauses. This greatly pleased our teacher. (adjective clause *or* noun clause as subject)

7. Every student understood the review. This made the teacher happy. (noun clause)

8. Jose said this. He had always had trouble with clauses. He was studying in his country. (noun clause as object + adverb clause)

9. The teacher wanted to know this. What had been the problem? (noun clause as object)

10. Now Jose understands very well. This makes him feel more confident. (noun clause as subject)

11. Using the clauses correctly and spontaneously is not easy to do. Nevertheless, everyone did well on the review. (adverb clause)

12. I am not worried about this. How well will I do on the test on this chapter? (noun clause as object of preposition)

Exercise 23 *Rewrite the sentences in the form of a paragraph. Use noun, adjective, and adverb clauses. You may also want to use coordinating conjunctions and conjunctive adverbs (see Part 2). Be careful not to overconnect.*

1. The grammar final was difficult. I took it last quarter.

2. I entered the room. I was a little nervous.

3. I didn't feel very confident. I had studied diligently.

4. The teacher gave us some directions before the exam. Her directions were poor.

5. I asked her a question. She answered the question very poorly.

6. I was supposed to do something. I didn't understand what.

7. Her explanation was so poor. I didn't understand what.

8. I do not like teachers. Their directions are not clear.

9. Everyone else had finished the exam. I completed it.

10. I went to her desk. She was correcting exams from an earlier class there.

11. She took my paper. She didn't even look up.

12. She didn't like me all quarter. I don't know why.

13. My grade will be high or low. I'm not certain.

Practice Exam

■ SECTION 1

Underline the noun clause in each sentence. Then identify the function of the noun clause: subject of the sentence, object of the sentence, object of a preposition, adjective complement.

1. Although I'm going to be an engineering student, I have always been interested in how people learn languages.

2. I don't know why this subject has always fascinated me.

3. That speaking a language always precedes writing it is obvious because children understand what their parents say before they learn to write.

4. Nevertheless, I am always surprised at how many words a one-year-old child knows.

5. Language learning research reports that all languages have a lot in common.

6. For example, I am certain that every language has a way to express time.

7. I really don't remember when I spoke my first word.

8. However, I am sure that I said something very interesting.

■ SECTION 2

Restate the sentences, using a noun clause as subject of each sentence.

1. My first word as a child was probably *mama*.

   _____

2. The reason most children learn this word first is obvious.

   _____

3. The way most small children pronounce the words of their language is always amusing.

   _____

4. The age at which a child speaks his or her first words is very important.

   _____

5. Einstein didn't speak until he was three years old. This surprises me.

   _____

■ **SECTION 3**

Answer the questions, using a noun clause as subject and a noun clause as object.

1. Why was our teacher's little boy in class yesterday?

_____

2. How long has she been married?

_____

3. Does her husband have a good job?

_____

4. Is she going to have more children?

_____

■ **SECTION 4**

Complete the sentences with -ever words.

1. _____ you decide to dress your children is up to you.

2. However, they simply cannot wear _____ they want to wear, in most private schools.

3. _____ wants more information on public versus private schools should visit each type of school.

4. _____ type of school you choose, public or private, should provide your children with a good education.

5. My parents moved a lot when I was a child, but I enjoyed _____ I was.

6. Furthermore, I made friends with _____ I met.

■ **SECTION 5**

Rewrite the sentences in the form of a paragraph. Use noun, adjective, and adverb clauses.

1. Einstein didn't speak until he was three years old. This surprises everyone. He grew up to be a genius.

2. I know the reason. He hated school.

3. He had a rebellious attitude toward his teachers. This caused him to behave disrespectfully in class.

4. I have a little cousin. He also has poor behavior in school.

5. We hope this. He will grow up to be another Einstein.

6. His parents have always been certain of this. He has a high I.Q.

PART 5

Passive Voice

INTRODUCTION TO PART 5 ■ ■ ■ ■ ■ ■ ■

The term "voice" refers to the relationship between the verb (or action) and the subject of a sentence. In an **active voice** sentence, we place the subject before the verb because we want to emphasize who or what performs the action. We want to emphasize the doer of the action.

In a **passive voice** sentence, we want to emphasize the **action**, what happened, rather than who or what performs the action. In the passive voice sentence, the subject (doer) of the active voice sentence is placed after the verb or is omitted entirely.

Active voice: ***The mechanic*** *discovered the problem.*

Passive voice: *The problem was discovered by* ***the mechanic.***

Active voice: ***The mechanic*** *repaired the brakes.*

Passive voice: *The brakes were repaired.*

Because the doer in a passive voice sentence is often not mentioned, a passive sentence often sounds impersonal and objective.

The passive voice is frequently used in written English. It is often found in textbooks, in scientific, business, technical and government reports, and in newspapers.

A sentence in the active voice is usually preferable to a sentence in the passive voice because an active voice sentence is shorter, stronger, and more direct.

LESSON ELEVEN

■ 11-1 FORMING THE PASSIVE

■ Simple Present ■

Active: *Many older citizens **use** the library.*
Passive: *The library **is used** by many older citizens.*

Active: ***Do** many older citizens **use** the library?*
Passive: ***Is** the library **used** by many older citizens?*

■ Simple Past ■

Active: *Many children **used** the library last summer.*
Passive: *The library **was used** by many children last summer.*

Active: ***Did** many children **use** the library last summer?*
Passive: ***Was** the library **used** by many children last summer?*

■ Present Continuous ■

Active: *Workmen **are painting** the third floor.*
Passive: *The third floor **is being painted**.*

Active: ***Are** workmen **painting** the third floor?*
Passive: ***Is** the third floor **being painted**?*

■ Past Continuous ■

Active: *Last week, they **were painting** the children's room.*
Passive: *Last week, the children's room **was being painted**.*

Active: ***Were** they **painting** the children's room last week?*
Passive: ***Was** the children's room **being painted** last week?*

▪ Future with *will* ▪

Active: *The library **will offer** many new programs next year.*
Passive: *Many new programs **will be offered** next year.*

Active: ***Will** the library **offer** many new programs next year?*
Passive: ***Will** many new programs **be offered** next year?*

▪ Future with *be going to* ▪

Active: *A local author **is going to organize** a children's story hour.*
Passive: *A children's story hour **is going to be organized** by a local author.*

Active: ***Is** a local author **going to organize** a children's story hour?*
Passive: ***Is** a children's story hour **going to be organized**?*

▪ Present Perfect ▪

Active: *The director **has ordered** a lot of new equipment.*
Passive: *A lot of new equipment **has been ordered**.*

Active: ***Has** the director **ordered** a lot of new equipment?*
Passive: ***Has** a lot of new equipment **been ordered**?*

▪ Past Perfect ▪

Active: *Workmen **had** already **installed** the new computer when I was there last week.*
Passive: *The new computer **had** already **been installed** when I was there last week.*

Active: ***Had** workmen already **installed** the new computer when you were there last week?*
Passive: ***Had** the new computer already **been installed** when you were there last week?*

▪ Future Perfect ▪

Active: *The library **will have started** the children's story hour by the end of next month.*
Passive: *The children's story hour **will have been started** by the end of next month.*

Active: ***Will** the library **have started** the children's story hour by the end of next month?*
Passive: ***Will** the children's story hour **have been started** by the end of next month?*

■ Present Infinitive ■

Active:	*I have **to renew** my library card.*
Passive:	*My library card has **to be renewed**.*
Active:	*Do you have **to renew** your library card?*
Passive:	*Does your library card have **to be renewed**?*

■ Modals ■

Active:	*You **should return** the book before June 1st.*
Passive:	*The book **should be returned** before June 1st.*
Active:	***Should** I **return** the book before June 1st?*
Passive:	***Should** the book **be returned** before June 1st?*
Active:	*You **should have returned** the book last week.*
Passive:	*The book **should have been returned** last week.*
Active:	***Should** I **have returned** the book last week?*
Passive:	***Should** the book **have been returned** last week?*

1. The passive is formed with a form of *be* + the past participle. Note the form of *be* for continuous tenses.

   *The third floor **is being painted**.*
   *Last week, the children's room **was being painted**.*

   Note the form of *be* for perfect tenses.

   *A lot of new equipment **has been ordered**.*
   *The new computer **had** already **been installed** when I was there last week.*

2. To make a verb in the passive voice negative, *not* is placed after the first auxiliary.

   *The second floor **is not being painted**.*
   *The book **should not be returned** after June 1st.*

3. Not every verb can be changed into the passive voice. Only transitive verbs (verbs that have an object) can be changed. Intransitive verbs (verbs that do not have an object) cannot be changed into the passive voice. For example, these sentences cannot be written in the passive voice because the verbs are intransitive.

   She seems tired.

   The dog disappeared.

   Verbs followed by reflexive pronouns also cannot be changed to the passive voice, as in *She picked **herself** up.*

4. The present perfect continuous, past perfect continuous, future continuous, and future perfect continuous tenses are not used in the passive voice.

5. When a transitive verb + preposition is put into the passive voice, the preposition remains immediately after the verb.

Active: *We must **put out** the fire.*

Passive: *The fire must **be put out**.*

Active: *The thief **locked** us **in** the closet.*

Passive: *We **were locked in** the closet.*

Exercise 1
Rapidly change the following active verbs to their passive forms. Do this exercise orally.

Examples: do *is done*   did *was done*   is doing *is being done*

1. tell
2. is telling
3. told
4. was telling
5. has told
6. had told
7. will tell
8. to tell
9. will have told
10. must tell
11. should write
12. to write
13. will write
14. had written
15. has written
16. was writing
17. wrote
18. is writing
19. writes
20. will have written
21. is fixing
22. will finish
23. sent
24. is giving
25. does
26. has seen
27. was correcting
28. is taking
29. will have finished
30. is going to fix

Exercise 2
Complete each sentence, using the correct passive form of the verbs in parentheses. Then work with another student and decide if the sentence is true or false.

1. Coffee (grow) _____ in France.

2. Dynamite (invent) _____ by Alfred Nobel, the man who was responsible for setting up the Nobel Peace Prize.

3. A cure for cancer (not find) _____.

4. A photograph of me and my classmates (take) _____ at the end of this course.

5. The classroom (not clean) _____ when students started arriving for class today.

6. Different actions (take) _____ these days to help deal with environmental problems.

7. Baseball (not play) _____ all over the world.

8. Computers (use) _____ more and more in the future.

9. A movie (not make) _____ in Hollywood right now.

10. A woman (elect) _____ president of the United States in the past.

Exercise 3 *Read the newspaper article. With another student, decide on an appropriate headline for the article. Then underline the verbs that can be changed into the passive voice. Finally, rewrite the paragraph, using the passive voice where possible.*

Something strange happened this past Sunday in Fairville. Numerous residents of the Pleasant Park area spotted a moose in gardens and on local streets. This was very unusual because people had never seen a moose in the town before. The sight must have really shocked Alice Meara, the owner of Serendipity Cards. At the sight of the moose in front of her store, she fell off the ladder on which she had been standing. After nearly two hours of excitement all over the area, the police, with the help of workers from the local zoo, caught the young male moose. It is now resting comfortably at the zoo. However, zoo officials will release it into the woods by the end of next week. As for Alice Meara, she's home in bed with an arm and a leg in casts. She broke both in the fall.

■ 11-2 USING THE PASSIVE

1. The passive voice is used in English in specific instances.

   a. When it is more interesting or important to emphasize *what happened* rather than who or what performed the action.

   *There was a terrible storm last night. Hundreds of houses **were destroyed**.*

    b. When the *doer* of the action is unknown. The subjects of such sentences in the active voice are words such as *they, people, someone, somebody,* etc.

       *Someone stole my car last night. My car **was stolen** last night.*

    c. When the *doer* of the action is known, but the speaker or writer does not want to name the person who made a statement or did something wrong.

       The teacher ruined the top of this desk accidentally.
       *The top of this desk **was ruined** accidentally.*

    d. When the *doers* of the action represent a large group of different individuals.

       *A lot of coffee **is grown** in Brazil.*

    e. When the *doer* of the action is obvious.

       *The letter **will be picked up** after 1:00.* (by the mailman)
       *Our tests **have already been corrected**.* (by the teacher)

2. The *by*-phrase is used only when it is important to know who performed the action.

Romeo and Juliet was written by William Shakespeare.

Often, *by* is used in an early statement but not in the statements that follow because the doer of the action has already been mentioned and is, therefore, obvious.

*Who gets a scholarship **will be decided by the scholarship committee**. Students **are judged** on grade point average, community activities, and financial need. All scholarship recipients **will have been announced** by the time classes begin next quarter.*

Exercise 4   *Change the sentences to the passive voice. Use* by *where necessary.*

1. A hurricane destroyed the small town.
2. The hurricane has left many people homeless.
3. The Red Cross is feeding the homeless victims.
4. The president is going to sign an emergency relief bill.
5. The citizens of the town have already organized cleanup crews.
6. Someone broke the pay phone on the third floor of the dormitory.
7. The dorm director had to notify the phone company immediately.
8. I hope the phone company will repair it soon.
9. The students on both the second and the third floors use it.
10. Phone company officials were interviewing all the students last night.

Exercise 5 ▪▪
▪▪▪▪▪▪▪▪▪▪ *With another student, write ten sentences to describe the accident scene in the picture below. Think about the immediate past, the present, and the future. Use the passive voice in as many sentences as possible.*

▪ 11-3 INDIRECT OBJECTS AND DIRECT OBJECTS AS PASSIVE SUBJECTS

1. Some sentences contain both a direct and an indirect object. Either the indirect or the direct object can become the subject of the passive sentence.

   *Someone gave **him a lot of money.***
   ***He** was given a lot of money.* (indirect object as subject)
   ***A lot of money** was given to him.* (direct object as subject)

2. When the direct object becomes the subject of the passive sentence, the sentence may need a preposition to make the sentence sound more natural.

   The salesclerk gave me a pen.
   *A pen was given **to** me by the salesclerk.*

The waiter found us a table.
*A table was found **for** us by the waiter.*

3. Remember that a noun clause may be the direct object of a sentence. The rules for changing the verb forms are the same. However, while the introductory verb that introduces the noun clause must be changed, the verb in the noun clause may be changed, or it may remain in the active voice.

Active: *Everyone applauded **what Bob said**.*
Passive: ***What Bob said** **was applauded** by everyone.*

OR

*What **was said** by Bob **was applauded** by everyone.*

Exercise 6   *Change the sentences to the passive voice in two ways.*

Example: The teacher gave Ann a perfect score on her composition.

Ann was given a perfect score on her composition.
A perfect score was given to Ann on her composition.

1. A local art club recently awarded Steve a four-year scholarship to study art.

   _____

   _____

2. Many different organizations have presented him awards for his artistic ability.

   _____

   _____

3. Steve will give a group of children art lessons next week.

   _____

   _____

4. The children's parents are paying him a lot of money.

   _____

   _____

5. They have already sent him their checks.

   _____

   _____

6. Steve is going to provide the children the necessary supplies.

_____

_____

7. Several department stores have offered him jobs.

_____

_____

8. Undoubtedly, some company will offer him a good job after graduation from art school.

_____

_____

Exercise 7 *Change the sentences to the passive voice. Use by where necessary. Remember to keep all modifiers next to the word they modify.*

Example: The police are going to question the two people who were near the building at the time of the robbery.

The two people who were near the building at the time of the robbery are going to be questioned by the police.

1. The police have caught the man who broke into the office last night.

2. The thief had completely destroyed some very important files.

3. They are holding him in the city jail until he can contact his lawyer.

4. They are going to schedule his trial for next month.

5. Officer Smith, chief of security, is studying the report of the break-in.

6. Because of the incident, the president of the company canceled the stockholder's meeting.

7. His secretary will send notices of the next meeting to everyone.

8. She typed the notices yesterday afternoon.

9. The company's security force is currently revising all security procedures.

10. The force is holding its meeting in Room 432 at the moment.

11. The chief of security was making some recommendations a few minutes ago.

12. By the end of the week, they will have revised all security procedures.

13. Since last year, people have burglarized the building five times.

14. Two months ago, someone locked a secretary, who had been working late, in a closet for eight hours.

15. They must maintain the safety of the employees working in the building.

16. The security force will present the new plan before the end of next week.

Exercise 8   *Complete each dialog, using a question in the passive voice. Use* by *where necessary.*

Example: **A:** A hospital orderly took Joanne down to the operating room.
  B: *When was Joanne taken down to the operating room?*
  A: About two hours ago.

1. **A:** One of the hospital's top surgeons is operating on Joanne at the moment.
   B: _____?
   A: Because she's had problems with her right knee ever since her skiing accident.

2. **A:** The hospital will send her husband the bill.
   B: _____?
   A: Next week.

3. **A:** Fortunately, their insurance company is going to pay part of the bill.
   B: _____?
   A: 70 percent.

4. **A:** The hospital admits visitors each evening.
   B: _____?
   A: From seven to nine.

5. **A:** However, you must notify the receptionist of your visit.
   B: _____?
   A: Because the hospital doesn't want too many people in a room at once.

6. **A:** Last night, Joanne had a slight fever, so the nurse had to take her temperature.
   B: _____?
   A: Every hour.

7. **A:** Someone was paging Joanne's surgeon. I hope everything is all right.
   B: _____?
   A: A few minutes ago.

8. **A:** The doctor will have released Joanne from the hospital by then.
   B: _____?
   A: By the time her parents arrive in Denver.

9. **A:** The hospital staff has provided Joanne with excellent care.

   B: _____?

   A: Since she arrived.

10. **A:** Joanne's husband had already packed when the doctor signed Joanne's release papers.

    B: _____?

    A: Her clothes.

Exercise 9 *Make* yes/no *questions in the passive voice, using the given words.*

Example: public transportation / use / a lot

   A: *Is public transportation used a lot?*

   B: No, unfortunately, a lot of people don't use public transportation.

1. more than twenty accidents / report / by 10:00 last night

   A: _____?

   B: No, by that time motorists had reported more than thirty.

2. all accident reports / record

   A: _____?

   B: No, the police are recording only the most serious ones.

3. many tickets / give out

   A: _____?

   B: No, the police haven't given out many tickets.

4. more than 350 tickets / write / last year

   A: _____?

   B: No, the police wrote more than 500 tickets.

5. you / give / a ticket / when / I / see / you / last night

   A: _____?

   B: No, the police officer was giving me a warning, not a ticket.

6. your driver's license / suspend / for thirty days last year

   A: _____?

   B: No, the judge suspended it for only ten days.

7. every accident / report

   A: _____?

   B: No, not all accidents are reported, only some.

8. many innocent people / kill / intoxicated drivers this year

   A: _____?

   B: One never knows, but it is hoped they won't.

9. careless drivers / punish / severely

   A: _____?

   B: Well, we hope the police are going to punish them severely.

10. good drivers / find

   A: _____?

   B: Of course you can find good drivers.

Exercise 10 *Find the ten mistakes in the article, which appeared in a college newspaper. Then correct the mistakes. There are no mistakes in tense.*

Library Vacancy

Many students are used the university library every day, but few who are being sat in its hundreds of chairs at this very moment are aware of what's been going on there lately. It has been learned that the director recently fired. However, the reason for his dismissal is concealing by the university. Since the director employed at the library for over twenty years, there is speculation that something scandalous has been happened. Rumors of every kind can hear behind closed doors.

It is not yet clear if another director has found. If not, one can only wonder whether the administration will finally hire a woman for a top position at this university. Surely, there are many highly qualified women who could interview, yet in view of this university's past hiring practices we can't help but be suspicious that the administration will be continued its discriminatory policy of filling all high positions with men only.

Exercise 11 *Decide which of the sentences should be used in the passive voice and which should remain in the active voice. Then write the sentences in the form of a paragraph. Remember not to overuse the passive voice. You should always have a specific reason for using it.*

1. This is Ed Scott, your reporter for the 6:00 news.
2. I'm at the airport waiting for the Denver Broncos football team to arrive.

3. Hundreds of fans meet the team's plane every time it returns to Denver.

4. Everyone knows that the fans in Denver are the most enthusiastic in the country.

5. Some T.V. sportscasters have even called them fanatics.

6. An unusually large number of people greeted the Broncos last weekend.

7. I see that their plane has just landed.

8. The police are pushing the crowd back.

9. Somebody has just lost a little boy in this mass of people.

10. I can hear his parents calling his name.

11. In the past, the pushing and shoving has hurt many people.

12. These fans must learn the rules of politeness and safety.

13. The Broncos have just gotten off their plane, and they're entering the airport now.

14. The ecstatic fans are shouting their congratulations.

15. The Broncos, as you know, defeated the mighty Dallas Cowboys last night.

16. They will play the championship team at Oakland next week.

17. After that important game, undoubtedly thousands will crowd the airport.

Exercise 12

Combine the sentences into one paragraph, using the passive voice where appropriate. Use the methods of coordination and subordination when you can, but do not overconnect. The accident scene is pictured on page 184.

Situation: Rita is in a phone booth. She's speaking to a friend and describing an accident she has just seen.

1. An accident happened just a few minutes ago.

2. A speeding minivan ran into a car.

3. The car was going though the intersection.

4. A large crowd is now standing around the car and the minivan.

5. A very tall police officer is inspecting the minivan driver's papers.

6. A short police officer is ordering the crowd to stand back.

7. A passer-by is talking to one of the drivers.

8. It seems that the collision hasn't injured either driver.

9. The collision didn't badly damage the minivan, but it totaled the car.

10. I know that the officers are going to question the driver of the minivan.

11. I can see that the driver is extremely nervous.

12. The officers have asked a few people if they would testify in court.

13. About ten people witnessed the accident.

14. The accident has backed up traffic.

15. A tow truck will eventually tow both vehicles away.
16. Now the driver of the minivan is getting into the police car.
17. The short officer is locking the driver's doors.
18. They are probably going to take the driver to the police station.
19. They are undoubtedly going to give him a breathalyzer test.
20. The state legislature should pass stricter laws to punish careless drivers.

Practice Exam

Write about a true event in your life. Use the passive voice when you think it is appropriate. Use as a model these paragraphs, which were written during the winter quarter of 1993.

On my wedding day, we had a small party at which our parents, relatives, and some of our friends were present and from whom we received many presents. After the marriage ceremony, my husband and I decided to leave on our honeymoon to London. The tickets **had been bought** for us by his parents; moreover, the journey **had been arranged** very well by my husband's friend, who drove us to the airport.

We took the airplane from Cairo to London. When we got on the plane, we **were directed** to our seats by a flight attendant, and as the plane was ready to take off, all the passengers **were asked** to fasten their seat belts and to stop smoking. Furthermore, we were given some advice on what to do in case of an emergency. After that we **were served** a delicious cocktail and **shown** a funny movie about teenagers on a bike tour. Later on, dinner **was served** to all the passengers while newspapers and magazines **were being distributed**.

When the plane landed, we **were met** by one of my husband's friends, who drove us to a very nice hotel. Although we stayed in London for only ten days, we had a wonderful time, and we felt as if we had just bought the whole world; hence, we still remember those days. We returned home to our new home, parents, and friends, hoping to live happily forever.

Jabria A. Jassim, Egypt

PART 6

Modal Auxiliaries

■ INTRODUCTION TO PART 6 ■ ■ ■ ■ ■ ■ ■

In English, modal auxiliaries are used to add meaning to a verb. The following are the modal auxiliaries in English.

can	*may*	*must*	*shall*	*will*
could	*might*	*ought to*	*should*	*would*

A modal auxiliary is used mainly to show the speaker's attitude to what he or she is saying. For example, a modal auxiliary can express possibility or impossibility.

> We ***could leave*** right now. (possibility)
> The dog ***might have gone*** upstairs. (possibility)
> That ***can't be*** their house. Their house is gray, not brown. (impossibility)
> That ***can't have been*** Michelle in the car. She's away on vacation. (impossibility)

Modal auxiliaries often indicate time, but their main job is to denote different shades of meaning. The grammatical construction of each of these sentences is the same. Are the meanings the same?

> I ***will go*** with you.
> I ***might go*** with you.
> I ***can go*** with you.
> I ***should go*** with you.
> I ***must go*** with you.

As the speaker or writer, only you know the meaning you want to express based on a particular situation, your knowledge about it, and your feelings toward it.

As students learning to speak English, you must learn the many different meanings that the modals express. In some instances the differences in meaning are easy to understand; in other instances the differences are very subtle. Nevertheless, it is important for you to learn these meanings because they will enable you to express precisely what you are thinking and feeling. They will help you to communicate what you mean.

In this part, you will practice using some of the meanings of modal auxiliaries; you will also practice using the modal auxiliaries to refer to the past, present, and future. For a summary of the meanings of the modal auxiliaries, see Appendix 2 on page 300.

LESSON TWELVE

■ 12-1 ADVISABILITY VS. NECESSITY

■ Advisability ■

A *My grandmother hasn't been feeling well. She should go to see her doctor.*
My grandmother hasn't been feeling well. She ought to go to see her doctor.

B *My grandmother should be living closer to her children.*
My grandmother ought to be living closer to her children.

C *My grandmother shouldn't spend so much time alone in her home.*

D *My grandmother shouldn't be living alone.*

E *Should we stop by my grandmother's place and say "hello"?*

1. The modals *should* and *ought to* express advisability. When giving advice, the speaker is expressing an opinion as to what to do or what not to do. (It is not necessary to follow the advice, however.)

2. The modals *should* and *ought to* are similar in meaning, but *ought to* is less common and is rarely used in negative and question forms.

3. To make a statement about an event in progress, *should/ought to* + *be* + present participle is often used. (See sentences **B** and **D**.)

4. In indirect speech, *should* does not change.
   She says, "You should go home and rest."
   She told me that I should go home and rest.

■ Moral Obligation ■

The modals *should* and *ought to* express obligation. The obligation is usually a moral one; it is the right or wrong thing to do.

Every society should take care of its senior citizens.
Every society ought to take care of its senior citizens.
People shouldn't ignore the senior citizens in their midst.

■ Necessity: *Must, Have to* ■

My grandmother **must take** several kinds of medicine.

My grandmother **has to take** several kinds of medicine.

My grandmother **will have to move** into a home for senior citizens when she is no longer able to take care of herself.

My grandmother **had to spend** a week in the hospital last year when she had pneumonia.

■ Absence of Necessity ■

I **don't have to visit** my grandmother often, but I like to spend time with her.

My grandmother **won't have to take** a taxi to the doctor's office next week because I'm going to take her.

My grandmother **didn't have to work** when she was younger because my grandfather had a well-paying job.

1. The modal *must* is used to express necessity.

   I'm afraid I **must work** late tomorrow.

   Soldiers **must obey** army regulations. (They have no choice.)

2. *Have to* is also used to express necessity. (*Have to* is actually not a modal auxiliary because it changes form—*I have to, She has to, You don't have to, He doesn't have to,* etc.)

   I'm afraid I **have to work** late tomorrow.

3. *Must* and *have to* are similar in meaning. *Have to* is more common in American English and is more informal in tone.

4. Be careful not to confuse *should/ought to* and *must/have to*. *Should/ought to* implies that there is a choice; *must/have to* implies that there is no choice.

   I **should go** to bed. I'm really tired. (It's a good idea for the speaker to go to bed. Maybe the speaker will; maybe the speaker won't.)

   Children, you **must go** to bed right now. (A mother or father is sending the children to bed. They do not have a choice.)

   Shouldn't implies that it is not a good idea to do something or that it is the wrong thing to do. *Don't/doesn't have to* means that it is not necessary to do something.

   You **shouldn't get up** early tomorrow if you don't feel well. (It's not a good idea for you to get up early.)

   You **don't have to get up** early tomorrow. It's a holiday. (It's not necessary to get up early tomorrow.)

5. *Don't have to,* not *must not,* expresses a lack of necessity.

    Correct: *We **don't have to do** any homework because the teacher is absent.*

    Incorrect: *We mustn't do any homework because the teacher is absent.*

Mustn't expresses prohibition. A prohibition is an order or a law against doing something.

*You **mustn't eat** or **drink** in the language lab.*

6. *Had to,* not *must,* expresses necessity in the past.

    Correct: *When I was in the army, I **had to obey** all regulations.*

    Incorrect: *When I was in the army, I must obey all regulations.*

Exercise 1

Complete each dialog with the correct form of have to *and a verb from the box. Add* not *where necessary.*

be	*come*	*give*	*pay*
bring	*exchange*	*move*	*work*

1. **A:** Lesley, you missed the party.
   B: I know. I'm sorry, but I _____ late.

2. **A:** These flowers are for you.
   B: They're beautiful, but you know you _____ anything.

3. **A:** Is Ms. Sacco in?
   B: No, I'm sorry she's not. You _____ back later.

4. **A:** Here are the nails you asked for.
   B: Oh, they're not the right ones. You _____ them.

5. **A:** How was your oral report?
   B: I was lucky. I _____ it. The school lost electrical power, and everyone was sent home early.

6. **A:** Look at this parking ticket I got! Well, they'll get their money when I'm good and ready.
   B: You know if you don't pay it on time, you _____ a penalty.

7. **A:** Why are you leaving for the airport now? You _____ there so early for a domestic flight.
   B: I know, but I don't want to rush at the last minute.

8. **A:** Aren't you living in the same place any more?
   B: No, we _____ because my wife changed jobs.

Exercise 2 ■■ *Complete the sentences, using* should *or* must. *In some sentences both* should *and* must *are possible.*

1. A father _____ take care of his family.

2. Parents _____ teach their children right from wrong.

3. Sylvia _____ visit her grandmother more often.

4. In the United States you _____ be at least 18 years of age in order to vote.

5. If you don't feel well, you _____ lie down.

6. If you want to become a lawyer, you _____ go to law school.

7. You _____ boil water if you want to make tea.

8. You _____ read this book. It's great.

9. It is unfortunate that teachers _____ give tests.

10. Foreigners visiting the United States _____ have a visa.

Exercise 3 ■■ *What might an English instructor say to his or her students at some point during a course? With another student, make sentences using* shouldn't *or* don't have to.

1. open your books during the test

2. do every exercise in the book

3. talk in your own language in class

4. look at the answer key when doing your homework

5. ask for permission to go to the restroom

6. arrive late to class

7. daydream in class

8. get my permission to stay home when you're sick

9. stand up when I walk into the room

10. forget to do your homework

11. write a 20-page paper

12. be rude to the other students in class

13. interrupt each other

14. raise your hand before speaking

Exercise 4 *With another student, make a list of at least six obligations that the members of a society have toward each other.*

Example: Every society should take care of its senior citizens.

Exercise 5 *With another student, make a list of the advice you would give the following people. When you finish, compare lists with other students.*

1. Someone who's going to come to the United States to study English
2. Someone who's planning to take the TOEFL
3. Someone who's going to get a roommate to share an apartment
4. Someone who's going to live with an American family
5. Someone who's planning to visit your country for a two-week vacation
6. Someone who's going to your country for a couple of years to teach English

Exercise 6 *In a group of three or four, discuss the advantages and disadvantages of each job—or of any other job you would like to discuss. Use (not) have to, and do not discuss money.*

1. surgeon
2. college professor
3. politician
4. police officer
5. salesperson
6. taxi driver
7. construction worker
8. journalist
9. fashion model
10. pilot

■ 12-2 PAST REGRETS AND CRITICISMS: *Should, Ought To*

A *I told you that we **should have turned** left.*
*I told you that we **ought to have turned** left.*

B *You **should have been paying** attention to the street signs.*
*You **ought to have been paying** attention to the street signs.*

C *We **shouldn't have gotten off** the highway at exit 22.*

1. *Should/ought to + have +* past participle is used to talk about past regrets or to criticize past actions. It is used to say that someone did the wrong thing and to state the opposite of what was done.

   I **should have left** *earlier.* (But I didn't.)

   I **shouldn't have waited** *for the bus.* (But I did.)

2. *Should/ought to + have been +* present participle is used to talk about an event in progress. It is used to say that someone was doing the wrong thing, an action lasting for a period of time.

   I **shouldn't have been talking** *during the test.* (But I was.)

3. The modals *should* and *ought to* are similar in meaning, but *ought to* is less common and is rarely used in negative and question forms.

Exercise 7   *Amanda had a terrible day yesterday. Make sentences about her problems using* should *or* ought to.

1. She overslept because she went to a party the night before and stayed up late.

2. She missed the bus because she had to go to a store to get exact change.

3. When she got to work, she realized that she didn't have her keys and couldn't get into her office.

4. Her boss got angry when he saw that she was still working on the report he had asked her for the day before.

5. She made a date to meet her friend at noon for lunch. When she got to the office, she found she had an eleven o'clock meeting. Her friend was angry when she showed up late for lunch.

6. She bought a new pair of jeans. When she got home, she tried them on and found that they were too tight.

7. While she was cooking dinner, she was talking on the phone with her sister. The potatoes burned.

8. She went out after dinner and left the windows open. There was a bad storm.

9. She was in a hurry to get home and was driving around 75 miles per hour when she was stopped by a police car. She got a speeding ticket.

10. In the afternoon, she had received notification in the mail that her power was going to be shut off because she had not paid her electric bill. When she got home last night, there was no power.

Exercise 8 *What are the following people probably saying to themselves? With another student, write at least two regrets for each person, one with should and one with shouldn't.*

1. A teenager who has been grounded for a month by his parents

2. A job applicant who has found out that she didn't get a job

3. A high-school graduate who didn't get into the three colleges he had applied to

4. A couple who have just come out of a casino after losing $500

5. An Olympic track star who came in second in the 500-meter race

6. A politician who lost an election

Exercise 9 *In a group of three or four, discuss each moral dilemma.*

1. A baby was born to a single woman. She put the baby up for adoption, and the baby was adopted by a childless couple. A year later the woman was reconciled with her boyfriend and told him about the baby. The couple married, and the father went to court to get the baby back. Now the child is three years old, and the judge has to decide whether the child should remain with the adoptive parents, the only parents the child has ever known, or be returned to the birth parents. What do you think the judge should do?

2. A terminally ill patient was in great pain and asked his young doctor to help him to die. At first the doctor was strongly against doing so, believing it was her duty to help patients get better, not to help them die. But as her patient's suffering became worse, she gave in to his wishes and gave him a lethal injection. The patient died peacefully. What do you think the doctor should have done?

3. A couple with ten-year-old identical twin daughters filed for divorce. The children, who were very close to each other and to both parents, were very upset. Both parents filed for custody of the twins. Because both parents were professionals and had very busy working lives, the judge tried to persuade the couple to accept joint custody. Nevertheless, each parent insisted on full custody of both children. At first, the judge ordered a six-month trial period in which one child went to live with her mother and the other child went to live with her father. After the trial period was over, the judge made a final custody decision. What do you think the judge should have done?

■ 12-3 LOGICAL CONCLUSION VS. EXPECTATION

■ **Logical Conclusion:** *Must* ■   ■ **Expectation:** *Should* ■

Present Time

Lee isn't home. He **must be** on his way.

Lee doesn't live far away. He **should be** here soon.

It's taking Lee a long time to get here. He **must be walking**.

I told Lee that he was the only person we invited for lunch. He **should be coming** alone.

Past Time

I wonder why Lee isn't here yet. He **must have decided** to walk.

Where is Lee? He **should have gotten** here by now.

I tried to call him, but his line was busy. His roommate **must have been talking**.

1. Both *must* for assumption and *should* for expectation involve making an intelligent guess. In sentences that refer to present or past time or to a present or past condition, either *must* or *should* is possible. However, *must* expresses a greater degree of certainty.

   *My wallet **should be** on the dresser. (I usually put it there.)*

   *My wallet **must be** on the dresser. (I always put it there.)*

   *My wallet **should have been** on the dresser. (I usually put it there.)*

   *My wallet **must have been** on the dresser. (Did you look carefully?)*

2. To make an intelligent guess about the future, only *should* can be used.

   *The check from my parents **should arrive** tomorrow. It was sent a few days ago.*

   Must means necessity when it refers to a future time.

   *The check from my parents **must arrive** tomorrow. I really need some money.*

3. To make a logical assumption about an event in progress, *must + be +* present participle is often used.

   *I don't hear any noise in the children's room. They **must be sleeping**.*

   To talk about an expectation of an event in progress, *should/ought to + be +* present participle is often used.

   *The train is scheduled to arrive at 11:00, and it's 10:58 now. The train **should be arriving** any minute now.*

4. To make a logical assumption about a past event, *must + have +* past participle or *must + have been +* present participle is used.

*Linda wasn't on the five o'clock train. She **must have decided** to take a later one.*

To talk about an expectation in the past, *should/ought to + have +* past participle or *should/ought to + have been +* present participle is used.

*The train **should have arrived** by now. Where is it?*

Exercise 10 *With another student, discuss the difference in meaning between Kurt's and Tina's responses.*

1. **Adam:** My roommate left Denver for Colorado Springs at 6:00. It's 7:00 now, and it takes only an hour to drive from Denver to Colorado Springs.
   Kurt: He **should be** in Colorado Springs now.
   Tina: He **must be** in Colorado Springs now.

2. **Adam:** Antonio studied for six straight hours last night. That's a long time to study without a break.
   Kurt: He **must have been** tired when he went to bed.
   Tina: He **should have been** tired when he went to bed.

3. **Adam:** During the summer months, it gets dark after 8:30 P.M.
   Kurt: It **should be** around 9:00 now because it's almost dark outside.
   Tina: It **must be** around 9:00 now because it's dark outside.

4. **Adam:** Cathy studied in France for three years. She has always enjoyed learning languages, and she learns them easily.
   Kurt: She **must speak** French very well.
   Tina: She **should speak** French very well.

5. **Adam:** Al has already drunk six cans of soda and eaten three hamburgers and two pieces of cherry pie.
   Kurt: He **must have had** very little to eat in the past few days.
   Tina: He **should have had** enough by now.

Exercise 11 *Find and correct the eight mistakes with the form of must in the dialog.*

Fay: Where's the mail?

Leo: Here it is. This letter must be from Flori. This is her handwriting, isn't it?

Fay: Leo, really. Do you have to ask about your own daughter's handwriting?

Leo: Well, how many times has she written us? She usually calls. She must forget to pay her phone bill, and the phone company cut off her phone. Or you must tell her that I've been complaining that she never writes.

Fay: No, I never said a thing. Besides, she knows you always complain. No, she must learn how to use her new computer these days. Actually, she says she's writing because she tried calling last Monday, but the line was busy for more than two hours.

Leo: Joey must talk to his girlfriend. I remember telling him to get off the phone at least five times last Monday. Anyway, what else does she say?

Fay: Well, she must have a great time because she says she's always going out.

Leo: Then she must make a lot of new friends since she arrived because you know that she never likes to go anywhere alone.

Fay: If she's going out a lot, she must need more money. Should we send her some?

Leo: I don't think so. She must earn enough money from her job last summer to keep her going for another month or so. Besides, I think we should be more concerned about her studies than her bank account. She must not study very much these days if she's going out all the time.

Fay: I wouldn't worry about her studies. She must know how to organize her studies. She's always gotten good grades.

Exercise 12 ▪ ▪
▪ ▪ ▪ ▪ ▪ ▪ ▪ ▪ ▪ ▪ ▪ ▪ ▪ *Complete the dialogs, using the correct form of* must *and* have to *and the verbs in parentheses.*

1. **A:** Why did Roseanne pay in cash? She _____ (not pay) in cash.

   B: She _____ (not know) that. She probably thought she couldn't pay by check.

2. **A:** Sorry I wasn't in when you called this morning. I _____ (go) to the dentist.

   B: That _____ (not be) fun.

3. **A:** You got home late from the party last night. You _____ (have) a good time.

   B: I had a great time, but that's not why I came home so late. I _____ (help) Marsha clean up. Her place was a mess!

4. **A:** Nina _____ (work) late last night because her boss gave her some extra work to do at the last minute.

   B: She _____ (be) upset. I know she was planning to go to her son's basketball game right after work.

5. **A:** You look terrible. The test _____ (last) a long time.

   B: It sure did. It was more than three hours long, and we all _____ (stay) until the end, even if we finished early.

6. **A:** We were lucky when we went to the theater. We _____ (not wait) a long time for tickets.

   B: You _____ (get) there early because by the time I arrived, there was a very long line.

Exercise 13 ■■ *Respond to the sentences, using* must *and the tense*
■ ■ ■ ■ ■ ■ ■ ■ ■ ■ ■ ■ *indicated in parentheses.*

Example: My brother was a star soccer player in high school.
   (present) He *must still be a good player.*
   (past)   He *must have started playing when he was very young.*

1. Two 747 airplanes crashed last week, and two hundred people died.

   (present) Their families _____

   (past)   The pilots _____

2. The men in the controller's tower were responsible for the crash.

   (present) Today, those men _____

   (past)   At the time of the accident, they _____

3. My friend's parents were aboard the plane, but they survived.

   (present) Today they _____

   (past)   When the accident occurred, they _____

4. My sister who is a stewardess was supposed to work that flight, but she was sick, so another flight attendant substituted for her.

   (present) Your sister _____

   (past)   When your sister heard about the crash, _____

5. The two captains were not aware of each other on their radar screens; nevertheless, both of them survived the crash.

   (present) Now, every time they fly, they _____

   (past)   Their equipment _____

Exercise 14 ■■ *Complete the sentence in each dialog, using* should *and the*
■■■■■■■■■■■ *correct form of the verb in parentheses. Add* not *where*
necessary.

1. **A:** Are the kids in their rooms?

   B: I hope so. They _____ (do) their homework. Why don't you go and check?

2. **A:** Do you want to go by car?

   B: No, let's walk. It _____ (take) too long.

3. **A:** I had to pay the dry cleaner with a credit card because the cleaning bill totaled more than $50. I didn't have that much money.

   B: That's strange. It _____ (cost) that much. Let me see the bill.

4. **A:** Where's Charlene? Didn't you pick her up?

   B: No, she _____ (wait) in front of her office building, but she wasn't there.

5. **A:** Do you have a copy of Mr. Murphy's schedule? I want to see if he's available at 2:00 this afternoon.

   B: I don't think he is. He _____ (hold) a meeting with the assistant directors at that time, but let me check his schedule.

6. **A:** Hasn't the check arrived yet?

   B: No. I'm going to call the company because we _____ (receive) the check by now.

7. **A:** Carol isn't back from class yet, is she?

   B: No. She _____ (finish) an hour ago. Maybe she went out for coffee with some of her classmates.

8. **A:** Did Mel Neville play in last night's game?

   B: Yeah. He _____ (play) because of his sore arm, but he was put in the game at the last minute.

9. **A:** The electricity's been cut off in the Rangers' apartment.

   B: That's strange. It _____ (be cut off). I'm sure they paid their bill.

10. **A:** Shall I go to the store and get some more flour?

    B: Don't bother. I have half a bag of flour. That _____ (be) enough.

Exercise 15 ▪▪ ▪ ▪▪▪▪▪▪▪▪▪▪▪▪ *Complete the sentences with* should *or* must. *Each speaker's reaction is included in the response. Be careful of the time response, and add* not *where necessary.*

1. **A:** I haven't eaten any sweets for two weeks.

   B: You _____ be on a diet, or you would not be giving up sweets.

   C: You _____ lose a lot of weight because sweets contain many calories.

2. **A:** I took two aspirins a half hour ago.

   B: Then your headache _____ go away soon because that brand of aspirin is very effective.

   C: *(A half hour later)* You _____ need something else beside aspirin if you're still in pain.

3. **A:** Look at the sky tonight. It's full of stars.

   B: We _____ have a beautiful day tomorrow because it's clear tonight.

4. **A:** Mansour is tying to sell his car.

   B: He _____ get a lot of money for it because it's in excellent condition.

   C: I wonder why he wants to sell it. It _____ be giving him a lot of trouble.

   D: It isn't, so he _____ seen another car that he liked better.

5. **A:** Pierre was elected president of the International Student's Organization.

   B: He _____ know a lot of people at the university because he received the largest number of votes.

   C: He _____ make a good president because he's very intelligent; also, he understands the concerns of foreign students.

   D: He _____ be an excellent student, too, because you have to have an "A" average to be a candidate for president.

6. **A:** I haven't received my parents' check for next quarter's tuition.

   B: Don't worry. It _____ arrive soon. Your parents have never been late with your tuition money.

   C: Your parents _____ have a lot of money. My parents don't, so I have to work and pay my own tuition.

7. **A:** I've been trying to solve this statistics problem for four hours.

    B: It _____ be very complicated; otherwise, it would not take so long to solve.

    C: The answer _____ be in the back of the book. Most statistics books contain the answers to the exercises.

    D: It _____ be in the back of the book. All statistics books contain the answers to the exercises.

8. **A:** Ali's best friend is a German student who doesn't speak English or Arabic, and Ali doesn't speak German.

    B: You're kidding! Then both of them _____ speak another language; otherwise, they couldn't communicate with one another.

Exercise 16   *Complete the sentences, using* must *or* should *and the correct form of the verbs in parentheses. In some sentences, either* must *or* should *is possible; in other sentences, only one can be used.*

1.   **Lin:**   I have only two more weeks of classes.

    Tom: You _____ (be) very happy. Will you have a final?

    Lin: Unfortunately, yes. We're going to have a two-hour grammar final, and the final _____ (be) difficult. A few students failed the grammar test last quarter.

    Tom: That final _____ (be) difficult. Has your teacher already written the final?

    Lin: Probably, but she wouldn't leave it at school. She _____ (take) it home.

    Tom: What's the test going to be like?

    Lin: Part I of the test is true/false, so it _____ (be) very easy. I wish I were as good a student as Maria. She has gotten an "A" on every test so far.

    Tom: Then she _____ (get) an "A" on the final.

    Lin: At least all of us understand adjective clauses now.

    Tom: Then everyone _____ (do) well on that part of the test.

2. **Keiko:** It's 9:20, and our teacher hasn't arrived yet.

   Krean: I'm a little worried. She's never late. She _____ (have) an accident.

   Carlo: Stop worrying. She _____ (be) here in a few minutes.

   Celia: She was sick yesterday afternoon, so she _____ (decide) to stay home today.

3. **Helen:** A fire engine is stopping in front of our building.

   Lucy: I smell smoke! There _____ (be) a fire somewhere in the building.

   Patty: Don't worry. These firefighters are experienced. They _____ (have) everything under control in a little while.

   Helen: The smoke is coming from the third floor. The fire _____ (start) there.

   Lucy: But I don't hear the fire alarm. It _____ (not work).

Exercise 17 *With another student, decide on a logical conclusion for each situation. Use* must. *When you finish, compare logical conclusions with other students.*

1. When Georgia died, her lawyer informed her relatives that Georgia had left her ten-room house and all her money to her five dogs and ten cats.

2. Matthew was in the hospital for almost a month. Now he's recuperating at home.

3. The automobile company had to recall all of its 1996 SX cars.

4. An hour ago Meg was bothering all the people in the office, asking if they had seen her glasses. Now she's wearing her glasses.

5. Susan doesn't usually mind hot weather, but last night even she had difficulty sleeping.

6. Mark was home fifteen minutes ago, but now nobody answers the doorbell and his car isn't in the driveway.

7. Nathan's very upset. His credit cards and money are missing from his wallet.

8. Lydia won more than $100,000 in last week's lottery!

9. Mimi's grandfather died many years ago, but she still thinks about him often. When she does, tears come to her eyes.

10. Daphne and Doug went to a party last night, and even at 3 A.M. they didn't want to leave.

Exercise 18 ▪▫   *With another student, answer each question, using* should.
▪ ▪ ▪ ▪ ▪ ▪ ▪ ▪ ▪ ▪ ▪ ▪

Example: Harris went to see a movie that all his friends had recommended. Why
was he disappointed at the end of the movie?

The movie should have been good, but it wasn't.

1. When Debbie accepted a job offer as an assistant manager with a computer
   software company, she expected to have a great career with the company. But
   after seven years with the company, her job was exactly the same as it had been
   when she first started working there. Why did she quit?

2. Ari worked very hard on his term paper. He thought it was very good. When he
   got his paper back, however, he saw that his grade was a "C+". Why was he
   disappointed?

3. Elisa bought a new TV, but she had nothing but trouble with it soon after she
   took it home. Why was she so annoyed about having to take the TV back to the
   store again and again for repairs?

4. Mr. and Mrs. Morales boarded an airplane for a flight to Madrid an hour and a
   half ago, but the plane is still on the ground. Why are they and all the other
   passengers so annoyed?

5. When Tess graduated from college last year, she hoped to find a great job and a
   place of her own to live in. It is unfortunate that things haven't worked out as
   she had hoped. She's had to move back home with her parents, and her parents
   are supporting her. Why is she disappointed?

6. When Miguel registered for a beginner's English class, he planned to enroll at a
   Canadian university in two years. It is now three years later, and Miguel's
   English still isn't good enough for him to begin his academic studies. Why is he
   disappointed?

7. Sandra told her elderly father that she would be taking her children to visit him
   this afternoon. She said she was leaving at 11:00. Sandra's home is a 45-minute
   drive from her father's place. It's 1:00 now, and they still haven't arrived. Why is
   Sandra's father worried?

▪ 12-4 SUGGESTIONS: *Could*

1. *Could* + verb is used to make suggestions about the present or future.

   A: I don't want to stay home tonight.

   *B: Well, we **could go** to the movies.*

   A: I don't have any money.

   *B: You **could borrow** some from your roommate.*

2. The expressions *why don't you*, *why don't we*, and *let's* are also used to express suggestions.

Why don't we go to the movies?

Let's go to the movies.

Note that *why don't we* and *let's* include the person making the suggestion.

Exercise 19 *With another student, take turns giving each other suggestions, using* could.

1. I don't know what to do this weekend.

2. I can't decide where to go on my next vacation.

3. I never have enough money.

4. I don't like where I'm living.

5. I sometimes have a hard time understanding people when they speak to me in English.

6. I'm having a hard time understanding how to use all these modal auxiliaries correctly.

7. A friend from home is coming to spend two weeks with me. I'm not sure how to entertain my visitor during that time.

8. I want to get a birthday present for the teacher.

Exercise 20 *Read the situation. In a group of three or four, make suggestions for a friend who is planning to get married in the near future.*

Over the past few years, many marriage ceremonies in the United States have become less and less traditional. Newspapers frequently report on couples who have said their marriage vows while riding motorcycles, deep-sea diving, dancing, or jumping out of airplanes. Although many marriages still take place in the traditional settings of the church and home, some couples prefer to plan their own personal ceremonies to reflect their personalities and the nature of their relationship. Such ceremonies are neither very different nor very traditional.

1. I don't want to get married in a formal ceremony because large, expensive weddings are a waste of money. Suggestion:

2. My fiancé and I have decided not to send out expensive wedding invitations, but we want our friends and relatives to know that we are getting married.

3. We do not feel that an expensive honeymoon is necessary, but we would like to go somewhere and be alone for a week. We both enjoy the outdoors.

4. We really do not want our friends and relatives to give us expensive gifts that we will never use.

5. We do not know what to serve during the party after the wedding, but we want to keep the menu simple.

6. I think my parents are going to ignore our preferences and plan a big wedding for us.

7. My fiancé's cousin wants to sing at our wedding, but she has a terrible voice.

8. You know, I'm not really sure that I'm ready for marriage.

■ 12-5 POSSIBILITIES: *May, Might, Could*

Present and Future Time

A *That woman **may know** where the building is. Why don't you ask her?*

B *The building **might be** on the next block, but I'm not sure.*
            could be

C *The line's busy. The manager **may be calling**   our office to find out where we are.*
            might be calling
            could be calling

Past Time

D *The repairman **may have gotten**   lost.*
            might have gotten
            could have gotten

E *The repairman **may have been talking**   about our other office.*
            might have been talking
            could have been talking

F *The repairman **could have asked** me for directions. I would have been happy to tell him how to get here.*

1. The modal auxiliaries *may, might,* and *could* all refer to possibility, that is, that something is happening or that something will happen. Sometimes the three modals are interchangeable, but usually they are different in meaning. *May* refers to a possibility that is more likely to happen. Compare:

   It ***may snow*** *tomorrow.* (I haven't listened to the weather report yet, but the air feels cold, and the sky looks the way it always looks before it snows.)

> *It **might snow** tomorrow.* (But I don't think it will.)
>
> *It **could snow** tomorrow.* (But I don't think it will.)

2. *May/might/could* + verb is used to talk about possibilities referring to present conditions or to future action. *May/might/could* + *be* + present participle is used to talk about an action in progress at the time of speaking. (See sentence **C**.)

3. *May/might/could* + *have* + past participle is used to talk about past possibilities, that is, that something happened, but one cannot be sure. For example, in sentence **D**, it is possible that the repairman got lost, but the speaker is not sure.

4. However, *could* + *have* + past participle can also be used to talk about past actions that were possible but did not happen. For example, in sentence **F**, it was possible for the repairman to ask me for directions, but he didn't. Compare:

   *Matt's sister **may have helped** him with his report.* (Maybe Matt's sister helped him; maybe she didn't. The speaker doesn't know for sure if.)

   *Matt's sister **could have helped** him, but he didn't want her help.* (It was possible for Matt's sister to help him, but Matt refused her offer.)

5. *May/might/could* + *have been* + present participle is used to talk about a possible event in progress at a specific time in the past. (See sentence **E**.)

6. *Might* is used as the past of *may* in indirect speech.

   *Stan said, "We **may get** married soon."*

   *Stan said they **might get** married soon.*

Exercise 21   *Complete the dialog, using* could *and the correct form of the verbs in parentheses.*

Bob: Where's Pete? He wanted me to give him a ride home.

Sue: I don't know for sure, but he wanted to talk to Professor Ray about his grades so far, so he *could be talking* (talk) to her right now.

Bob: You're probably right. He's probably talking about his lateness, too.

Sue: I know. He doesn't have to come to class late every morning. He _____ (come) to class on time if he tried.

Bob: Why was he late this morning?

Sue: Don't ask me. He _____ (stay) up late last night to study.

Bob: Or he _____ (go) to a party.

Sue: He has passed only one test so far this quarter. He _____ (fail) this course if he doesn't get serious.

Bob: Professor Ray _____ (tell) him that right now.

Sue: You're his best friend. You _____ (talk) with him and see if he has any big problems.

Bob: That's a good suggestion. Pete _____ (have) trouble with his girlfriend this quarter.

Sue: That's right. They _____ (have) an argument last night.

Bob: They _____ (plan) to break up soon.

Sue: They _____ (discuss) this all last night.

Bob: Well, whatever the problem is, I'll talk to him.

Sue: Good. Who knows? Just your concern _____ (make) him feel better.

Bob: I _____ (say) something to him earlier, but I have been so busy during the past few weeks.

Sue: Well, better late than never.

Exercise 22 ▪▪ *Restate the underlined part of each sentence, using* may, might, *or* could.

1. It was possible for Cindy to come, but she didn't want to.
2. Perhaps Cindy came, but I'll check with her secretary to find out for sure.
3. It's possible Cindy arrived late, but if she did, nobody noticed.
4. It was possible for Cindy to call, but she didn't think it was necessary.
5. Maybe Cindy called, but her secretary forgot to tell us.
6. It was possible for Cindy to attend the meeting, but she thought it would bore her, so she decided not to come.

Exercise 23 ▪▪ *With another student, answer the questions. Give at least two possible explanations for each picture, using* may *or* might.

1. Why is the baby crying?

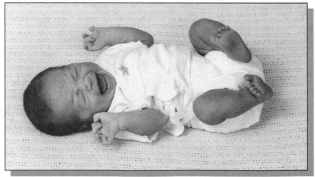

2. Why is the coyote howling?

3. Why is the woman tired?

4. Why did the building collapse?

5. Why is the man happy?

6. Why is the man being arrested?

7. Why is the woman frightened?

Exercise 24 *With another student, take turns asking and answering the questions.*

1. What could you be doing right now if you were not in class?

2. When was the last time you saw a terrible movie? What could you have done instead?

3. What could you be doing these days if you weren't studying English?

4. Could you take a test on this lesson tomorrow and pass it with a high grade?

5. What could you have done to get a higher grade on the last test?

6. What could you have been doing last week if you hadn't had to come to class?

7. Where could you go this weekend if you had the time and the money?

8. Which mode of transportation could you have used to come to the United States instead of coming by airplane?

■ 12-6 NEGATIVE POSSIBILITIES AND IMPOSSIBILITIES

■ Negative Possibilities ■

Present and Future Time

A *The baby **may not have** a temperature, but there's definitely something wrong with her.*

B *The baby **might not be** better by tomorrow, so I may have to stay home.*

C *The baby **might not be sleeping**. Why don't you check?*

Past Time

D *The baby **might not have had** enough to eat. See if she wants some more.*

E *The baby **may not have been feeling** well.*

1. *May/might* + *not* + verb is used to say that it is possible that something in the present is not the case or that something in the future will not happen. (See sentences **A** and **B**.) *May/might* + *not* + *be* + present participle is used to say that it is possible that something in progress at the time of speaking is not the case. (See sentence **C**.)

2. *May/might* + *not* + *have* + past participle is used to say that it is possible that something in the past did not happen or was not the case. (See sentence **D**.)

3. *May/might* + *not* + *have been* + present participle is used to say that it is possible that something in progress at a specific time in the past did not happen or was not the case. (See sentence **E**.)

4. *May not* and *might not* cannot be contracted.

■ Impossibilities ■

Present Time

A *That **can't be** Rebecca. Rebecca isn't so tall.*

B *Rebecca **couldn't be** here yet. Her classes don't finish for another half hour or so.*

Past Time

C *Rebecca **couldn't have driven** that car. She doesn't know how to drive a stick shift.*

D *That **can't have been** Rebecca at the store. Rebecca went away for the weekend.*

1. *Can/could + not + verb* is used to say that it is impossible for something to be the case. *Can/could + not + be + present participle* is used to say that it is impossible for something in progress at the time of speaking to be the case. (See sentences **A** and **B**.)

2. *Can/could + not + have + past participle* is used to say that it was impossible for something in the past to have happened or to have been the case. (See sentence **C**.)

3. *Can/could + not + have been + present participle* is used to say that it is impossible for something in progress at a specific time in the past to have happened. (See sentence **D**.)

4. Be careful not to confuse *can/could + not* and *may/might + not*. Compare:

   Jerry **might not have done** the report. He wasn't sure he would have the time. (It's possible Jerry didn't do the report, but the speaker isn't sure.)

   Jerry **couldn't have done** the report. He wasn't in the office all week. (It was impossible for Jerry to have done the report.)

Exercise 25

Circle the words that make the best completion for each sentence.

1. He _____ the doctor. He's only 20 years old.
   a. can't be
   b. might not be

2. The woman _____ the crime. She has an alibi.
   a. couldn't have committed
   b. may not have committed

3. William's wife didn't tell me why he wouldn't go to Disney World, but he _____ to go to such a crowded place.
   a. can't have wanted
   b. may not have wanted

4. I don't know why the children overslept, but I guess their alarm clock _____.
   a. couldn't have gone off
   b. might not have gone off

5. The elderly man _____ of natural causes. The police are looking into the matter.
   a. can't have died
   b. may not have died

6. Henry _____ such a delicious meal. He doesn't even know how to boil an egg.

   a. can't have made
   b. might not have made

7. What she said _____ true. I just don't believe it!

   a. can't be
   b. might not be

8. You _____ new brakes. I'll let you know after I've had a chance to look at the car.

   a. can't have to get
   b. may not have to get

9. The dog _____ hungry again. She just ate half an hour ago.

   a. couldn't be
   b. might not be

10. Rosa _____ to school today. School's closed.

   a. can't have gone
   b. might not have gone

Exercise 26   *With another student, read the sentences and cross out any that are true about your teacher. Then make complete sentences, using* can't *or* couldn't, *about why it is impossible for the remaining sentences to be true.*

Example: Someone heard your teacher holding a conversation in your language.

     My teacher couldn't have been holding a conversation in my language because she (or he) doesn't speak my language.

1. Somebody saw your teacher on the island of Jamaica the day before yesterday.

2. Somebody saw your teacher driving a Rolls Royce a couple of days ago.

3. Somebody says that your teacher spoke to your mother on the phone a couple of days ago.

4. Somebody saw your teacher in a news report on TV last night.

5. Somebody says that your teacher won a million dollars in the lottery last week.

6. Somebody heard that your teacher quit working last week.

7. Somebody saw your teacher talking to the president of the United States.

8. Somebody says that your teacher wrote this book.

Exercise 27 ▪▫ *With another student, answer the questions about other*
▪▪▪▪▪▪▪▪▪▪▪ *people in the class. If you are not sure of the answers, be*
sure to use may *or* might.

1. Who didn't want to come to class today?

2. Who didn't do all the homework?

3. Who sometimes played hooky from class as a high school student?

4. Who had a hard time learning how to drive?

5. Who didn't wear jeans in high school?

6. Who didn't like to go to parties in high school?

7. Who in the class was the first to go out on a date?

8. Who was naughty as a child?

9. Who got into a lot of fights as a child?

10. Who wasn't good at sports as a child?

▪ 12-7 DEGREES OF CERTAINTY

	Affirmative	Negative
Present Time		
A 100% sure	Eve *is* upset.	Eve *isn't* upset.
B 99% sure	xxxxxxxxxxxxxx	Eve *can't be* upset.
C 95% sure	Eve *must be* upset.	Eve *mustn't be* upset.
D 50% sure	Eve *may be* upset. Eve *might be* upset. Eve *could be* upset.	Eve *may not be* upset. Eve *might not be* upset. Eve *couldn't be* upset.
Past Time		
A 100% sure	Eve *was* upset.	Eve *wasn't* upset.
B 99% sure	xxxxxxxxxxxxxx	Eve *can't have been* upset.
C 95% sure	Eve *must have been* upset.	Eve *mustn't have been* upset.
D 50% sure	Eve *may have been* upset. Eve *might have been* upset. Eve *could have been* upset.	Eve *may not have been* upset. Eve *might not have been* upset. Eve *couldn't have been* upset.

1. In sentence **A**, the speaker is sure. The speaker is stating a fact.

2. In sentence **B**, the speaker is stating a strong probability.

3. In sentence **C**, the speaker is stating a logical conclusion.

4. In sentence **D**, the speaker is stating a possibility.

Exercise 28   *Complete the dialogs, using* might *or* must *according to how certain the speakers are and the correct form of the verbs in parentheses.*

1. **A:** Look how late it is. Warren and Cheryl were supposed to be here more than an hour ago. Something _____ (happen). They _____ (have) a car accident.

   B: Or they _____ (leave) their place late. Stop worrying!

2. **A:** How do you think the burglars got in?

   B: I don't know. They _____ (make) a special key.

   A: Don't be ridiculous! Such things only happen on TV. I'm going to check the basement. *(Several minutes later)* Come on down and see. They _____ (come) in through the basement window. It's wide open.

   B: But we've never been able to open that window.

   A: Then they _____ (have) some special tools.

3. **A:** How was your daughter's graduation ceremony?

   B: It was wonderful. She won several awards.

   A: You _____ (be) very proud of her.

   B: We were.

4. **A:** Why isn't the telephone working?

   B: Do you need to ask? You _____ (forgot) to pay the bill—again.

   A: No, you're wrong. I paid it in plenty of time. Do you want to see the canceled check?

   B: No, I believe you. I guess I should go to a pay phone and call the telephone company to find out what has happened.

   A: Wait a minute. Let me go upstairs and check the phone in the bedroom. One of the kids _____ (leave) the phone off the hook.

5. **A:** Gee, Lieutenant, it doesn't look like anybody's been here for a while. We
_____ (come) to the wrong house.

B: Sergeant, don't be so quick to jump to conclusions. Have a look around the house.

A: Hey, lieutenant, look here in the kitchen! The coffee machine's warm. Someone
_____ (be) here just a short time ago.

B: You're right. Let's check the rest of the house. Check everything, even the closets.

A: Yes, sir.

Exercise 29

With one or two other students, decide on at least two explanations for the news in each headline. Use could, may, might, *or* must *according to how certain you are.*

1.

PRESIDENT WINS RE-ELECTION

2.

FIRE DESTROYS APARTMENT
Family Left Homeless

3.

TRAGIC ACCIDENT ON ROUTE 108
Truck Crashes Into Car

4.

FAMOUS ACTOR FOUND DEAD
Police Conduct Investigation

5.

Thelma Myers Breaks World Long-Jump Record

6.

WITNESS IN MURDER TRIAL DISAPPEARS
Police in Nationwide Search

7.

POLICE NAB MAJOR DRUG DEALER

8.

VAN GOGH AT RECORD PRICE
Painting Sold for $20 Million

Practice Exam

■ SECTION 1

Identify the meaning of each modal in the sentences. The meanings are listed in the box.

advice	criticism	necessity	suggestion
assumption	expectation	possibility	

1. You should have put snow tires on your car last week.
2. Snow tires aren't cheap, but they shouldn't be very expensive.
3. If new tires are very expensive, and you don't have enough money, you could buy a set of used tires.

4. I saw several accidents on the freeway yesterday. Many people must not have had snow tires on their cars.

5. My next-door neighbor is coming over in a few minutes to help me put on my new snow tires. Someone's at the door now. It must be my neighbor.

6. Driving in the snow is very dangerous. You must get some new snow tires before the next storm.

7. You should buy your tires at the discount store. It has good tires that are not very expensive.

8. That store might be having a sale on tires now.

9. You could call to see if it is having a sale.

10. The store ought to be open now.

■ SECTION 2

Respond to each statement as indicated in parentheses.

Example: The sky is very dark.

(State a possibility about a future action.)

It might rain this afternoon.

(Give some advice.)

You should roll up your car windows.

(Make a suggestion.)

We could go to the museum instead of the park.

1. The director doesn't seem to be in a good mood this morning.
   a. (State a possibility.)
   b. (Make an assumption about the past.)
   c. (Give another student some advice.)

2. The leader of any country has many responsibilities.
   a. (State an obligation.)
   b. (State a necessity.)
   c. (Make an assumption.)

3. Tetsuo is more than six feet tall.
   a. (Make an assumption about Tetsuo when he was in high school.)
   b. (Give Tetsuo some advice.)
   c. (State a possibility about his future.)

4. Rosa's brother has just entered the army for three years.
   a. (State an obligation.)
   b. (State an expectation.)
   c. (Make an assumption.)
   d. (Give some advice for Rosa's brother.)

5. Margaret suddenly decided not to finish her Master's degree.
   a. (State a possibility about a present condition.)
   b. (State a possibility about a future action.)
   c. (State an expectation.)
   d. (Make an assumption.)

6. Our teacher is twenty-five minutes late this morning.
   a. (Make a statement of assumption about the past.)
   b. (Make a statement of expectation.)
   c. (Make a statement of possibility about the past.)
   d. (Make a suggestion to the other students.)

■ SECTION 3

Write two paragraphs. In the first, tell about a correct decision you made in the past. Tell some things you could have done, and then tell why you did not do them. In a separate paragraph, tell about a decision you made in the past that you now regret. Tell what you should have done instead. Before you begin, read these student paragraphs.

1. In 1991, I graduated from high school. I decided to register at the College of Engineering. I could have registered at the Medical College, but I like the subjects that depend on mathematics. The first two years I took general engineering courses. In the beginning of the third year, I could have studied electrical engineering, but I preferred mechanical engineering because I like thermodynamics and the strength of material subjects. In the summer of 1994, I worked with the Royal Saudi Air Force, and I could have worked there the next summer, but I worked with an oil company to get different knowledge.

   After graduation, I could have worked at a research center in Saudi Arabia, but I worked at the University of Riyadh because they give students a chance to continue studying after graduation. I could have gone to England for my Master's and Ph.D., but I preferred American universities because they are on the credited course system. I could have gone to Oklahoma to study English, but I came to Denver because it is a nice place.

2. Last Friday night, I went to the movies with my friend. I think we should have gone to the movies in the afternoon instead of at night. Because neither I nor my friend had a car, we had to take a bus to go to and return from the theater. After we had waited twenty minutes, the bus came. We should have known the bus schedule before we left. When we reached the theater, the movie had started. We should have had time to spare. The movie was over at 11:30, and it was snowing outside. It was too cold to stand at the bus stop; so we dropped into a coffee shop and drank a cup of coffee. We should not have taken that break. After we had waited thirty minutes, we started to walk home. It took about thirty minutes, and I caught a cold. Now, my friend and I are talking about last Friday. We agree that we should not have gone to the movies at night, and we should have learned the bus schedule before we left.

■ SECTION 4

Complete the dialog, using the modals and the correct form of the verbs in parentheses.

Ray: This quarter is almost finished, and I'm really disgusted with myself.

Mia: Why do you say that?

Ray: I _____ (could, study) much harder than I did.
1

Mia: I agree _____ (should, pass) the last two tests.
2
You _____ (must, feel) very bad right now about all the
3
time you wasted.

Ray: I do feel bad. I _____ (should, look forward to) the break right
4
now, like everyone else. Instead, I'm worrying about my grades.

Mia: Don't give up yet. Who knows? You _____ (might, pass) all
5
your courses.

Ray: There's always a chance, I guess. I probably _____ (should,
6
attend) all the review lectures.

Mia: SHOULD? You _____ (must, attend) all the review lectures.
7
That's your only hope. If you want, you can study with me and my
roommate tonight. We can help you prepare for the review lectures.

Ray: That's impossible tonight. I have a date.

Mia: You have a WHAT! You _____ (must, be) crazy!
8

Ray: Why do you say that?

Mia: You _____ (should not, think) about dates right now. You
9
_____ (should, plan) to use your time for studying.
10

Ray: I _____ (could, get) better grades on the last two tests if the
11
chemistry professor liked me.

Mia: That's a poor excuse. You were always late, and you never studied for the
tests. For example, three weeks ago you _____ (must, be) crazy
12
to come to the test thirty-five minutes late.

Ray: I'll tell you what happened on that day.

Mia: Don't bother. I'm going to the library now. See you later.

■ **SECTION 5**

Complete the dialog, using appropriate modals and the correct form of the verbs in parentheses.

Son: Mom, do you mind if I use the car tonight?

Mother: I don't know. I _____ (let) you use it. I'm not sure. After all, last
$\underset{1}{}$
week the police gave you a ticket for speeding. And you were lucky you

didn't lose your driver's license. You _____ (lose) it, you know.
$\underset{2}{}$

Son: It won't happen again. I realize now that I _____ (drive) more
$\underset{3}{}$
carefully last week.

Mother: Last week? You _____ (drive) carefully every week, every day,
$\underset{4}{}$
and every minute. A car is not a toy. Do you understand?

Son: Yes, Mom, I do.

Mother: Okay. Take the car, and leave now before I change my mind.

Son: Thanks, Mom. Oh, by the way, Mom, I need the car keys and some money
for gas.

Mother: I don't have my handbag with me. It _____ (be) in the
$\underset{5}{}$
bedroom on the dresser. Get it and bring it to me.

Son: Mom, it's not in the bedroom.

Mother: Then I _____ (leave) it in the kitchen. Go look there.
$\underset{6}{}$

Son: Here it is.

Mother: Here's ten dollars. You _____ (pay) me back by next week.
$\underset{7}{}$

Son: But Mom, I lost my part-time job, so I _____ (be able to) pay
$\underset{8}{}$
you back by next week.

Mother: Then you _____ (take) a bus tonight instead of the car. It's a
$\underset{9}{}$
beautiful evening.

Son: But, Mom, my date hates buses. You don't want her not to like me, do you?

Mother: That's not my problem. You _____ (think) about that before
$\underset{10}{}$
you lost your job. A car doesn't run on soda pop, you know. It uses gas, and
gas costs money.

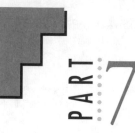

PART 7 Conditional Sentences

◼ INTRODUCTION TO PART 7 ■ ■ ■ ■ ■ ■ ■ ■

There are three basic types of conditional sentences in English. Each type

- expresses a different meaning.
- refers to a different time.
- uses a different combination of tenses.

Type 1 ■ Future Real

Meaning:	Refers to a situation that may or may not happen in the future.
Form:	**If** + simple present . . . , **will** + base form of verb

*If I have any free time, I **will meet** with you.*
(I may have some free time, but I'm not sure I will.)

Type 2 ■ Present or Future Unreal

Meaning:	Refers to a situation that does not exist in the present and/or will not exist in the future.
Form:	**If** + simple past . . . , **would** + base form of verb

*If I **had** any free time, I **would meet** with you.*
(I'm sorry. I do not have any free time.)

Type 3 ■ Past Unreal

Meaning:	Refers to a situation that did not happen.
Form:	**If** + past perfect . . . , **would have** + past participle

*If I **had had** any free time, I **would have met** with you.*
(I'm sorry that I didn't have any free time.)

Conditional sentences enable a speaker or writer to communicate many different ideas. Among them are

1. To make predictions.

   If I study hard this quarter, I will get "A"s in every class.

2. To discuss mistakes in the past.

   If I had studied more last quarter, I would have gotten better grades.

3. To express dreams.

    If I were rich, I would travel around the world.

4. To give advice.

    If I were you, I would save money instead of wasting it.

    If I were you, I would not take the TOEFL test this quarter.

5. To make apologies.

    If I had known you were waiting for a call, I would not have stayed on the phone so long. I'm sorry to have kept you waiting.

LESSON THIRTEEN

■ 13-1 FUTURE REAL VS. PRESENT/FUTURE UNREAL

■ Forming the Future Real (Type 1 Conditional Sentence) ■

***If*-Clause (Dependent Clause)**

If +
- simple present — *If John **studies**, . . .*
- present continuous — *If John **is studying**, . . .*
- present perfect — *If John **has studied**, . . .*
- present perfect continuous — *If John **has been studying**, . . .*
- modals — *If John **can study**, . . .*

Main Clause (Independent Clause)

will (='ll)
be going to
should
may
might
ought to
+ base form of the verb

*he **will**/'**ll** pass the test.*
*he **is going to pass** the test.*
*he **should pass** the test.*
*he **may pass** the test.*
*he **might pass** the test.*
*he **ought to pass** the test.*

1. Even though the time reference in the *if*-clause is the future, future verb forms are not used in the *if*-clause.

    Correct: *If it **rains** tomorrow, we'll stay home.*

    Incorrect: *If it will rain tomorrow, we'll stay home.*

    Will can be used in the *if*-clause only when the meaning is "don't mind."

    If you will have a seat (If you don't mind sitting down), I'll see if the doctor is ready to see you.

2. The choice of tense in the *if*-clause depends on the specific time referred to.

   *If he **is studying** (present), . . .*

   *If he **has been studying** (present perfect continuous), . . .*

3. The modal you choose for the independent clause depends on the specific meaning you want to communicate.

   he will pass the test. (There is no doubt in my mind.)

   he might pass the test. (I'm not sure, but I think he will.)

   he should pass the test. (I expect him to pass the test.)

4. In writing, a comma follows an *if*-clause when it is at the beginning of a sentence. Do not use a comma when the *if*-clause follows the main clause.

   If John studies, he will pass the test.

   John will pass the test if he studies.

   These punctuation rules also apply to type 2 and type 3 conditional sentences.

Exercise 1   *With another student, complete the following sentences.*

1. If it snows, _____.
2. If the streets are icy, _____.
3. If I have to wait for the bus in the cold weather, _____.
4. I might not go to class if _____.
5. If it has stopped snowing by morning, _____.
6. If the highway department is sanding the roads now, _____.
7. If the landlord doesn't turn on the heat in my apartment, _____.
8. If he has already turned the heat on, _____.
9. If it's still snowing when class is over, _____.
10. I'll walk home from class if _____.

Exercise 2 ▪▪ *With another student, suggest solutions to each problem,*
▪ *using* if. *Think of as many solutions as you can.*

1. You need a loan, but your bank probably won't give you one.
2. Your teacher assigns so much homework that you have time for little else.
3. You sent in your college application a while ago and were supposed to hear by now whether you had been admitted. However, you haven't received any correspondence from the college.
4. For the past month a strange-looking man has been standing outside your building when you leave every morning. You don't know who he is or why he is always there.
5. A friend borrowed $100 from you a month ago and still hasn't paid you back.
6. One of your neighbors is a music student, and she practices the violin at all hours, even late at night.
7. Your car had been making a strange noise. You took it to a mechanic, but he couldn't find anything wrong with it. The car is quieter now, but you still hear the noise.
8. You're in a foreign country, and you don't speak the language. You think you can find your way back to your hotel, but you're not sure.

▪ Forming the Present/Future Unreal (Type 2 Conditional Sentence) ▪

If-clause (Dependent Clause)

If + { simple past
        past continuous
        modals

If John **studied,** . . .
If John **was studying,** . . .
If John **could study,** . . .

Main Clause (Independent Clause)

would (='d)
could   } + base form of the verb
should
might

he **would** /**'d pass** *the test.*
he **could pass** *the test.*
he **should pass** *the test.*
he **might pass** *the test.*

1. Even though the time reference in the *if*-clause is the present or future, past verb forms are used in the *if*-clause.

   Correct: *If we* **had** *the money, we would buy a car today.*

   Incorrect: *If we have the money, we would buy a car today.*

Would can be used in the *if*-clause only when the meaning is "be willing to."

If you would take the time to study (If you were willing to take the time to study), *you could be an excellent student.*

2. The subjunctive *were* is used for all persons.

   *If I **were** rich, I would quit my job immediately.*
   *If she **were** rich, she would quit her job immediately.*
   *If they **were** rich, they would quit their jobs immediately.*

   In informal speech, *If I was rich* is sometimes heard.

3. The modals in the independent clause are in the forms they take in indirect speech.

4. Remember that with type 2 conditional sentences, you are stating the opposite of present truths.

   [Present truth: I don't have any money, so I can't lend you any.]
   *If I **had** some money, I **could lend** you some.*

   [Present truth: I'm not concentrating, so this page is difficult to understand.]
   *If I **were concentrating**, this page **would not be** difficult to understand.*

5. *If* may be omitted in the *if*-clause when it is followed by an auxiliary verb such as *should* and *were*. Note that the auxiliary precedes the noun when *if* is omitted.

   ***Should I see** him today, I'll tell him to call you.* (If I should see him today, . . .)
   ***Were he** home now, you could call him.* (If he were home now, . . .)

Exercise 3   *Restate each statement in a type 2 (present or future unreal) conditional sentence.*

1. The weather is terrible today, so we can't have the party in the park.

2. It is raining, so the grass in the park is wet.

3. We can't have the party in my apartment because it is too small.

4. The university will not permit us to have the party in the dorm; otherwise, we could have it downstairs in the recreation room.

5. None of our friends is renting a house this quarter. Let's forget about the party.

6. I don't know how to ski, so I am not going to go to Colorado during the break.

7. You aren't an experienced skier, so you are not able to teach me.

8. Besides, I don't have any money, so I can't go.

9. I have to finish a term paper during the break, so I won't have a real vacation anyway.

10. My roommate is gone, so I will have plenty of peace and quiet.

Exercise 4 *With another student, complete the sentences.*

1. I'd get a car if _____.

2. If I had a car, _____.

3. If I were rich, _____.

4. If I knew where to buy a good used car, _____.

5. I'd have fewer problems if _____.

6. If my roommate had a car, _____.

7. If this city had a good system of public transportation, _____.

8. It wouldn't take me so long to get to class if _____.

9. If I didn't live so far from the university, _____.

10. If I could get a single room in the dorm, _____.

Exercise 5 *In a group of three or four, ask and answer questions based on the given words. Answer in complete sentences.*

1. What / you / do / differently from the leader of your country / if / you / be / the leader?

2. If / you / can go / anywhere in the world tomorrow / where / you / go?

3. If / you / win / ten thousand dollars / what / you / do / with it?

4. How often / you / give / tests / if / you / be / the teacher of this class?

5. If / you / can have / dinner with a famous person / with whom / you / like / to have dinner?

6. What / you / do / if / you / find / a very expensive watch?

7. If / you / be / on a desert island / what three things / you / want / to have with you?

8. What three pieces of advice / you / give / if / your teacher / be planning / to visit your country?

■ 13-2 PAST UNREAL

■ **Forming the Past Unreal** (Type 3 Conditional Sentence) ■

If-clause (Dependent Clause)

If + $\left\{\begin{array}{l}\text{past perfect}\\\text{past perfect continuous}\\\text{past perfect passive}\end{array}\right.$

If John had studied, . . .
If John had been studying, . . .
If John had been told about the exam, . . .

Main Clause (Independent Clause)

$\left.\begin{array}{l}\textit{would}\\\textit{could}\\\textit{should}\\\textit{might}\end{array}\right\}$ + *have* + past participle

he would have passed the test.
he could have passed the test.
he should have passed the test.
he might have passed the test.

1. Remember that type 3 conditional sentences state the opposite of what actually happened in the past.

   If John had studied, he would have passed the test. (He hadn't studied, and he didn't pass the test.)

   If Leslie hadn't studied, she wouldn't have passed the test. (She had studied, and she did pass the test.)

2. The word *if* may be omitted in the *if*-clause. Note the position of *had* and *not* when *if* is omitted.

   Had I known *you wanted to talk with her, I would have told her yesterday.* (If I had known you wanted to talk with her, . . .)

   We would have gone for a walk **had it not been** *so cold.* (. . . if it hadn't been so cold.)

3. The passive voice can be used in either the *if*-clause or the main clause.

   If I **had mailed** *my application on time, I could have taken the TOEFL test last week.*
   If my application **had been mailed** *on time, I could have taken the TOEFL test last week.*

   We **wouldn't have canceled** *the picnic if it hadn't rained in the morning.*
   The picnic **wouldn't have been canceled** *if it hadn't rained in the morning.*

   The passive voice can also be used in type 1 and type 2 conditional sentences.

Exercise 6   *With another student, complete the sentences.*

1. If Pat had arrived on time for work, _____.
2. Had Pat not missed the bus, _____.
3. She wouldn't have missed the bus if _____.
4. If her son hadn't been sick most of the night, _____.
5. Her son wouldn't have been sick most of the night if _____.
6. Had this been the first time Pat was late for work, _____.
7. If her boss hadn't been in the office when Pat arrived, _____.
8. Pat wouldn't have been upset about what her boss said if _____.
9. Pat would have had lunch with some of her colleagues had _____.
10. If Pat had known the day was going to turn out so badly, _____.

Exercise 7   *Write an explanation of the meaning of each sentence.*

Examples: If he has time, he'll meet with you.
Maybe he will and maybe he won't have time. I'm not sure.

If he had time, he could meet with you.
I'm sorry. He doesn't have any time, so he can't meet with you.

If he had had time, he could have met with you.
But he didn't have any free time, so he could not meet with you.

1. If I see your roommate, I'll tell him to buy a six pack of soda.

2. Had I known you wanted some soda, I would have bought it for you.

3. If you lived closer to the supermarket, you could walk there and get a six pack yourself.

4. If you had made a shopping list before you went to the store, you wouldn't have forgotten to buy soda.

5. If you're really thirsty, you can get some soda from the vending machine.

6. If my parents come to the States this summer, I'll have a party for them.

7. They could come sooner if my mother were not afraid to fly.

8. She might have agreed to fly last year if there had not been so many airplane accidents.

9. Had my mother traveled more when she was younger, she might not have acquired such a fear of flying.

10. If my parents decide to come by ship, the trip will take three weeks.

Exercise 8   *Restate each sentence, using if.*

Examples: I didn't hear the phone, so I didn't answer it.
If I had heard it, I would have answered it.

I don't know her number, so I can't give it to you.
If I knew her number, I would give it to you.

I don't think I will have time to call you tomorrow.
But if I have time to call, I will.

1. I didn't take a vacation last summer because I didn't have enough money.

2. I hope I'll have enough money to take a vacation next summer.

3. I don't even have enough money to go home next month during the spring break.

4. I didn't know you were going to visit Colorado, so I didn't invite you to stay at my house.

5. I won't get an opportunity to take a vacation next year, so you're welcome to stay with me instead of in a hotel.

6. I don't have a very big house, so your friends will have to stay in a hotel.

7. Another friend might come to Colorado next year, and I think she'll like it too.

8. My roommate's cousin was in Denver last year, but he didn't write and tell us he was coming, so when he arrived we were out of town.

9. We learned later that he had lost our address and telephone number, so he couldn't notify us of his visit.

10. I doubt that he's coming to Denver again this year.

Exercise 9 *Complete each sentence, using the correct form of the verbs in parentheses.*

1. If the final exam _____ (be) easy, I might get an "A" in grammar.

2. I will certainly get a "B" if I _____ (review) all the lesson.

3. Of course, If I _____ (have) a quiet roommate, I could study more.

4. During finals, I'll go to the library if my roommate _____ (continue) to make a lot of noise.

5. If I _____ (can) move to a single room, I would.

6. I _____ (apply) to Harvard University for the fall quarter if I get a score of 600 on the TOEFL exam.

7. I might have worked harder at the beginning of this quarter if I _____ _____ (not, be) so homesick.

8. If I had received more money from home, I _____ (get) an apartment.

9. After this quarter ends, I'm going to go to Canada if I _____ (have) enough money for a ticket.

10. I would drive to Canada if I _____ (own) a car.

11. If I had saved my money last year, I _____ (buy) a new car at the beginning of this quarter.

12. I would buy a used car if I _____ (trust) used cars.

13. If my parents _____ (be) rich, I wouldn't be worrying about all of this.

14. My roommate has a car, so if he decides to go to Canada, I _____ (not, have) any problems.

Exercise 10 *Change the underlined verbs to the passive voice and make the other necessary changes in each sentence. Use* by *where needed.*

1. Bob would not be riding the bus these days if someone <u>had not stolen</u> his car.

2. If Bob <u>hadn't left</u> the door unlocked, the car wouldn't have been so easy to steal.

3. If Bob <u>had reported</u> the theft right after it happened, the police <u>might have found</u> his car.

4. The thief <u>might not have taken</u> the car if Bob <u>had locked</u> it.

5. If someone <u>had seen</u> the thief, he might not have gotten away.

6. Bob still might get his car back if some garage <u>is not painting</u> it a different color.

7. If the police <u>can catch</u> the thief, he will certainly spend time in jail.

8. If every citizen <u>reported</u> car thefts promptly, we <u>could solve</u> this problem.

9. We <u>would discourage</u> many criminals if some people were not afraid to report crimes.

10. If the police <u>patrolled</u> more neighborhoods regularly, we <u>would see</u> fewer crimes.

11. If Bob has to buy a new car, I believe that his insurance company <u>will pay</u> for it.

12. If I ever see anyone doing anything illegal, I <u>will make a report</u> immediately.

■ 13-3 REPLACING *If*

1. It is possible to replace *if* with *unless*.

   unless + affirmative verb = *if* + negative verb

   Unless *you hurry, we're going to miss the movie.* (**If you don't** hurry, . . .)

2. It is possible to replace *if* with *provided* or *provided that* when the idea of restriction is very strong.

   I will lend you fifty dollars **provided that** *you repay me as soon as your check arrives.*

3. It is possible to replace *if* with *suppose* or *supposing*. (*suppose/supposing* = what will happen if . . . /what would happen if . . . / what would have happened if . . .?)

   Suppose *you fail the final exam?* (**What will happen if** you fail the final exam?)

   Supposing *you failed the final exam?* (**What would happen if** you failed the final exam?)

   Suppose *you had failed the final exam?* (**What would have happened if** you had failed the final exam?)

4. It is possible to replace *if* with *in case. In case* means that someone has something or someone does something in order to deal with an event that might happen.

   We'll eat inside **in case** *it rains.*

Exercise 11 ■ ■   *Complete each sentence, using* unless, provided that, supposing, *or* in case.

1. We're going to rent a car when we travel to San Juan _____ we decide to visit some places outside the city.

2. We're going to rent a car when we travel to San Juan _____ we can get a mini-van.

3. _____ there's a lot of traffic, shouldn't we get there in time?

4. _____ we leave now, will we get there in time?

5. I'll take some extra money _____ we need it.

6. I'll take some extra money _____ you do, too.

7. I'll go out with you for dinner _____ my roommate has already cooked dinner.

8. I'll go out with you for dinner _____ we don't go anywhere expensive.

Exercise 12 *Restate the sentences, using* unless, provided that, suppose, *or* in case.

1. I won't be able to go to Mexico if air fares don't go down.

2. I'll be happy to drive you to Mexico if you promise to help me pay for gas.

3. What will happen if we run out of fuel in the middle of the desert?

4. Don't worry. I'll have some extra gas in the trunk of my car if we run out of fuel.

5. If you don't remember to put an extra can of gas in the trunk, we could be stranded in the middle of nowhere.

6. Stop worrying. If that happens, we can call for help on my car phone.

7. That's a good idea if someone is around to hear our call.

8. What would have happened if we had not had the car phone last year on our way to Alaska?

9. If you don't stop worrying, I'll cancel the whole trip.

10. All right, but if you discover that your car can't make such a long trip, I'm going to find out about the cheapest air fares.

11. If Tom decides to go with us, we should agree on what to charge him for gas.

12. He can go with us if he promises to leave his dog at home.

13. You know that he won't leave his dog if he can't find a responsible person to take care of him.

14. That's not our problem. We will simply tell him that he can't go with us if he insists on taking his dog.

■ 13-4 MIXED CONDITIONAL SENTENCES

1. Both type 2 and type 3 conditionals can appear in the same sentence when one part of the sentence refers to past time and the other part of the sentence refers to present or future time.

   type 3   type 2
   *If I **hadn't failed** the road test last week, I **would have** my driver's licence now.*

   type 2   type 3
   *If I **weren't going** to their house tomorrow, I **wouldn't have bought** them a gift.*

2. Two or more individuals may respond to a statement made in a conversation or in writing in a number of different ways. For example, one person may use a type 1 conditional sentence, another a type 2 sentence, and another a type 3 sentence. A fourth person's response may mix type 2 and type 3 sentences.

Exercise 13 ■ *Identify the type of conditional form(s) used in each sentence.*

Examples: You **would be finished** now if you **had used** the computer.
<u>*Type 2 and Type 3*</u>

I know, but there were no computer terminals available. If there **had been**, I **would have used** one.
<u>*Type 3*</u>

It's Thursday night, and six friends are talking about their plans for the coming weekend.

Jim: Last night the weatherman said that the temperature was going to be in the '90s this coming weekend.

Bob: If it **is**[1] that hot Sunday, I'**ll**[2] spend the afternoon in the park.

Sue: I **would go**[3] to the mountains this weekend if I **didn't have**[4] an exam on Monday.

Gail: If I **had heard**[5] the weather report last night, I **wouldn't have promised**[6] to help my roommate with her chemistry assignment on Saturday.

Tom: Jim, I **would plan**[7] to play soccer with you in the park this weekend if I **had already completed**[8] my composition, which is due on Monday.

Rita: I don't believe anything the weatherman says anymore. If I **hadn't listened**[9] to him last weekend, I **wouldn't have**[10] this terrible cold now.

Exercise 14 *With another student, write responses to the sentences, using as many different types of conditional forms as possible. In some responses, only one type of conditional may be possible. Be careful of meaning and time reference.*

1. You have a friend who wants to work in Spain next year, but he doesn't speak Spanish. What would you say to him?

2. Your alarm didn't go off, so you got up late and missed your final exam in grammar. What would you say to your teacher?

3. You were invited to Ali's party, but you stayed home. Three days later a friend tells you that it was really a good party. What would you say to him?

4. a. A friend is going with you to a party next Saturday night. He wants you to introduce him to some women when you get there. You don't know for certain if you will see anyone you know. What would you tell him?

   b. At the party you discover that you don't know anyone there, but your friend is still begging you to introduce him to some of the women. What would you tell him?

   c. The party is over. You are on your way home. Your friend is angry because you didn't introduce him to any women. What would you tell him?

5. You brought a used car that you found was not in the condition the salesperson stated. You went back to the used-car lot to tell the salesperson that you were going to make a report to the police, but the salesperson had quit. What would you say?

6. Your friend was driving 90 miles per hour and was caught by the police. Now she has to pay a $350 speeding ticket. What would you say?

7. The tuition at the college you are attending has risen three times in the last year. What would you say?

8. You need a specific book to use as resource material for your Master's thesis.

   a. You can't afford to buy the book at present. What would you say?

   b. The book is difficult to find. What would you say?

   c. You found a copy of the book, but it is written in a language you don't know. What would you say?

Practice Exam

■ SECTION 1

Complete the following sentences.

1. If the airline pilots go on strike, _____

   _____

2. If the pilots weren't so dissatisfied with their working conditions. _____

   _____

3. If I'd known they were planning to strike at this time, _____

   _____

4. If the pilots get the changes they are asking for, _____

   _____

5. Had the public been notified of the possibility of a strike, _____

   _____

6. If the strike didn't affect people's travel plans, _____

   _____

■ SECTION 2

Restate the sentences, using if.

Example: I really don't understand economics, so I can't explain why inflation is so high.

If I could understand (OR If I understood) economics, I could explain (OR I would be able to explain) why inflation is so high.

1. Saleh didn't get to the cleaners before it closed, so he couldn't pick up his suit.

   _____

   _____

2. I don't think I will have time this afternoon to help you review the work that you missed yesterday, but I might.

   _____

   _____

3. I won't have time to help you review the work you missed. I'm sorry.

_____

_____

4. Rafael has not been taking the medicine his doctor prescribed, so he's going to have to spend a few days in the hospital.

_____

_____

5. You were speeding again, so naturally the police officer gave you a ticket.

_____

_____

6. I might have a party next weekend, but I'm not sure. My roommate hasn't agreed to the idea yet.

_____

_____

■ SECTION 3

Restate the sentences, using unless, provided that, suppose, *or* in case.

1. If the cost of new houses doesn't go down, we'll have to stay in our apartment.

_____

_____

2. We might be able to buy a house if we can get a large down payment.

_____

_____

3. What will happen if the landlord raises our rent?

_____

4. We'll start looking for a smaller apartment if that happens.

_____

5. If I get a good raise next year, we might be able to afford a small house.

_____

6. However, we had better start saving more money if I don't get a large enough raise.

_____

_____

■ SECTION 4

Read the situation and write an appropriate response for each speaker. Use the type of conditional sentence indicated in parentheses.

All the students are sitting in class waiting for the grammar teacher to arrive with the tests. Instead, the director walks in and announces that the teacher is very sick and will not be able to come to class and give the test. He tells the students that they cannot leave the class, but they may use the time for additional study before their next class begins.

Student 1: (type 1 response) _____

_____

Student 2: (type 2 response) _____

_____

_____

Student 3: (type 3 response) _____

_____

_____

Student 4: (mixed response, types 2 and 3) _____

_____

_____

PART 8 Verbals

INTRODUCTION TO PART 8 ■ ■ ■ ■ ■ ■ ■

In English a verb form may sometimes function in a sentence as another part of speech. Verb forms that are used as other parts of speech are called "verbals." The infinitive and gerund forms of a verb are two examples of verbals. Look at these sentences.

    A **To exercise** is good for your health.

    B **Exercising** is good for your health.

    C Some people really like **to exercise**.

    D Some people really enjoy **exercising**.

In the sentences, the infinitive and gerund forms are used as nouns. In sentence **A**, the infinitive is the subject of the sentence. In sentence **B**, the gerund is the subject of the sentence. In sentences **C** and **D**, the infinitive and gerund forms are used as the direct objects of the statements. In addition to functioning as a noun, the infinitive may also be used as an adjective or an adverb.

In this part, you will study infinitive and gerund constructions and the ways they are used in English sentences.

LESSON FOURTEEN

■ 14-1 SIMPLE INFINITIVES AND INFINITIVE PHRASES

Simple Infinitives

A *Most people want **to work**.*

B *We stopped our work **to rest**.*

C ***To succeed** is difficult.*

Infinitive Phrase

D *My father wants* **me to succeed**.

E *I have always liked* **to study business**.

F *He advised* **my brother to take economics**.

G *Many people like* **to live dangerously**.

H *Professor Jeffers is the person* **to see about scholarships**.

1. A simple infinitive is formed with *to* + the simple form of a verb (sentences **A–C**).

2. The makeup of an infinitive phrase varies. In sentence **D**, *me* is the subject of the infinitive. In sentence **E**, *business* is the object of the infinitive. In sentence **F**, *my brother* is the subject of the infinitive, and *economics* is the object of the infinitive. In sentence **G**, *dangerously* modifies the infinitive. In sentence **H**, *about scholarships* modifies the infinitive.

3. In a negative infinitive, *not* immediately precedes the infinitive. Compare:

   Natalie **agreed not to help** *me.*

   Natalie **did not agree to help** *me.*

   In the first sentence, the infinitive phrase is negative. In the second sentence, the verb *did not agree* is negative. In some sentences, however, the meaning is the same. Compare:

   I **didn't want to take** *the test.*

   I **wanted not to take** *the test.*

   Not all verbs can be made negative. It depends on the meaning of the verb that precedes the infinitive.

4. The verbs *help, have, let, make* and verbs of sense such as *feel*, *see*, and *hear* are followed by nouns or object pronouns and the simple form of the verb without *to*.

   The instructor **helped us organize** *our outlines.*

   He **had the students write** *the composition in class.*

   He **let us use** *our dictionaries.*

   He **saw me open** *my dictionary several times.*

   I **made myself write** *as neatly as I could.*

Exercise 1 ■ ■ *Read the letter and underline all the infinitives and infinitive phrases.*

Dear Sir or Madam:

I am writing to complain about your customer service department. When I received an incorrect bill last week, I decided to call a representative from your customer service department rather than write to you. This turned out to be a mistake. I tried to get through all day, but the line was constantly busy. Clearly, the phone had been taken off the hook—or else many other customers were also calling to complain.

It's hard to believe, but it wasn't until 9:30 at night that I finally got through, and the conversation turned out to be a complete waste of time. I spoke to your customer service representative for about ten minutes, but she refused to do anything about the problem. She insisted that the computer never makes mistakes. After I explained the mistake and told her that I could prove it, she said that I would have to go the main office and see one of the supervisors. When I mentioned that the lines at the main office are always long, she told me that that was my problem, not hers. Is this the way you train your representatives to speak to customers?

It is unfortunate that I never got the name of this representative, but I hope you will look into the matter and remind all your representatives that "customer service" means it is their job to serve the customer. I look forward to receiving a response from you regarding this matter.

Sincerely yours,

G. Gomez

G. Gomez

Exercise 2 ■ ■ *With another student, practice asking and answering questions, using negative infinitive phrases.*

Example: A: Did your roommate agree *not to keep the TV on all the time?*
  B: *Yes, she agreed not to keep it on all the time.*

1. Because of the bad weather a few days ago, did you decide _____?

2. After your last argument with a friend, did you promise yourself _____?

3. After spending so much time studying English, have you finally learned _____?

4. In the face of danger, do you usually pretend _____?

5. In class, do you try _____?

6. Since the grades on the last test were so low, has the teacher agreed _____?

7. Has anybody today told you _____?

8. If a friend isn't doing well in school, do you persuade _____?

9. Do you think the teacher is going to continue _____?

10. Since nobody in the class likes to do a lot of homework, has the teacher been persuaded _____?

■ 14-2 INFINITIVE/INFINITIVE PHRASE FUNCTIONING AS SUBJECT AND SUBJECT COMPLEMENT

Subject of the Sentence

A *To study* takes a lot of time.

B *To learn another language* is not easy.

C *To be a student* is a difficult job.

Subject Complement

D *My goal* is *to get good grades*.

E *His desire* has been *to enter graduate school*.

F *Her job* last summer was *to answer the phone*.

1. An infinitive or infinitive phrase functions as a noun when it is the subject of the sentence or is the subject complement. (A subject complement renames or refers to the subject of the sentence, as in sentences **D–F**.)

2. An infinitive or infinitive phrase can be used as the subject of the sentence (**A – C**, above). Nevertheless, speakers of English usually use the word *it* as the "false" subject of the sentence and place the "true" subject after the verb. In these sentences, the true subjects are underlined and the infinitive subjects follow adjectives.

   It is not easy to save. (To save is not easy.)

   It is fun to read. (To read is fun.)

   It is fun to read a good mystery story. (To read a good mystery story is fun.)

   In these sentences, the infinitive structures follow nouns.

   It takes a lot of money to buy a house. (To buy a house takes a lot of money.)

   It took a lot of time to furnish our new home. (To furnish our new home took a lot of time.)

3. Sometimes the false subject *it* is followed by *for* + noun/pronoun + infinitive construction. In these sentences, the true subjects are underlined.

   It is difficult <u>for me to learn a second language</u>. (<u>For me to learn a second language</u> is difficult.)

   It will be easy <u>for Ana to pass this class</u>. (<u>For Ana to pass this class</u> will be easy.)

4. In sentences where *it* is used as the false subject, certain adjectives may be followed by the preposition *of* + noun/pronoun + infinitive construction.

   It *was nice of you to visit me* in the hospital.

   It *was foolish of me to ski* without any lessons.

   It *was considerate of the class to send me* flowers.

   With some adjectives *for* is also possible.

   It *was foolish for me to ski* without any lessons.

Exercise 3   *Answer the questions, using* it *as the false subject of the sentence.*

Example: When someone is studying for a driver's license, what usually takes a lot of time?

   It usually takes a lot of time to learn the rules in the driver's manual.

1. When a person is taking the road test, what is sometimes difficult?

2. After you had been driving for a while, what was easy?

3. When you drive, what is against the law?

4. Before you take a long trip by car, what is important to do?

5. If you were on a long trip by yourself, what would be necessary?

6. When you take a long trip by car, what is enjoyable?

7. If a traffic light is yellow, what can be dangerous?

8. If you are behind an inexperienced driver, what is very frustrating?

9. Before you turn a corner, what is necessary?

10. When you drive in an unfamiliar city, what takes a lot of time?

11. Concerning the care of a car, what is essential?

12. Before you buy a new car, what is advisable?

Exercise 4 ▪▪ ▪ *Complete each sentence, using an infinitive phrase as subject complement.*

Example: My goal is *to be a lawyer.*

1. When I graduated from high school, my ambition was _____.

2. Before I return to my country, my plan is _____.

3. A medical doctor's highest purpose should be _____.

4. In every country in the world, the police officer's main job is _____.

5. My father believes that his responsibility has always been _____.

6. Before I can pass this level, my problem will be _____.

7. Our grammar teacher's main goals is _____.

8. Before many people get married their one desire is _____.

9. In the library, the information clerk's duty is _____.

10. When I was a child, my dream was _____.

11. The teacher said that the assignment for tomorrow was _____.

12. The purpose of this exercise has been _____.

Exercise 5 ▪▪ ▪ *With another student, take turns asking and answering questions using* for *+ noun/pronoun + infinitive/infinitive phrase.*

Example: A: When you first came to the States, was it difficult *for you to make new friends?*

B: *Yes, it was difficult for me to make new friends when I first came here.* OR

No, it wasn't difficult for me to make new friends when I first came here.

1. When you were at home in your country, was it fun _____?

2. When you were in high school, did it take much time _____?

3. On the weekends, is it relaxing _____?

4. Before the next test, will it be necessary _____?

5. Concerning learning to speak English fluently, is it taking a lot of time _____?

6. I would like to visit your country one day. Would it cost much money _____?

7. Since you've been living in a foreign country, has it been exciting _____?

8. When you go to a restaurant for the first time, is it difficult _____?

9. When you are watching American television, is it sometimes hard _____?

10. Since you've been living away from your family, has it been almost impossible _____?

Exercise 6   *Complete the sentences with of.*

Example: It was considerate *of her to help me.*

1. It was really foolish _____.

2. It was very smart _____.

3. It is generous _____.

4. It was very kind _____.

5. It was extremely disrespectful _____.

6. It is rude _____.

7. Actually, it was stupid _____.

8. It is very impolite _____.

9. It was friendly _____.

10. It is wise _____.

11. It was intelligent _____.

12. It is very nice _____.

13. It was wrong _____.

14. It is inconsiderate _____.

14-3 INFINITIVE/INFINITIVE PHRASE FUNCTIONING AS DIRECT OBJECT

■ GROUP 1: Verb + Infinitive/Infinitive Phrase ■

afford[1]	come	happen	offer	remember
agree	consent	hesitate	plan[3]	seem
appear	decide	hope	prepare	struggle
arrange	demand	intend	pretend	swear
be	deserve	learn	proceed	tend
care	endeavor	manage	prove	threaten
choose[2]	fail	mean	refuse	volunteer
claim	forget	neglect	regret	wait

[1] The verb *afford* is always used with a form of *can* or *be able to.* (*They **can afford** to buy a house, but they **aren't able to afford** a new car, too.*)

[2] The verb *choose* is followed by an infinitive when it means *prefer.* (*I **chose to buy** that car because it is more fuel-efficient.*)

[3] The verb *plan* indicates future time when used in the simple present tense. (*We **plan** to leave **soon**.*)

1. An infinitive or infinitive phrase functions as a noun when it is the object of the verb.

   She **refused to tell me** *what happened.*

   I **chose not to do anything** *about it.*

2. Additional information may appear between the main verb and the infinitive or infinitive phrase.

   *I did not come **to this country as a student** to waste time.*

   Several words may separate the main verb and the infinitive, as in the sentence above, but the infinitive is <u>never</u> separated.

   Correct: *You need **to work** carefully.*

   Incorrect: *You need to carefully work.*

Exercise 7 ▪ ▪
▪
■ ■ ■ ■ ■ ■ ■ ■ ■ ■ ■ ■

Check (✓) the sentences in which the infinitive phrase is the object of the verb. Then identify the tense of the main verb in each checked sentence.

1. I must get a roommate; otherwise, I can't afford to rent an apartment.

2. My cousin has agreed to live with me.

3. She seems to be happy about our decision.

4. We have arranged to share the cooking and the cleaning.

5. It will be my job to cook.

6. I don't mind cooking, but I don't care to clean.

7. It is also my responsibility to do the grocery shopping.

8. My cousin and I are hoping to have a really nice apartment.

9. Our landlord has finally consented to paint the apartment.

10. To live with a roommate is not easy, but it is not too difficult to live with my cousin.

Exercise 8 ▪ ▪
▪
■ ■ ■ ■ ■ ■ ■ ■ ■ ■ ■ ■

Complete each item, using appropriate infinitives or infinitive phrases. In some sentences there may be more than one correct answer.

1. Although the hitchhiker seemed _____ cold and tired, we hesitated _____, so we pretended not _____ him. Before we began our trip, we had decided not _____ any strangers along the road.

2. There are good universities in every part of the world; however, many students choose _____ in another country because they hope _____ another language in addition to studying in their particular major. After I complete my studies, I am preparing _____ to my country where I intend _____.

3. My roommate, Ana, and I had forgotten _____ our door before we left our apartment, so when we returned, the door was open and we heard noises inside. Ana, who is afraid of everything, hesitated _____ the apartment first, and I agreed _____. I was pretending not _____ afraid, but I was very nervous. Finally, I volunteered _____ the apartment. Turning on the hall light, I looked around but

saw no one. Whoever was there refused _____, so I quickly returned outside into the hall where Ana was waiting _____ what had happened. We heard a loud noise, which came from the living room, and both of us proceeded _____ down the hall as quickly as we could to the manager's office. We endeavored _____ to him why we were knocking so loudly on his door, but we weren't speaking very calmly. Finally he consented _____ to our apartment with us. As we entered the apartment, the lights came on, and twenty of our friends shouted, "HAPPY BIRTHDAY, ANA!"

4. **Advisor:** You were an excellent undergraduate student. Do you intend _____ graduate school?

   Student: I hope to, but because of the expense, I don't think I will be able to this year.

   Advisor: I have been aware of your financial troubles, so I managed _____ you a scholarship for the entire four years of study.

   Student: I don't know how to thank you.

   Advisor: Don't worry about it. You have proven yourself _____ a serious young man, so you deserve _____ some help.

   Student: I don't mean _____ a problem, but how will I pay for books and other supplies?

   Advisor: Don't worry about that either. The department has arranged for you _____ as a lab assistant three days a week.

   Student: Thank you, but will I make enough to pay for an apartment?

   Advisor: I failed _____ you that my wife and I would like you to live with us. We have plenty of room.

   Student: I can't thank you enough for your kindness.

■ GROUP 2: Verb + Object + Infinitive/Infinitive Phrase ■

advise	compel	get	oblige	show . . . how
allow	convince	help[1]	order	teach
appoint	direct	hire	permit	tell
cause	enable	implore	persuade	tempt
caution	encourage	instruct	remind	urge
challenge	forbid	invite	request	warn
command	force	motivate	require	

[1]The verb *help* is followed by nouns or object pronouns and the simple form of the verb without *to*. (*Can you **help me find** my jacket?*)

1. These verbs must be followed first by an object, then by the infinitive.

   The doctor **advised me to take** a long vacation.
   The doctor **advised Bill to take** a long vacation.
   My friend **encouraged me to take** some time off.
   I **invited my friend to spend** a few days at a ski resort with me.

2. These verbs can be used with an infinitive alone only when the main verb is in the passive voice.

   Bill and I **were advised to take** a long vacation.

Exercise 9 ■■ *Put the words in order so that they make logical sentences.*

1. smoking / me / The / doctor / stop / to / advised

2. smoke / rooms / allow / This / their / patients / hospital / in / not / to / does

3. the / smoker / head nurse / hospital director / to / appointed / report / The / any

4. cough / Smoke / sister / to / my / causes

5. smoking / Anticigarette ads / anyone / stop / cannot / to / compel

6. The / ordered / cigarettes / its / hospital / staff / give up / to

7. this / protest / people / smoke / order / encouraged / The / who / each other / to

8. regulation / director / anyone / ignore / forbids / this / The / to

9. dangers / to / smoking / doctor / finally / me / the / of / about / got / think / My

Exercise 10 *Complete the sentences, using an appropriate noun or pronoun object + infinitive/infinitive phrase. In some sentences there may be more than one correct answer.*

1. On the airplane, the hijacker forced ＿＿＿＿＿＿＿＿ ＿＿＿＿＿＿＿＿
                                                     (object)   (infinitive)
   in their seats.

2. The man beside John helped ＿＿＿＿＿＿＿＿ ＿＿＿＿＿＿＿＿ calm.
                                       (object)   (infinitive)

3. The flight attendant instructed ＿＿＿＿＿＿＿＿ ＿＿＿＿＿＿＿＿
                                       (object)   (infinitive)
   the hijacker's commands.

4. A little boy was crying, so John invited ＿＿＿＿＿＿＿＿
                                              (object)
   ＿＿＿＿＿＿＿＿ with him.
         (infinitive)

5. The hijacker commanded ＿＿＿＿＿＿＿＿ ＿＿＿＿＿＿＿＿
                                 (object)   (infinitive)
   talking.

6. His accomplice ordered ＿＿＿＿＿＿＿＿ ＿＿＿＿＿＿＿＿.
                             (object)   (infinitive phrase)

7. They didn't permit ＿＿＿＿＿＿＿＿ ＿＿＿＿＿＿＿＿.
                        (object)   (infinitive phrase)

8. The captain finally persuaded ＿＿＿＿＿＿＿＿ ＿＿＿＿＿＿＿＿
                               (object)   (infinitive)
   the women and children.

9. The captain warned ＿＿＿＿＿＿＿＿ ＿＿＿＿＿＿＿＿
                        (object)   (infinitive)
   all the passengers with care.

10. The airlines should hire ＿＿＿＿＿＿＿＿ ＿＿＿＿＿＿＿＿ every flight.
                          (object)   (infinitive)

Exercise 11 ■ ■ *In a group of three or four, answer the questions in complete*
■ ■ ■ ■ ■ ■ ■ ■ ■ ■ ■ ■ ■ *sentences.*

1. What did your parents advise you to do before you left home for the first time?

2. When you were a child, what were some of the things your father did not allow you to do?

3. What did your father show you how to do when you were a child?

4. What have your parents always encouraged you to be?

5. What are some of the adjustments a new culture has forced you to make?

6. Have you been able to help another student adjust to a new culture?

7. What was the last thing a friend tried to get you to do?

8. If you were the director, what would you require the teachers to do?

9. On an airplane, what won't the stewardesses permit the passengers to do?

10. If a burglar broke into your apartment, what would you persuade him to do?

11. What do you frequently have to be reminded to do?

12. Has a friend ever challenged you to do anything risky? What?

13. Have you ever urged anyone to do anything silly, just for fun? What?

14. What would a million dollars tempt you to do?

■ **GROUP 3: Verb + Infinitive/Infinitive Phrase or Verb + Object +
Infinitive/Infinitive Phrase** ■

ask	dare[1]	need	want
beg	expect	prefer	wish
choose	like	promise	

[1] In negative and interrogative statements, the verb *dare* is used without *to* if no object follows the verb. (*Don't you* **dare jump** *off that building! Do you* **dare me to jump** *off that building?*)

1. These verbs have two patterns. They may be followed by an object and infinitive, or they may be followed by an infinitive only. The meaning of each pattern is different.

I **want you to help** *him.*
I **want to help** *him.*

Only the verb *promise* keeps the same meaning in both patterns.

*She **promised us to be** on time.*
*She **promised to be** on time.*

2. The verbs *expect, hope, need, promise, want,* and *wish* may indicate future time even when they are in the simple present or past tense.

*My neighbor **needed someone to help him**.*
*I **didn't expect him to pay me**.*

Exercise 12 *With another student, discuss the difference in meaning between the sentences.*

1. a. I have asked to see the doctor.

    b. I have asked my husband to see the doctor.

2. a. The little girl begged to go home.

    b. The little girl begged her friend to go home.

3. a. The committee chose to investigate the hospital.

    b. The committee chose Jim Hopkinton to investigate the hospital.

4. a. I expected to be in the hospital for a couple of days.

    b. I expected my friend to be in the hospital for a couple of days.

5. a. I promised to take better care of myself in the future.

    b. I promised my mother to take better care of myself in the future.

6. a. Most people don't like to be in the hospital.

    b. Most people don't like their relatives to be in the hospital.

7. a. My sister dared to leave the hospital without the doctor's permission.

    b. My sister dared me to leave the hospital without the doctor's permission.

8. a. I prefer to have an older doctor.

    b. I prefer you to have an older doctor.

9. a. I want to get a checkup next week.

    b. I want you to get a checkup next week.

Exercise 13 *Complete the sentences, using either an infinitive/infinitive phrase or an object + infinitive/infinitive phrase, as indicated in parentheses.*

Example: Yesterday I spent three hours in the ladies department of the store. I was trying to find a birthday present for my mother. Finally I asked *the clerk to give me some suggestions.* (object + infinitive phrase)

1. Our grammar teacher puts a check by our incorrect answers, but she never gives the correction. She expects _____. (object + infinitive)   I completed yesterday's grammar assignment very carefully, so I expect _____. (infinitive phrase)

2. When Jackie took her two nephews to the zoo, the older brother dared _____ (object + infinitive) the lion's cage. The younger boy, however, didn't dare _____ (infinitive without *to*) it.

3. When the dentist entered the room, Linda's son begged _____ (infinitive) home. The dentist begged _____ (object + negative infinitive) while he was trying to pull his tooth.

4. My father has always worked hard to save money so that I could study at a university. Because of his hard work, I promised _____. (infinitive phrase)   I promised _____. (object + infinitive)

5. I missed the last week of classes because I was sick. Before the next test, I really need _____ (object + infinitive) with me. I especially need _____ (infinitive) the chapters I missed.

6. I'll help Mary review the material because I would like _____ (object + infinitive) a good grade. Besides, I like _____ (infinitive) with Mary.

7. Paul expects _____ (infinitive) well on the next test. The teacher expects _____ (object + infinitive) all sections of the test carefully.

8. Louisa met with the director last week because she wanted _____ (object + infinitive) her permission to take her finals one week early. Her parents are coming to the States, and Louisa wants _____ (infinitive) around America with them.

9. Louisa prefers _____ (infinitive) by train. Her mother prefers _____ (object + infinitive) by car so that they can stop whenever they wish.

10. Excuse me, I wish _____ (infinitive) with the manager.

■ 14-4 INFINITIVE/INFINITIVE PHRASE FUNCTIONING AS ADJECTIVE AND ADJECTIVE COMPLEMENT

Adjective

A *I have a lot of work **to do**.*

B *Dr. Soto gave us five problems **to solve**.*

C *The assignment **to do for tonight** is on page 83.*

D *I won't have time **to go anywhere tonight**.*

Adjective Complement

E *This problem is difficult **to do**.*

F *I'm glad **to see you in class today**.*

G *We were eager **to hear about his trip**.*

1. An infinitive or infinitive phrase functions as an adjective when it modifies the noun before it. In sentence **A**, *to do* modifies the noun *work;* in sentence **B**, *to solve* modifies *problems;* in sentence **C**, *to do for tonight* modifies *assignment;* in sentence **D**, *to go anywhere tonight* modifies *time.*

2. As an adjective complement, the infinitive/infinitive phrase completes the meaning started by the adjective. In sentence **E**, *to do* complements *difficult;* in sentence **F**, *to see you in class today* complements *glad;* in sentence **G**, *to hear about his trip* complements *eager.*

3. As complement, the infinitive/infinitive phrase is usually used after **adjectives expressing emotion,** such as these:

amazed	delighted	glad	relieved	upset
angry	disappointed	happy	sad	
anxious	disgusted	horrified	sorry	
ashamed	disturbed	pleased	shocked	
astonished	eager	proud	surprised	

Exercise 14 *Complete the sentences, using a simple infinitive (to + verb) that will modify the underlined nouns and complete the meaning of each sentence.*

Example: The best <u>place</u> _____ is Wilson's Lake.

The best <u>place *to fish*</u> is Wilson's Lake.

1. In 1995, the top children's <u>movie</u> _____ was *Pocohantas*.

2. When we entered the theater, the only <u>places</u> _____ were in the front row.

3. The first ten <u>people</u> _____ the theater received free *Pocohantas* T-shirts.

4. The first time we went to see *Pocohantas*, the <u>line</u> _____ tickets was all the way around the block.

5. Because of the long line, we made the <u>decision</u> _____ and see it on a weekday.

6. The best <u>time</u> _____ to a movie is during the week when there aren't large crowds.

7. My husband couldn't go to the movies with us because he had a <u>report</u> _____ for the following day.

8. Our son's <u>desire</u> _____ every *Pocohantas* record, book, poster, and toy was unbelievable.

9. He tried to learn the words in every book, but he had a lot of <u>words</u> _____.

10. He was so interested in learning the words that he didn't have <u>time</u> _____ with his friends.

Exercise 15 *Restate each sentence, using an infinitive or infinitive phrase.*

Example: I was surprised when I got an A on my last composition.

I was surprised to get an A on my last composition.

1. The students in the Section 1 grammar class were glad when they learned they would not have a grammar final.

2. The students had done so well all quarter that their instructor was happy that he did not have to give the class a final.

3. The director, however, was disturbed when he heard about this decision.

4. The students in Section 2 were angry when they found out about this.

5. In fact, they were shocked when they discovered it.

6. Don't be surprised if you see them protest this decision.

7. The grammar teacher for Section 1 said that he would be delighted if he had a class like Section 1 every quarter.

8. I really don't blame the students in Section 2 for getting angry. I'd be happy if I could forget about taking a final, too.

Exercise 16 *Complete the sentences, using an infinitive phrase. When you finish, compare sentences with another student.*

1. When my mother called last night, I was happy _____.

2. When I finished talking to her, I was sad _____.

3. When I got a letter from my friend the other day, I was surprised _____

_____.

4. While watching the news on television, I am often disgusted _____

_____.

5. When I read the newspaper the other day, I was shocked _____

_____.

6. Although our last test was difficult, our teacher said that she was pleased _____

_____.

7. When I looked at my test, however, I was disappointed _____

_____.

8. Even though I was disappointed with my grade, I was relieved _____

_____.

■ 14-5 INFINITIVE/INFINITIVE PHRASE FUNCTIONING AS ADVERB

A *We came here **to work**.*

B *I'm leaving now **to get to class on time**.*

C ***To keep warm at night**, you should buy an electric blanket.*

D *To be honest*, *I hate the cold weather.*

E *To tell the truth*, *I miss the beautiful weather in my country.*

F *To be frank*, *snow has never excited me.*

1. An infinitive or infinitive phrase functions as an adverb when it modifies a verb or an entire sentence. In sentence **A**, *to work* modifies the verb *came*; in sentence **B**, *to get to class on time* modifies *am leaving*; in sentence **C**, *to keep warm at night* modifies *should buy*. In sentences **D**, **E**, and **F**, the infinitive phrases modify the entire sentence.

2. As an adverb modifying a verb, the infinitive or infinitive phrase expresses purpose. It answers the question "Why?"

   Why is he going to Spain? He's going there **to study***.*

   Why did she quit her job? She quit it **to get a better one***.*

3. When an infinitive or infinitive phrase is used as an adverbial to modify a verb, it is usually a substitution for a prepositional phrase beginning with *in order*.

   He's going to Spain **to study***.* (He's going to Spain **in order to study**.)

   She stopped **to talk** *to me.* (She stopped **in order to talk** to me.)

Exercise 17 *Answer each question, using an infinitive or infinitive phrase.*

1. Why did Mr. Turner make an appointment with his banker?

2. Why is he planning to borrow five thousand dollars?

3. Why does he want to open his own business?

4. Why has he been talking to real estate brokers?

5. Why do many people keep their money in savings accounts?

6. Why do other people invest in the stock market?

7. Why did you decide to learn English?

8. Why did you choose to study in another country?

9. Why are you returning home next quarter?

10. Why did you call your parents the other day?

■ 14-6 REDUCTION WITH INFINITIVE PHRASES

Adverb Clauses ──────────▶ Infinitive Phrases

*We arrived at the ticket office early **so that we could be sure to get tickets**.*	*We arrived at the ticket office early **to be sure to get tickets**.*
*Basketball fans must often stand in line for long hours **if they want to get good seats**.*	*Basketball fans must often stand in line for long hours **to get good seats**.*
*I took my camera to the game **because I wanted to take pictures of my favorite players**.*	*I took my camera to the game **to take pictures of my favorite players**.*

1. Infinitive phrases are commonly used in place of adverb clauses beginning with *so that, if,* and *because.*

2. An adverb clause cannot be changed to an infinitive phrase if the subjects of the dependent and independent clauses are different, as in this sentence:

   You have to sign this paper so that the lawyer can take care of the problem.

■

Exercise 18 ▀▀ ▀▀▀▀▀▀▀▀▀▀▀ *Change the underlined adverb clause in each sentence to an infinitive phrase.*

1. In the United States, candidates for the presidency campaign <u>so that they can present their views to the public</u>.

2. Most candidates buy T.V. time <u>because they can reach a large number of people at one time</u>.

3. All candidates ask for money <u>so that they can pay for campaign expenses</u>.

4. Many private citizens must make financial contributions to their favorite candidate <u>if they want to keep their candidate in the race</u>.

5. A candidate has to study national and international issues <u>if he wants to address the voters knowledgeably</u>.

6. All presidential hopefuls hire campaign workers in each state <u>because they want to have good publicity on the local level</u>.

7. These workers have to hold many meetings <u>if they expect to establish a good local organization</u>.

8. Campaign volunteers often go from door to door in their cities <u>so that they can tell voters about their candidates</u>.

9. These people must work hard <u>if they want to get the people to vote for the candidate</u>.

10. Voters should listen to all the individuals running for office <u>if they want to be able to make intelligent decisions</u>.

11. One year, I read three different newspapers every day <u>so that I could learn the candidates' views on various issues</u>.

12. During an election, T.V. stations cancel their regular shows <u>because they present the election results to the public</u>.

13. At this time, many people listen to the radio <u>because they can get relief from the many hours of election reporting</u>.

14. Most people would be surprised <u>if they knew how much money many presidential hopefuls spent to get elected</u>.

Noun Clauses   ⟶   Infinitive Phrases

*Sue asked me **which store she should shop in** for inexpensive but good clothes.*

*She was thinking about **how much she ought to spend** on a new coat.*

*I finally decided **where I would take him.***

*In the store, a friendly clerk explained **where we should look for certain clothing items**.*

*Sue asked me **which store to shop in** for inexpensive but good clothes.*

*She was thinking about **how much to spend** on a new coat.*

*I finally decided **where to take him**.*

*In the store, a friendly clerk explained **where to look for certain clothing items**.*

Infinitive phrases are often used to replace noun clauses beginning with the words *who, what, where, when, which, how, how often, how much,* and *how long*.

Exercise 19   *Change the underlined noun clause in each sentence to an infinitive phrase.*

1. While my friend and I were talking with the clerk in the department store, we discovered <u>how we could find good bargains</u>.

2. During our discussion, we also learned <u>when we should check the newspapers for sales</u>.

3. The clerk also told us <u>how anyone can tell good shoes from poorly made ones</u>.

4. Now I know <u>what I have to do before I make a purchase</u>.

5. I am wondering <u>whom I can talk to about getting a part-time job in the department store</u>.

6. I'm going to ask my doctor <u>what I can take for my cold</u>.

7. It's difficult to know <u>which cough syrup I should buy</u>.

8. I can never remember <u>when I have to take medicine</u>.

9. Everyone would love to discover <u>how he could avoid catching a cold</u>.

10. Most people don't really know <u>how long they should stay in bed</u>.

Exercise 20   *With another student, take turns asking and answering the questions. In the questions, use the words in parentheses and an infinitive phrase.*

Example: A: You look very worried. What are you thinking about? (how)
           B: *I'm thinking about how to earn some extra money.*

1. The next vacation begins in two weeks. What are many students considering? (where)

2. Most students know all the tenses in English. What don't they often understand about tenses? (when)

3. Ana will complete her English studies this semester. Concerning next semester, what must she decide? (which)

4. Some professors in university classes speak very quickly. What must students learn? (how)

5. While Dave was making spaghetti sauce last night, what was he wondering? (how much)

6. After the counselor's lecture on visa information, what do you know? (who)

7. When people buy a new car, they receive an operating manual. What is one of the things it tells the driver? (how often)

8. We will soon have final exams. What are most of us worrying about? (how many)

9. Penny's going away for two weeks, and she doesn't want to leave her dog alone. What is she wondering? (what)

10. Since Chris has been taking a course in public speaking, what has she learned? (how)

11. Ricardo wants to have a party. His apartment is small, but he has a lot of friends. What must he decide? (whom)

12. His friend Monica is responsible for the refreshments for the party. What has she been trying to figure out? (how much)

Adjective Clauses   ⟶   Infinitive Phrases

*I have a lot of dirty clothes **that I must wash.***	*I have a lot of dirty clothes **to wash.***
*Carla is the person **whom you can trust**.*	*Carla is the person **to trust**.*
*Can you lend me a good book **which I can read on the plane?***	*Can you lend me a good book **to read on the plane?***

1. An infinitive or infinitive phrase is often used in place of an adjective clause.

2. The infinitive or infinitive phrase is also used after *the first, the second, the last,* and *the only* to replace an adjective clause.

   *The first student **who finished the exam** was Rina.*
   *The first student **to finish the exam** was Rina.* OR
   *The first student **to finish** was Rina.* OR
   *The first **to finish** was Rina.*

   *The only person **who didn't finish** was Marc.*
   *The only person **not to finish** was Marc.*

   *Of course, the last person **who left the room** was the teacher.*
   *Of course, the last person **to leave the room** was the teacher.* OR
   *Of course, the last person **to leave** was the teacher.* OR
   *Of course, the last **to leave** was the teacher.*

Exercise 21   *First, underline the adjective clauses in the dialog. Then, with another student, repeat the dialog, replacing the adjective clauses with infinitives or infinitive phrases.*

Student: Does this store have a manager whom I can complain to about my problem?

Clerk: On Saturdays there is usually no one here who can help you with a complaint.

Student: I have a defective typewriter that I must replace.

Clerk: Just a minute. Perhaps I can find someone from that department who can talk to you.

Student: I must talk to someone. I have a lot of work that I must complete this weekend.

Clerk: Have a seat over there. I shouldn't be too long. There are some
            magazines that you can read while you're waiting.

Student: Am I the first person who has had trouble with this brand?

Clerk: No. But you're the only one who has an immediate need for repair.

Exercise 22 ▪▪ *Change the underlined adjective clause in each sentence to*
▪▪▪▪▪▪▪▪▪▪▪▪ *an infinitive phrase.*

1. Before Maria returns to Venezuela, she has a lot of presents <u>that she must buy</u>.

2. Can anyone suggest a nice gift <u>that she could get for her father</u>?

3. She wants to get him something <u>that he can put in his office</u>.

4. Her father is a businessman <u>whom you have to admire</u>.

5. He was the first businessman in his country <u>who established a successful exporting business</u>.

6. He is a good person <u>whom you can consult if you have any questions about trade</u>.

7. Maria doesn't have a lot of money <u>that she can spend on a present</u>.

8. She is from Caracas, and there are many beautiful places <u>that you can visit there</u>.

9. She hasn't taken final exams yet, so she has a lot of work <u>that she must do before she goes shopping</u>.

10. Before she returns to Caracas, she is going to Mexico <u>where she will spend two weeks with her aunt Carla</u>, <u>who is her mother's sister</u>.

11. Her aunt has a beautiful ranch and plenty of horses <u>that she can ride</u>.

12. The ranch is a good place <u>where she can relax after finals</u>.

13. Because she will have two entire weeks, she will have plenty of time <u>in which to enjoy herself</u>.

14. Maria's aunt is the only member of her family <u>who has a ranch</u>.

■ 14-7 INFINITIVE/INFINITIVE PHRASE WITH *Enough* AND *Too*

▪ Infinitive with *Enough* ▪

adjective + *enough* + infinitive/infinitive phrase

*The map we had wasn't excellent, but it was **good enough to get us to our destination**.*

*Sam's car isn't very big, but it is **big enough to hold five people comfortably**.*

adverb + *enough* + infinitive/infinitive phrase

*We were driving **slowly enough to enjoy the beautiful scenery**.*

*At times, the kids played the radio **loudly enough to burst our eardrums**.*

enough + noun + infinitive/infinitive phrase

*We only went on a short trip because we didn't have **enough money to take a long one**.*

*What's more, we didn't have **enough time to stay away for more than four days**.*

1. *Enough* comes after an adjective or adverb and before a noun.

2. *For* + noun/pronoun may appear before the infinitive or infinitive phrase.

   *Sam drove slowly enough **for all of us to see the beautiful scenery**.*

Exercise 23 ▪▪ Combine each pair of sentences, using enough.

Example: The bicycle isn't strong. It can't hold two people.

The bicycle isn't strong enough to hold two people.

1. The candidate for president of the foreign student association doesn't have many friends. She can't get the majority of the votes.

2. She doesn't have much time. She won't make many speeches.

3. She hasn't been on campus a long time. She doesn't know many people.

4. Most of the students don't know her well. They won't give her their support.

5. She really isn't very interested in the position. She won't campaign very hard.

6. For her, winning isn't important. It won't make her lose time from her studies.

7. Ahmed's embassy didn't give him very much time. He couldn't finish his English studies.

8. Six months was not long. He couldn't complete all the levels.

9. He didn't realize the problem early. He didn't get permission to study longer.

10. This problem is not serious. It won't make him forget about beginning academic work.

11. His English is good. He can at least start part-time academic work.

12. Besides, he learns quickly. He will do well during his first semester.

■ **Infinitive with** *Too* ■

too + adjective + infinitive/infinitive phrase

When we returned from our trip Sunday night, we were **too tired to attend classes on Monday morning.**

When I got home, my apartment was **too cold to sleep in.**

too + adverb + infinitive/infinitive phrase

I woke up **too late to eat breakfast with her the next morning.**

She left **too early for me to say goodbye.**

1. *Too* has the meaning of a negative result. In this sentence, the speaker didn't catch the 5:30 train.

   I arrived at the train station **too late to catch the 5:30 train.**

2. *For* + noun/pronoun can be used before the infinitive construction.

   I'm too tired **for you to come over tonight.**

Exercise 24 *Combine each pair of sentences, using* too *(and* for, *where necessary).*

Example: Many big cities have become dangerous. Citizens cannot walk alone at night.

   Many big cities have become too dangerous for citizens to walk alone at night.

1. When I lived in Paris a few years ago, I was afraid. I didn't go out alone after dark.

2. Some people in large urban areas have become very suspicious. They don't trust anyone except their close friends.

3. In a big city, the pace of life is very fast. I would not enjoy it.

4. Many people are busy. They don't speak to their neighbors.

5. In most large cities, the cost of living is very high. The average citizen cannot have a comfortable life.

6. I am very happy in my small town. I would not move to a big city.

7. My brother, on the other hand, is restless. He will not stay here forever.

8. He says that our town is small. It is not interesting.

9. He says he's young. He will not die of boredom.

10. At the moment, however, he is broke. He cannot leave until he has saved some money.

11. I am very satisfied here. I don't worry about money.

12. Life is very short. I do not want to spend it living in fear.

Exercise 25 *Complete each sentence, using an infinitive phrase that is true for you. Then compare sentences with another student.*

1. I'm too old _____.

2. It's not warm enough _____.

3. I don't have enough money _____.

4. Sometimes I don't wake up early enough _____.

5. I never seem to have enough time _____.

6. I was too busy the other day _____.

7. My place doesn't have enough space _____.

8. Sometimes Americans speak too fast _____.

9. My English is good enough _____.

10. I might be too tired tonight _____.

11. My place is too small _____.

12. This exercise has been easy enough _____.

Practice Exam

■ SECTION 1

Identify each underlined infinitive phrase according to its function in the sentence. The functions are listed below. Be careful of the false subject it.

Subject = **S**	Adjective = **A**	Object = **O**
Subject complement = **SC**	Adjective complement = **AC**	Adverb = **AV**

_____ 1. Because of the complexity of the world's problems today, <u>to find proper solutions</u> is a difficult task.

_____ 2. Today's world leaders have an extremely difficult job <u>to do</u>.

_____ 3. Indeed, it is not easy for any leader <u>to govern his or her country wisely</u>.

_____ 4. Every head of state needs <u>to have well-informed advisors</u>.

_____ 5. The president of one country recently fired his defense minister <u>to get someone more knowledgeable</u>.

_____ 6. He was anxious <u>to have someone who could look at the subject of defense rationally</u>.

_____ 7. His chief concern was <u>to have a strong yet rational policy of defense</u>.

_____ 8. It is disturbing <u>to think about the effects of war today</u>.

_____ 9. Few individuals want <u>to see their country engaged in war</u>.

_____ 10. Every sane person's desire is <u>to live in peace</u>.

■ SECTION 2

Use each verb in a short sentence. Remember that some verbs require an object before the infinitive.

Examples: afford *I cannot afford to buy a new car.*

advise *My friend advised me to get a used car.*

1. allow _____

2. command _____

3. decide   _____

4. demand   _____

5. direct   _____

6. encourage   _____

7. forget   _____

8. hesitate   _____

9. intend   _____

10. neglect   _____

11. offer   _____

12. order   _____

13. persuade   _____

14. refuse   _____

15. seem   _____

■ SECTION 3

Change the underlined adjective, noun, and adverb clauses in each sentence to an infinitive phrase.

> **Example:** Rosa registered for the TOEFL exam early <u>so that she would be sure to have a seat</u>.
>
> *Rosa registered for the TOEFL exam early to be sure to have a seat.*

1. Before the test, she asked her grammar teacher <u>which points of grammar she should review</u>.

   _____

   _____

2. Her teacher gave her the lesson <u>that she should study</u>.

   _____

   _____

3. As she was reviewing, she realized there were many rules <u>that she had to remember</u>.

_____

_____

4. After she had talked with her teacher again, she discovered <u>how she could review quickly yet thoroughly</u>.

_____

_____

5. Most students have to review a little <u>if they want to get a high score</u>.

_____

_____

6. Next quarter, the director is giving a special class once a week <u>because he wants to help the students review before the test</u>.

_____

_____

7. In this class, he will explain <u>how the students should prepare for the test</u>.

_____

_____

8. Last quarter, Mirko was the only person <u>who received a score above 550</u>.

_____

_____

9. Mirko had spent a lot of time preparing for the test <u>so that he would get a high score</u>.

_____

_____

10. Since he had taken the practice tests in the TOEFL book, he knew <u>what kind of questions he should expect on the test</u>.

_____

_____

LESSON FIFTEEN

■ 15-1 GERUNDS

1. A gerund is a noun that has been formed from a verb. Any verb can be turned into a gerund by adding *-ing* to the simple form of the verb.

   walk, walking   *play, playing*   *be, being*

   When changing some verbs into gerunds, changes in spelling may be necessary.

   lie, lying

   Be careful not to confuse gerunds with present participles.

   Gerund: *Swimming is good for you.*
   Present participle: *Why aren't you swimming with the others?*

2. Gerunds function as nouns in a sentence.

   Jogging *is good exercise.* (subject of the sentence)
   My favorite form of exercise is **jogging***.* (subject complement)
   I have always enjoyed **jogging***.* (direct object)
   My roommate is against **jogging***.* (object of a preposition)
   His favorite form of exercise, **dancing***, is more enjoyable.* (appositive)

3. A gerund phrase is formed with an object, a complement, and/or other modifiers. In the first sentence, *children* is the direct object of the gerund *interviewing*. In the second sentence, *tennis* is the direct object of the gerund *playing*.

   Interviewing small children *is amusing.*
   Playing tennis *is fun.*

4. To make a gerund negative, *not* is placed immediately before the gerund. Compare:

   Betty **regretted not seeing** *that movie.*
   Betty **did not regret seeing** *that movie.*

   In the first sentence, the gerund *seeing* is negative. Betty did not see the movie, and she regretted having missed it. In the second sentence, the verb *regret* is negative. Betty saw the movie, and she was not sorry that she had gone to it.

Exercise 1   *Read the story and underline all the gerunds and gerund phrases.*

I always thought I loved flying—until the other day, that is. First, the plane was delayed for more than three hours because of bad weather, and finding somewhere to sit in the airport was very difficult. I ended up sitting near a bunch of teenagers who were playing loud music and making so much noise that nobody else wanted to be near them.

When we were finally allowed to board the plane, getting to my seat proved to be difficult. First, some little kids were running up and down the aisle, and nobody wanted to tell them to stop doing so. When I did, the kids looked at me like I was nuts and then went back to doing what they had been doing before. Only the flight attendant was able to get them to sit down. When I got to my seat, I saw that two of the teenagers who had been torturing me for nearly three hours were sitting next to me. I said to myself, "At least, it's a short flight."

That turned out not to be the case. When we were ready to take off, the pilot announced that there was a failure in the flight controllers' computer system, and taking off wouldn't be possible until the system was fixed. We sat on the runway for two hours without being told anything, and believe me, sitting in a hot plane—the air conditioning system wasn't working—for two hours next to two fun-loving teenagers is about the worst way you can imagine spending your time.

"So how was the flight?" you want to know. There was no flight. The passengers ended up taking the train, courtesy of the airline. We arrived twelve hours late, and getting a taxi in the middle of the night was no fun. But we did arrive, and I guess we should be thankful for small favors. It will be a long time before I consider flying anywhere again.

Exercise 2   *With another student, practice asking and answering questions containing negative gerund phrases.*

Example: A: When you were small, did you regret <u>not always listening to your parents?</u>

  B: <u>I sometimes regretted not listening to my parents, but not always.</u>

1. Please, would you mind _____?

2. Have your parents ever regretted _____?

3. Do you sometimes miss _____?

4. Can you imagine _____?

5. As a child, did you hate _____?

6. When you get married, will you consider _____?

7. Do you enjoy _____?

8. If your friends want to go out tonight, will you suggest _____?

9. If a new student talked to you about the school, would you advise _____?

10. When you were a child, do you remember _____?

■ 15-2 GERUND/GERUND PHRASE FUNCTIONING AS SUBJECT AND SUBJECT COMPLEMENT

Subject of the Sentence

Traveling is enjoyable.

Traveling with young children can be difficult.

Finding a good hotel is not always easy.

Subject Complement

My mother's hobby is **gardening**.

My father's favorite pastime is **collecting foreign stamps**.

What he really enjoys is **getting rare stamps**.

Exercise 3   *Replace it + the infinitive phrase in each sentence by a gerund phrase.*

Example: My grandparents loved children, so it was an enjoyable experience to spend weekends with them.

My grandparents loved children, so spending weekends with them was an enjoyable experience.

1. It really annoys most mothers to have to tell their children to clean up their rooms all the time.

2. If it is raining and they can't go outside, it appeals to most children to play video games.

3. My parents didn't have a television when they were young, so their way of relaxing after school was to play in the garden.

4. It takes a lot of time for parents to help their children with their homework.

5. It is a big responsibility for every parent to make sure children learn right from wrong.

6. It demands a lot of patience from both parents to answer children's questions all the time.

7. In many families, it has always been the father's job to earn a living.

8. In many countries, it has usually been the woman's responsibility to take care of the children.

9. As children grow up, it becomes more difficult to get them to obey.

10. It is not easy for children to please their parents.

Exercise 4 *Complete each sentence, using a gerund or gerund phrase as subject of the sentence.*

Examples: <u>*Listening to the news*</u> really depresses me sometimes.

<u>*Sleeping*</u> is my favorite pastime.

1. _____ is an excellent form of exercise.

2. _____ has changed my life.

3. _____ is going to be very difficult for me.

4. _____ has always been important to me.

5. _____ is not easy in a foreign country.

6. _____ will be the most difficult thing for me to do when I return home.

7. _____ is foolish, considering the price of gasoline.

8. _____ seems to be a favorite American pastime.

9. _____ has never made me comfortable.

10. _____ will be a difficult job for the next U.S. president.

Exercise 5 *In a group of three or four, discuss how you would complete the sentences. Use a gerund or gerund phrase as subject complement.*

Example: One solution to the large number of cars on the roads is *car pooling*.

1. My biggest problem during this course is _____.

2. My favorite form of recreation is _____.

3. If I were the leader of my country, my main concern would be _____.

4. After five hours of classes every day, my one thought is _____.

5. One of my major goals in life has always been _____.

6. Before I left my country, my one fear was _____.

7. When driving in a downtown area of a city, a big frustration is always _____.

8. Mankind's highest aim should be _____.

9. My mother's biggest fault is _____.

10. If I had a million dollars, my one desire would be _____.

■ 15-3 GERUND/GERUND PHRASE FUNCTIONING AS DIRECT OBJECT

■ Verb + Gerund/Gerund Phrase ■

admit	detest	keep[2]	recall
appreciate[1]	discuss	mention	recommend
avoid	enjoy	mind[3]	resent
can't help	escape	miss	resist
consider	excuse[1]	postpone	risk
defer	finish	practice	suggest
delay	forgive	prevent	tolerate
deny	imagine	quit	understand[1]

[1] The verbs *appreciate, excuse,* and *understand* are always followed by the possessive before the gerund. (*Do you **understand her wanting** to live alone?*)

[2] The verb *keep* is followed by a gerund when it means *continue.* (*George **keeps doing that** even though I've told him to stop.*)

[3] The verb *mind* is followed by a gerund when it means *dislike.* (*I **don't mind going** there alone.*)

1. The gerund or gerund phrase may follow a verb and function as the direct object, but not every verb in English can take a gerund or gerund phrase as the direct object. The verbs in the box above are among the most commonly used verbs that can be followed by a gerund or gerund phrase.

2. In formal English, the possessive is often used before a gerund/gerund phrase.

   Formal: *I couldn't understand **his** coming late.*
   *I couldn't understand **Norman's** coming late.*

   In informal usage, however, speakers of English often use the object form of a personal pronoun or the noun without the possessive inflection.

   Informal: *I couldn't understand **him** coming late.*
   *I couldn't understand **Norman** coming late.*

   When a possessive is used before a gerund/gerund phrase, there is often a change in meaning.

   We enjoyed singing. (We were singing.)
   We enjoyed the choir's singing. (We were listening to the choir.)

Exercise 6   *Complete the sentences, using a possessive + a gerund/gerund phrase made of the words in the box.*

come late	*interrupt her explanation*
excuse them for being late	*not wait for their turn*
do some extra review	*tell them off*
go to the language lab more often	*visit a museum*
get a low grade	

Example: The teacher did not appreciate <u>*my interrupting her explanation.*</u>

1. Because of the bad weather, Maria's instructor excused _____.

2. Maria and her classmates really appreciated _____.

3. Maria studied very hard for the last test, so she couldn't understand

   _____.

4. Because so many students did poorly on the test, the instructor suggested

   _____.

5. Although Maria has a good class, a few students constantly speak out of turn.
   She hates _____.

6. Maria's instructor told two students that she wasn't happy with their behavior. They didn't like _____.

7. Maria talked to her instructor about her pronunciation problems. Her instructor recommended _____.

8. The students in Maria's class would like to do something different next week. The instructor has discussed _____.

Exercise 7 ▪▪ ▪ *With another student, complete the sentences, using a gerund or gerund phrase as direct object. Then write a news report of the trial. First decide whether your report will be for a newspaper article or for a TV broadcast.*

1. In the courtroom, the defendant admitted _____.

2. The defendant's lawyer couldn't avoid _____.

3. The defendant had always been a quiet man, but on the night of the crime he could not help _____.

4. Because he had never been in trouble with the law, the judge considered _____.

5. The jury needed more time, so it delayed _____.

6. The defendant's wife detested _____.

7. That night he and his wife discussed _____.

8. The trial was interesting, but I don't really enjoy _____.

9. Actually, many times the defendant could not finish _____.

10. I have never been in jail, so I can't imagine _____.

11. While the defendant's lawyer was speaking, the lawyer for the prosecution kept _____.

12. Because the jury could not agree on the defendant's innocence or guilt, the judge postponed _____.

13. Finally, the judge gave his verdict, and the defendant's wife quit _____.

14. The defendant seemed to be such a quiet man that I can't resist _____.

15. Nevertheless, I really don't understand (his) _____.

■ 15-4 GERUND AS DIRECT OBJECT VS. INFINITIVE AS DIRECT OBJECT

■ Verbs Followed by Gerunds or Infinitives ■

1. Some verbs are followed by a gerund <u>or</u> gerund phrase. (For a complete list of these verbs, see Appendix 4 on page 305.)

   *Why haven't you **finished cleaning**?*

   *I **resent** his **talking** to me like that.*

   *Richard cannot **risk losing** his job.*

2. Some verbs are followed by an infinitive <u>or</u> infinitive phrase. (For a complete list of these verbs, see Appendix 3 on pages 302–304.)

   *My parents always **encouraged** me **to do** my best.*

   *I **warned** you **not to go** there.*

   *The police officer **ordered** me **to stop**.*

Exercise 8 *Make a sentence with each pair of words. Use any subject and tense.*

Examples: deny/break

<u>*Both of them denied breaking the window.*</u>

tell/clean

<u>*My father will tell me to clean my room before I go to the movies.*</u>

1. finish/study
2. recommend/go
3. offer/drive
4. promised/do
5. admit/write

6. mind/walk
7. afford/stay
8. avoid/make
9. hope/hear
10. keep/talk

11. discuss/find
12. manage/get
13. deserve/win
14. detest/work
15. consider/take

Exercise 9 *In a group of three or four, take turns completing the sentences truthfully.*

1. When I'm 45, I hope I'll be able to afford _____.

2. When I'm 45, I'll probably miss _____.

3. When I'm 45, I don't think I'll enjoy _____.

4. When I'm 45, I'll refuse _____.

5. When I'm 45, I hope I'll have finished _____.

6. When I'm 45, I might detest _____.

7. When I'm 45, I won't be able to escape _____.

8. When I'm 45, I would like to be able to quit _____.

9. When I'm 45, I'll advise _____.

10. When I'm 45, I'll need _____.

11. When I'm 45, I won't mind _____.

12. When I'm 45, I hope I'll have learned _____.

13. When I'm 45, I expect _____.

14. When I'm 45, I'll probably consider _____.

Verbs Followed by Gerunds or Infinitives with No Change in Meaning

advise	can't bear	intend	neglect
allow	continue	like	permit
attempt	forbid	love	prefer
begin	hate	need	start

I love **traveling.**   *Nonsmokers hate **sitting** near smokers.*

I love **to travel.**   *Nonsmokers hate **to sit** near smokers.*

1. The verbs *advise, allow, forbid,* and *permit* are followed by a noun or pronoun object before the infinitive. Compare:

   *Our travel agent advised **us to take** a European vacation.*

   *Our travel agent advised **taking** a European vacation.*

   *Professor Muraki doesn't allow **anyone to leave** the room during an exam.*

   *Professor Muraki doesn't allow **leaving** the room during an exam.*

*My father forbids **me to smoke** in his house.*
*My father forbids **smoking** in his house.*

*The landlord doesn't permit **any resident to have** a pet in the apartment building.*
*The landlord doesn't permit **having** a pet in the apartment building.*

2. The verbs *begin* and *start* take either a gerund or an infinitive. But if the verb following *begin* or *start* is a verb of "knowing" or "understanding" (such as *reflect, contemplate, perceive*), the infinitive is more common.

   *After a few minutes, we **started to understand** the explanation.*
   *As I watched the report of the earthquake victim, I **began to perceive** the horror of such a disaster.*

3. After the verbs *attempt* and *intend*, gerunds are possible, but infinitives are more common.

   *Ron attempted **moving** the piano by himself.*
   *Ron attempted **to move** the piano by himself.*

4. With the verb *need*, the gerund is similar in meaning to the passive infinitive.

   *My car **needs washing**.*
   *My car **needs to be washed**.*

Exercise 10 *Answer the questions. If the question contains an infinitive, use a gerund. If the question contains a gerund, use an infinitive.*

Examples: If it begins to rain, are you going to cancel the picnic?
          Of course, we'll cancel it if it begins raining.
          Did the radio announcer continue asking for donations?
          Yes, he continued to ask for donations.

1. I understand that Miriam is looking for a new job. Doesn't she like to work here anymore?

2. Wouldn't she prefer to have a job where she could travel once in a while?

3. Hasn't she neglected doing much of her work lately?

4. When will she start looking for another job?

5. Did you advise going to an employment agency or checking the want ads in the newspaper?

6. She has excellent sales experience. Couldn't she begin working as a salesman?

7. Does she intend leaving before she finds another job?

8. Doesn't our company policy forbid quitting without giving at least two weeks notice?

9. She really looks depressed. Don't you agree that she needs cheering up?

10. She is such a nice person. Don't you hate to see her so depressed?

■ Verbs Followed by Gerunds or Infinitives with a Change in Meaning ■

forget	regret	try
mean	remember	used to/be used to
propose	stop	

1. After the verbs *forget, remember,* and *regret,* the infinitive is used if it refers to an action that happens after the action of the main verb. If the action happens before the action of the main verb, a gerund is used. Compare the pairs of sentences.

*I was really annoyed that my sister **forgot to show** up for the party.* (She didn't show up. *Forgetting* occurred before *showing up.*)

*My sister **forgets** ever **being** in the hospital.* (She has forgotten that she was ever in the hospital. *Being in the hospital* occurred before *forgetting.*)

*I **remembered to write** down the assignment, so I was able to do it.* (First I remembered; *remembering* occurred before *writing.*)

*I **remember writing** down the assignment. Where is it?* (*Writing* occurred before *remembering.*)

*I **regret to tell** you that you are not going to get the promotion.* (I'm going to tell you news. *Regretting* occurs before *telling.*)

*I **regret telling** you the bad news.* (*Telling* occurred before *regretting.*)

2. An infinitive follows the verb *mean* when the meaning is *to intend.* A gerund follows the verb *mean* when it means *to result in; mean* + gerund is used only with an impersonal subject.

*The police detective **means to solve** this crime even if it **means forgetting** about his other work.*

*I'm tired of working such long hours. I **mean to quit** my second job even if it **means having** less money.*

3. When the verb *propose* means *to plan* or *intend*, the infinitive follows. When the verb *propose* means *to suggest*, a gerund follows.

   *We **propose to leave** early tomorrow morning.* (We plan to leave early.)

   *I **propose leaving** before 6:00 A.M.* (I suggest leaving before 6:00 A.M.)

4. When the verb *stop* means *in order to do something*, an infinitive follows. When the verb *stop* means *to quit*, a gerund follows.

   *I **stopped to talk** to Jamilla.* (I stopped in order to talk to Jamilla.)

   *I **stopped talking** to Jamilla.* (I don't talk to Jamilla anymore.)

5. When the verb *try* means *to make an effort*, an infinitive follows. When the verb *try* means *to experiment*, a gerund follows.

   *I've been looking for an apartment for several weeks. I **tried to go** to a real estate agent, but the office was closed.* (I made an effort to go to a real estate agent.)

   *I've been looking for an apartment for several weeks. I **tried going** to a real estate agent, but she couldn't help me.* (I went to a real estate agent as one way of finding an apartment.)

6. When *used to* refers to a habitual past action, an infinitive follows. When *be used to* means *to be accustomed to*, a gerund follows.

   *We **used to drive** to Chicago from Nevada every other month to see our parents.* (We did this again and again, but we don't anymore.)

   *We **were used to driving** long distances, so the trips didn't bother us.* (We were accustomed to driving long distances.)

Exercise 11   *Circle the word or words that best complete the following sentences.*

1. I tried _____ you, but the line was always busy.
   a. calling
   b. to call

2. My father stopped _____ a few years ago. He has felt much better ever since then.
   a. smoking
   b. to smoke

3. I hope you remembered _____ the windows. It looks like it's going to rain.
   a. closing
   b. to close

4. I'll never forget _____ the president of the United States. It was a memorable day.

   a. meeting
   b. to meet

5. I forgot _____ my book. Can I go back to my room and get it?

   a. bringing
   b. to bring

6. I'm used to _____ grammar exercises like these, but it wasn't easy when I first started learning English.

   a. doing
   b. to do

7. You should try _____ the baby. That may make him stop crying.

   a. holding
   b. to hold

8. Don't you remember _____ to that restaurant the last time we came here?

   a. going
   b. to go

9. I stopped _____ a drink because I was very thirsty.

   a. to get
   b. getting

10. We regret _____ you that you have not been granted a scholarship.

    a. informing
    b. to inform

11. I know it may mean _____ her angry, but I'm still going to tell her what I think.

    a. making
    b. to make

12. The university proposes _____ new housing on the outskirts of the campus.

    a. building
    b. to build

Exercise 12 ▪▪   *Find and correct the ten mistakes in the text.*
▪▪▪▪▪▪▪▪▪▪▪

Do you enjoy to play the lottery? Did you ever stop to think what a bad idea it actually is? First, the people who can least afford playing are the ones who do. Even if it means to have difficulty paying for rent and food, and even if they have little chance of ever winning much money, these unfortunate people don't seem to mind to spend their time waiting in line to buy those tickets and being disappointed every time they lose—which is always.

I knew that before I read a recent article about the lottery. What I didn't know was how playing the lottery actually ruined the lives of those who saw their dreams come true: they won millions. I hate to tell all of you lottery players this, but money not only fails buying happiness; it also doesn't even buy a good time. It turns out that most of those big winners who lottery players so envy are actually miserable once the initial joy of winning fades.

First, there's the world of work. If the lottery winners continue working, their co-workers start to resent their take the job of someone who really needs the work. Eventually, the winners are forced to stop to work. That leads to new misery: what to do with all their free time?

Next are the friends and relatives who expect the winner to lend them money and pick up all the checks. They pretend liking the winner when all they really like is all the winner's money. This wouldn't be so bad if the recipients of the generosity showed some gratitude; unfortunately, all they show is jealousy and contempt and eventually disappear just like the jobs do.

What is the moral of this story? Playing the lottery is a bad idea not only because you have almost no chance of winning it but because you may win. How will the knowledge of the evils of the lottery affect me? I guess I'm going to keep to play it, but I'm certainly going to stop to hope that I win. I'm doing too well in my ordinary life to risk being successful.

Exercise 13 *In a group of three or four, discuss how you would complete the sentences. If you are already married, you will have to change the tense of most of the sentences.*

1. When I get married, I will begin _____.

2. I will allow my spouse _____.

3. As a parent, I will attempt _____.

4. When I get married, I hope _____.

287

5. As a spouse, I'll refuse _____.

6. Before I get married, I intend _____.

7. If my spouse and I have trouble, I will consider _____.

8. When I get married, I will quit _____.

9. When I get married, I will promise _____.

10. A single person can't imagine _____.

11. Even when I am married, I will continue _____.

12. When I am married, I will enjoy _____.

13. When I have children, I will try _____.

14. When I first get married, I won't be used _____.

15. Some people will never get married even if it means _____.

16. Before people get married, they need _____.

Exercise 14 *Read the dialogs. With another student, discuss possible answers to each question. Use a gerund or infinitive phrase.*

1. **Dina:** Isn't this wonderful?
   Nora: Oh, it's absolutely spectacular.
   What are Dina and Nora enjoying? _____

2. **Nick:** Didn't Jack look awful?
   Anna: He certainly did. He really needs to make some changes in his life.
   What should Jack stop? _____

3. **Carl:** It's really hard to make a decision.
   Fred: Why don't you talk to your father?
   What is Carl considering? _____

4. **Nick:** Look at the car. How could that have happened?
   Dina: Don't look at me. I didn't do it.
   What did Dina deny? _____

5. **Carl:** Do we have enough money?
   Nora: Probably, but are you sure you like that one?
   What do Carl and Nora intend? _____

6. **Anna:** Why don't you come with me? There will be a lot of people for you to meet.
   Fred: No, that kind of thing isn't for me.
   What does Fred dislike? _____

7. **Bill:** Will you ever forget that day?

   Joni: Never! It was a terrible experience.

   What will Joni never forget? _____

8. **Nick:** It was a terrible mistake. How I could have done something so stupid?

   Nora: It's not the end of the world. You'll find something else.

   What does Nick regret? _____

9. **Joni:** This is awful!

   Dina: I know. But what can we do about it?

   What can't Dina and Joni bear? _____

10. **Fred:** It's at 8:00, right?

    Neal: Yeah. Don't forget.

    What shouldn't Fred forget? _____

■ 15-5 GERUND/GERUND PHRASE FUNCTIONING AS OBJECT OF A PREPOSITION

■ GROUP 1: Verb + Preposition + Gerund/Gerund Phrase ■

adjust to	comment on	look forward to
agree with	complain about	object to
apologize for	concentrate on	plan on
apologize to (someone) for	consist of	refer to
approve of	deal with	see about
argue about	depend on/upon	talk about
believe in	dream about	think about
blame (someone) for	forget about	warn (someone) about
care about	forgive (someone) for	worry about
care for	insist on	

1. Some verb + preposition combinations are always followed by a gerund. The combinations in the box above are among the most commonly used ones.

   *The children **insisted on going** to the zoo.*

   *I'm **looking forward to going** on vacation.*

   *We don't **object to our daughter's living** alone.*

2. The verb + preposition combinations in the box can be used in these patterns.

   Pattern 1: subject + verb + preposition + gerund phrase
   She apologized for being late.

   Pattern 2: subject + verb + preposition + possessive + gerund phrase
   Bruce worries about his daughter's living alone.

   Pattern 3: subject + verb + object + preposition + gerund phrase
   The police officer accused me of speeding on the freeway.

3. These verbs can be used only in pattern 3.

accuse . . . of	pay . . . for
congratulate . . . on	prevent . . . from
devote . . . to	thank . . . for

Exercise 15 *Complete each question with the correct preposition. Try to complete the sentences without looking at the list of verbs + prepositions on the previous page.*

Example: After class today, what do you have to see *about?*

1. What are you devoting yourself _____ these days?

2. What did your parents prevent you _____ doing when you were a child?

3. Who was the last person you paid? What did you pay this person _____?

4. Who was the last person you thanked? What did you thank this person _____?

5. When was the last time you apologized? What did you apologize _____?

6. When you first came to the United States, what did you have to adjust _____?

7. Have you argued with anyone recently? What did you argue _____?

8. What doesn't your father approve _____?

9. Before you left your country, what did your mother warn you _____?

10. What do you plan _____ doing this weekend?

11. What does the teacher always insist _____?

12. What are you trying to forget _____?

13. What did you dream _____?

14. What have you been concentrating _____ since this course began?

15. As a student, what do you really care _____?

Exercise 16   *With another student, practice asking and answering the questions in Exercise 15. Use gerund phrases.*

Example: A: After class today, what do you have to see about?

　　　　　　B: *I have to see about finding an apartment.*

■ GROUP **2: Adjective + Preposition + Gerund/Gerund Phrase** ■

accustomed to[1]	excited about[1]	proud of
afraid of	famous for	responsible for
angry at	generous about	sorry about
appropriate for	good at	sure of/about
ashamed of	grateful to (someone)	surprised at[1]
concerned about[1]	grateful for (something)	tired of [1]
content with	incapable of	used to[2]
delighted at[1]	interested in[1]	worried about[1]
essential to	lazy about	

[1] These verbs are past participles used as adjectives.

[2] The adjective *used to* is followed by a gerund when it means *accustomed to*. (*I'm not **used to eating** such spicy food.*)

1. The adjective + preposition combinations listed in the box above are among the most commonly used ones.

　　*My aunt was **concerned about leaving** too early.*

　　*However, she was not **interested in staying** all day.*

2. The adjective + preposition combinations in the box often follow after the verbs *be, seem, appear, remain, look, become.*

Exercise 17 *With another student, practice asking and answering the following questions. Use gerund phrases. If you've already done Exercise 16, do this exercise with a different student.*

1. Since you've been away from home, what have you become accustomed to?
2. When you were a small child, what were you afraid of?
3. Before you left your country, what was your mother concerned about?
4. What do you usually feel excited about?
5. What would you like to become famous for?
6. What have you always been interested in?
7. The last time you were ashamed of yourself, what were you ashamed of?
8. What are you grateful to your parents for?
9. What are you good at?
10. What are you responsible for these days?

GROUP 3: Noun + Preposition + Gerund/Gerund Phrase

difficulty in	interest in
in addition to	in the course of
in charge of	in the middle of
in danger of	need for
in favor of	reason for
in return for	technique for
instead of	the point of

1. The noun + preposition combinations in the box above are among the most commonly used ones.

   *We're not sure of her **reason for leaving**.*

   *It was a problem because she was **in charge of organizing the meeting**.*

   *She probably wanted more money **in return for working extra hours**.*

2. All the noun + preposition combinations in the box above may be followed by a possessive form + gerund, **except**:

difficulty in	*He has **difficulty in understanding the directions**.*
in charge of	*Who is **in charge of looking after the baby**?*
in danger of	*The building's **in danger of falling**.*
technique for	*I can't figure out the **technique for hitting the ball**.*

Exercise 18 ∎∎ *Complete the sentences.*

1. As they were driving to the mountains, Sue told Bob to slow down because she did not see the need for _____.

2. She also warned him that they were in danger of _____.

3. Because the road was clear, Bob said he did not see the point of _____.

4. Sue reminded him that in addition to _____, they could get a ticket.

5. When Bob saw a police car in his rear-view mirror, he was suddenly in favor of _____.

6. It was too late. After the police officer had checked Bob's license, he asked him if he had difficulty in _____.

7. The officer sarcastically asked if he had an interest in _____.

8. The officer also reminded Bob that as an officer of the law, he was in charge of _____.

9. Surprisingly, instead of _____ the police officer told Bob to report to the police station every Wednesday night for safe driving lessons.

10. Sue mentioned that because of his poor driving record, Bob really needed to review the techniques for _____.

Exercise 19 ∎∎ *Complete the paragraphs, using the correct preposition and an appropriate gerund. Use the gerund form of the verbs in the box, and try to use a different gerund for each blank.*

ask	contact	have	look for	serve
assist	correct	help	mug	solve
be	do	improve	rear up	spend
bring up	enforce	insure	reside	use
change	fight	keep	rob	wait
combat	find	live	see	walk

Few would deny that the quality of life has changed in many big American cities. Many people can remember a time when it was very safe to walk to the corner store after dark; however, today they are afraid _____ alone. Store owners

find that they are always in danger _____ robbed. Some of them have

2

been threatened in the course _____ their customers. Many people

3

agree that a big city is no longer suitable for _____ children.

4

People who live in the big cities are concerned _____ these

5

conditions. They say that the city governments do not really seem interested

_____ solutions to the problems. On the other hand, the city officials

6

maintain that they are incapable _____ very much without money from

7

the state and national governments. The mayors of the big urban areas admit that

they, too, are worried _____ the quality of life in their cities. The

8

majority of citizens believe that their police forces have not been good

_____ law and order. Everyone feels that a good police force is

9

essential _____ a safe environment.

10

The citizens in these areas are also tired _____ such high taxes.

11

Again they complain that the city and state governments are responsible for not

correctly _____ the money available to them. Violence and high taxes

12

are only two of the problems that city dwellers face. Many Americans who move to

the big cities from small towns have been used _____ in an atmosphere

13

that is friendly and quiet; therefore, they are not accustomed _____ in

14

an environment that is cold and impersonal. No American is proud

_____ about these conditions, and all agree that there is a need

15

_____ the situation. Everyone feels that the problems are very serious,

16

but no one seems to know the best technique _____ these problems.

17

Some officials are in favor _____ the law enforcement officials of

18

certain European cities for advice.

While it is true that many European cities, as well as others around the world,

have some of the same problems, it is also true that they seem to have found

successful solutions to many of them.

Exercise 20 *Read the headlines. Then, with another student, discuss possible answers to the questions. In some answers, you may need a possessive before the gerund/gerund phrase.*

STRIKE ENDS
Mayor's Talks with Teachers Successful

1. What did the mayor succeed in doing?
2. What did the mayor probably concentrate on during the talks?
3. What did students' parents probably disapprove of?
4. What are teachers looking forward to?

NATIONALS LOSE FINAL GAME, 3–0
COACH BLUM FIRED

5. What did the owner of the team blame the coach for?
6. What will fans never forgive one of the players for?
7. What did the players object to?
8. What do the Nationals need to concentrate on for next year?

PROTEST TURNS VIOLENT
10 ARRESTS MADE

9. What had the protesters planned on?
10. What did the police warn protesters about?
11. What did the police prevent the protesters from doing?
12. What did the protesters insist on?

Practice Exam

■ SECTION 1

Identify each underlined gerund phrase according to its function in the sentence.

Subject = **S**   Object = **O**   Appositive = **A**
Subject complement = **SC**   Object of preposition = **OP**

_____   1. <u>Having a summer job</u> is the only way many students can pay for their college tuition.

_____   2. When my father was in college, his favorite summer job was <u>working in a restaurant</u>.

_____ 3. He has often said that he didn't mind <u>serving the customers</u>, but he
_____ disliked <u>removing the dirty dishes</u> from the tables.

_____ 4. After only two weeks at one restaurant, however, he was fired for
<u>eating too much on the job</u>.

_____ 5. A waiter doesn't make a large salary, but <u>being polite to customers</u> can
_____ result in <u>getting big tips</u>.

_____ 6. The best part of his job was <u>waiting on attractive girls</u>.

_____ 7. My father and mother often recall <u>meeting each other for the first time</u>.

_____ 8. My mother's job, <u>working as a cashier</u>, was in the same restaurant.

■ SECTION 2

Use each of the following verbs in a short sentence.

Examples: admit   <u>*My father admitted eating on the job.*</u>
           agree   <u>*After the manager had spoken to him, he agreed to stop.*</u>

1. appear   _____

2. avoid   _____

3. can't help _____

4. consider   _____

5. choose   _____

6. consent   _____

7. deny   _____

8. discuss   _____

9. finish   _____

10. forget   _____

11. miss   _____

12. offer   _____

13. postpone   _____

14. practice   _____

15. refuse   _____

16. resent   _____

17. seem   _____

18. suggest   _____

■ SECTION 3

Complete each sentence, using the correct preposition followed by a gerund phrase.

1. Most employers do not approve   _____

2. Last week, two secretaries were arguing   _____

3. When interviewing for a job, I have never believed   _____

   _____

4. In a noisy office, it is difficult to concentrate   _____

5. I have often dreamed   _____

6. Al worked in a dentist's office last summer, and he will never forget   _____

   _____

7. Last summer, I had two good job offers, and I had a lot of difficult   _____

   _____

8. I finally made up my mind in the course   _____

9. Next summer, I am looking forward   _____

10. Since I have always been a good employee, I have never worried   _____

    _____

11. Some people are lazy, but most people devote   _____

    _____

12. Understanding the rules in an office is essential   _____

    _____

13. The manager of an office is responsible   _____

14. Since a five-day workweek is very long, most employees would be in favor   ____

    _____

Appendix 1 Irregular Verbs

NOTE: Some verbs have two past forms: -ed *and* -t, *as in* burned, burnt. *The* -ed *form is usually used.*

Present and Infinitive	Past	Past Participle
awake	awoke	awaked
be	was/were	been
bear (bring forth)	bore	born
bear (carry)	bore	borne
become	became	become
begin	began	begun
bend	bent	bent
bite	bit	bitten
bleed	bled	bled
blow	blew	blown
break	broke	broken
bring	brought	brought
build	built	built
burn	burned, burnt	burned, burnt
burst	burst	burst
buy	bought	bought
catch	caught	caught
choose	chose	chosen
cling	clung	clung
clothe	clothed, clad	clothed, clad
come	came	come
cost	cost	cost
creep	crept	crept
cut	cut	cut
deal	dealt	dealt
dig	dug	dug
dive	dived, dove	dived
do	did	done
draw	drew	drawn
dream	dreamed, dreamt	dreamed, dreamt
drink	drank	drunk
drive	drove	driven
eat	ate	eaten
fall	fell	fallen
feed	fed	fed
feel	felt	felt
fight	fought	fought
find	found	found
flee	fled	fled
fling	flung	flung
fly	flew	flown
forbid	forbade, forbad	forbidden
forget	forgot	forgotten

Present and Infinitive	Past	Past Participle
forsake	forsook	forsaken
freeze	froze	frozen
get	got	got, gotten
give	gave	given
go	went	gone
grind	ground	ground
grow	grew	grown
hang (suspend)	hanged, hung	hung
hang (kill)	hanged, hung	hanged
have	had	had
hear	heard	heard
hide	hid	hidden, hid
hit	hit	hit
hold	held	held
hurt	hurt	hurt
keep	kept	kept
kneel	knelt	knelt
know	knew	known
lay (put, place, prepare)	laid	laid
lead	led	led
leap	leaped	leaped, leapt
leave	left	left
lend	lent	lent
let	let	let
lie (tell a falsehood)	lied	lied
lie (recline, be situated)	lay	lain
light	lighted, lit	lighted, lit
lose	lost	lost
make	made	made
mean	meant	meant
meet	met	met
pay	paid	paid
prove	proved	proved, proven
put	put	put
read	read	read
rid	rid	rid
ride	rode	ridden
ring	rang	rung
rise	rose	risen
run	ran	run
say	said	said
see	saw	seen
seek	sought	sought
sell	sold	sold
send	sent	sent

Present and Infinitive	*Past*	*Past Participle*
set (place, put)	set	set
shake	shook	shaken
shine	shone	shone
shoot	shot	shot
show	showed	shown, showed
shrink	shrank	shrunk, shrunken
shut	shut	shut
sing	sang	sung
sink	sank	sunk, sunken
sit	sat	sat
sleep	slept	slept
slide	slid	slid
sling	slung	slung
speak	spoke	spoken
speed	sped	sped
spend	spent	spent
spin	spun	spun
spread	spread	spread
spring	sprang	sprung
stand	stood	stood
steal	stole	stolen
stick	stuck	stuck
sting	stung	stung
stink	stink, stank	stunk
strike	struck	struck
string	strung	strung
swear	swore	sworn
sweep	swept	swept
swell	swelled	swelled, swollen
swim	swam	swum
swing	swung	swung
take	took	taken
teach	taught	taught
tear	tore	torn
tell	told	told
think	thought	thought
throw	threw	thrown
understand	understood	understood
wake	woke	woken
wear	wore	worn
weep	wept	wept
wet	wet	wet
win	won	won
wind	wound	wound
wring	wrung	wrung
write	wrote	written

Appendix 2   Modal Auxiliaries

Modal	*Meanings*	*Examples*
Can	a. ability	Pam **can ski** very well.
	b. strong possibility	Don't stop your car suddenly. You **can cause** an accident.
	c. suggestion	**Sue:** My roommate is a nuisance. **Bob:** You **can get** a single room.
	d. permission	**Jim:** **Can** I **see** you again? **Pat:** Yes, I would like that.
Could	a. past ability	When I was ten years old, I **could pat** my head and rub my stomach at the same time.
	b. ability based on certain conditions	You **could be** a good pianist if you practiced more.
	c. possibility	Be careful with those matches! You **could start** a fire.
	d. permission	**Could** I **use** your eraser?
	e. polite request	**Could** you please **be** quiet?
	f. suggestion	You **could get** your father a pen for his birthday.
	g. past of *can* in indirect speech	Gail said she **could drive** us to the airport.
May	a. permission	Dr. Smith, **may** I **borrow** your lecture notes?
	b. possibility	
	(1) about a future action	I **may go** home during the next break.
	(2) about a present condition	Min-Jung **may be** homesick. She has been very depressed for two weeks.
Might	a. possibility	
	(1) about a future action	I **might go** home during the next break.
	(2) about a present condition	Min-Jung **might be** homesick.
	b. past of indirect speech	She said she **might go** home before the break is over.
Should	a. advice	You really **should read** more.
	b. moral obligation	A teacher **should have** patience.
	c. expectation	That police officer **should know** where the downtown area is.

Modal	Meanings	Examples
Ought to	a. advice	You really **ought to read** more.
	b. moral obligation	A teacher **ought to have** patience.
	c. expectation	That police officer **ought to know** where the downtown area is.
Must	a. necessity	You **must get** to work on time.
	b. assumption	He **must be** a good writer because he has won so many awards.
	c. prohibition	You **must not smoke** in this section of the hospital.
Will	a. simple future	I'**ll see** you tomorrow.
	b. promise	I **will be** there on time. (Intonation distinguishes between a future tense and a promise.)
	c. determination	I **will get** an A in this course if it kills me. (Intonation distinguishes between a future tense and determination.)
Shall	a. an offer to do something for someone	**Shall I** put these papers on your desk?
	b. first-person question asking for agreement	**Shall** we **leave** now? (Are you ready to leave now?)
Would	a. polite request	**Would** you **hold** my books for a moment?
	b. willingness to do something	**Would** you **like** to eat out tonight?
	c. past habitual action	My last roommate **would play** music until 3:00 in the morning.
	d. past of *will* in indirect speech	She said Noah **would help** me.
	e. result of a condition	If I had time, I **would meet** with you.

Appendix 3   Verbs Followed by Infinitives

■ GROUP 1: Verbs + infinitive/infinitive phrase as direct object ■

afford	We can't **afford to take** a vacation this year.
agree	The family **agreed to wait** until next year.
appear	The children **appear to be** happy about this decision.
arrange	We'll **arrange to go** to Hawaii.
be (am, is, are)	We **are to leave** some time in July.
care	I really don't **care to eat** out tonight.
choose (prefer)	I certainly didn't **choose to come** to this restaurant.
claim	It **claims to serve** the best Italian food in town.
come	We **came to see** if the food is really good.
consent	Everyone **consented to try** it tonight.
decide	I **have decided to order** a chicken dish.
demand	Why **is** that customer **demanding to see** the manager?
deserve	Every customer **deserves to receive** good service.
endeavor	That student **has** always **endeavored to do** well.
fail	He **has** never **failed to get** a good grade on a test.
forget	He never **forgets to complete** his assignments.
happen	I **happen to like** him very much.
hesitate	I don't know why the other students **hesitate to talk** to him.
hope	He **hopes to receive** a scholarship for next year.
intend	His teachers **intend to help** him all they can.
learn	My children **are learning to ski**.
manage	I **have managed to remain** calm so far.
mean	I'm sorry. I didn't **mean to interrupt** you.
neglect	You **neglected to tell** me that you had to study tonight.
offer	Don't worry. The teacher **has offered to give** a review.
plan	Many students **are planning to take** the review.
prepare	The teacher **is prepared to spend** three hours on the review.
pretend	At my surprise birthday party, **I pretended to be** surprised.
proceed	I **proceeded to act** and **look** as if I hadn't known about it.
prove	Your decision **proved to be** the wrong one.
refuse	Never **refuse to tell** the truth.
regret	I **regret to tell** you that your luggage is missing.
remember	Did you **remember to put** an address label on each suitcase?
seem	You don't **seem to be** very worried about it.
struggle	The students **struggle to stay** awake in that history class.
swear	The defendant **swore to tell** the truth in court.
tend	Your child **tends to be** a little noisy at times.
threaten	She **threatened to call** the police.
volunteer	Who **will volunteer to help** us?
wait	Have a good trip. I'**ll be waiting to hear** from you.

■ GROUP 2: Verbs + object + infinitive/infinitive phrase ■

advise	Who **advised you to join** this soccer team?
allow	Does the coach **allow the players to smoke**?
appoint	Who **appointed John to be** the captain?
cause	Bill's injury **caused him to play** poorly yesterday.
caution	The referee **cautioned the members of both teams to play** fairly.
challenge	The losing team **has challenged our team to meet** again.
command	The police officers **commanded the thief to stop**.
compel	They **compelled him to drop** his weapon.
convince	I can't **convince you to do** anything you don't want to do.
direct	The usher **directed us to sit** in the third row.
enable	His strong desires **have enabled him to succeed**.
encourage	Parents should **encourage their children to do** their best.
forbid	Her mother **forbids her to tell** a lie.
force	Her son's refusal to obey **forced her to spank** him.
get	I **got my neighbor to take** me to the hospital.
*help	The police officer **helped me find** the address.
hire	He **has hired me to work** in his store this summer.
implore	I **implore everyone to help** the tornado victims.
instruct	Our teacher **instructed us to read** the directions carefully.
invite	After the exam, she **invited the class to come** to her house.
motivate	I don't know what **motivates some people to hurt** others.
oblige	Human decency **obliges us to treat** all people equally.
order	The court **ordered him to pay** for his parking tickets.
permit	The coach **permitted the players to take** a short break.
persuade	She **persuaded me to go** with her.
remind	I **reminded her not to forget** her driver's license.
request	The invitation **requested all guests to be** on time.
require	Does this school **require new students to take** a placement test?
show . . . how	Who **showed you how to do** that?
teach	My father **taught my brothers and me to play** chess.
tell	He **told us to concentrate** on the game.
tempt	You know that was wrong. What **tempted you to do** it?
urge	I **urge you to think** before you act.
warn	She **warned me not to do** it again.

*Help is followed by a noun or object pronoun and the simple form of the verb, without to.

GROUP 3: Verbs + infinitive/infinitive phrase (Group 1 pattern) OR + object + infinitive/infinitive phrase (Group 2 pattern) ■

Remember that the sentences in each pair differ in meaning.

ask	She **asked to talk** with the manager. She **asked me to talk** with the manager.
beg	He **begged to come** with us. He **begged us to come** with him.
choose	The director **chose to investigate** the problem. The director **chose a committee to investigate** the problem.
*dare	They **dared to ask** the teacher for an answer during the test. They **dared me to ask** the teacher for an answer during the test.
expect	We **expected to be** on time. We **expected you to be** on time.
like	I **like to meet** new people. I **like you to meet** new people.
need	We **need to help** your roommate with his math class. We **need your roommate to help** us with our math class.
prefer	The children **prefer to tell** stories. The children **prefer their teacher to tell** stories.
†promise	My brother **promised not to tell**. My brother **promised me not to tell**.
want	The nurse **wants to give** the injection. The nurse **wants the doctor to give** the injection.
wish	I **wish to consult** with my lawyer. I **wish you to consult** with my lawyer.

* In interrogative and negative statements, *dare* is used without *to* if no object follows the verb. ("Do you **dare jump** off that building?" "No, I **don't dare** do that." "Do you **dare me to jump** off that building?")

†Only the verb *promise* keeps the same meaning in both patterns.

Appendix 4   Verbs Followed by Gerunds

▪ Verbs + gerund/gerund phrase ▪

admit	He **has admitted taking** the money.
appreciate	We **appreciated his telling** the truth.
avoid	Sue **avoids having** a conversation with Jim whenever she can.
can't help	Sometimes, however, she **can't help asking** him a question.
consider	We **are considering moving** to Hawaii.
defer	We **have deferred making** a final decision until next month.
delay	I **can't delay telling** you the truth any longer.
deny	Why **did** you **deny being** at the party?
detest	Most people **detest waiting** in long lines at the movie.
discuss	We **discussed going** to the mountains for the weekend.
enjoy	Everyone **enjoys being** in the fresh air.
escape	How **did** you **escape taking** the makeup test?
*excuse	The teacher **excused** my **being** late.
finish	**Has** everyone **finished doing** the assignment?
forgive	She **forgave** my **shouting** at her yesterday.
imagine	**Can** you **imagine winning** a thousand dollars?
keep (continue)	**Keep working** until you finish page thirty-four.
mention	I **didn't mention seeing** you yesterday.
mind (dislike)	**Do** you **mind not smoking** in class?
miss	**Do** you sometimes **miss being** with your high school friends?
postpone	Susan **had to postpone taking** her trip.
practice	I'm **going to practice giving** this speech all night.
prevent	Sometimes it's impossible **to prevent fighting** among children.
quit	Please, children! **Quit shoving** and **pushing**.
recall	I don't **recall promising** to have lunch with you.
recommend	She **recommended getting** a tutor.
resent	I really **resent being** the last one in line.
resist	I'm on a diet, but who can **resist eating** your good cooking.
risk	I will not **risk failing** tomorrow's test, so I won't go out tonight.
suggest	The football coach **suggested swimming** as a means of relaxation.
tolerate	Be quiet. Professor Smith does not **tolerate talking** during a test.
*understand	I can't **understand** your **getting** angry with me.

*These verbs are always followed by the possessive before the gerund.

Appendix 5 Verbs Followed by Gerunds or Infinitives

These verbs are followed by either a gerund <u>or</u> an infinitive construction with no change in meaning.

advise
Jim's high school counselor **advised going** to a small college.
Jim's high school counselor **advised him to go** to a small college.

allow
Most restaurants **allow smoking** only in certain sections.
Most restaurants **allow diners to smoke** only in certain sections.

attempt
To forget our fear, we **attempted singing**.
To forget our fear, we **attempted to sing**.

begin
It **has begun raining**. Roll up the car windows.
It **has begun to rain**. Roll up the car windows.

cannot bear
I'm taking you to the hospital. I **can't bear seeing** you in pain.
I'm taking you to the hospital. I **can't bear to see** you in pain.

continue
Although we were tired, we **continued working**.
Although we were tired, we **continued to work**.

dislike
Most people **dislike hearing** about their faults.
Most people **dislike to hear** about their faults.

dread
I really **dread being** alone in a big house at night.
I really **dread to be** alone in a big house at night.

forbid
The law **forbids driving** over the speed limit.
The law **forbids motorists to drive** over the speed limit.

hate
I **hate asking** such a big favor from you, but I need help.
I **hate to ask** such a big favor from you, but I need help.

Index